D1707626

ASHGATE NEW CRITICAL THINKING IN THEOLOGY & BIBLICAL STUDIES

Ashgate New Critical Thinking in Theology & Biblical Studies presents an open-ended series of quality research drawn from an international field of scholarship. The series aims to bring monograph publishing back into focus for authors, the international library market, and student, academic and research readers. Headed by an international editorial advisory board of acclaimed scholars, this series presents cutting-edge research from established as well as exciting new authors in the field. With specialist focus, yet clear contextual presentation, books in the series aim to take theological and biblical research into new directions, opening the field to new critical debate within the traditions, into areas of related study, and into important topics for contemporary society.

Series Editorial Board

Hope in Barth's Eschatology

Interrogations and transformations beyond tragedy

JOHN C. McDOWELL

Ashgate

Aldershot • Burlington USA • Singapore • Sydney

Published by
Ashgate Publishing Ltd
Gower House
Croft Road
Aldershot
Hants GU11 3HR
England

Ashgate Publishing Company
131 Main Street
Burlington, VT 05401-5600 USA

Ashgate website: http://www.ashgate.com

British Library Cataloguing in Publication Data
McDowell, John C.
    Hope in Barth's eschatology : interrogations and
    transformations beyond tragedy. - (Ashgate new critical
    thinking in theology & biblical studies)
    1. Barth, Karl, 1886-1968 - Contributions in eschatology
    2. Hope - Religious aspects - Christianity
    I. Title
    236

Library of Congress Control Number: 00-134820

ISBN 0 7546 1542 1

Printed and bound by Antony Rowe Ltd, Chippenham, Wiltshire

To Sandra and my sons, Archie and Jonathan

Without whom this could not have been possible ...

Contents

Acknowledgements

During my research I have come to appreciate the wisdom of John Donne's comment that "no man is an island, intire of it selfe". I have been fortunate to have had the support and encouragement of many people. A particular debt is owed to my doctoral supervisor at the University of Cambridge, Professor Nicholas Lash, whose guidance and continual critique have generated so much of the inspiration behind the shaping of this study. Professor David Ford's supervisions during Professor Lash's sabbatical leave (Michaelmas term 1994), and his subsequent enthusiasm for my project, have also been invaluable. Professor John Webster, one of my doctoral examiners, has also provided a vital source of encouragement in bringing the thesis to publication.

I am grateful to Professor Trevor Hart, whose enthusiastic support did much to direct me into research on Karl Barth's theology. Dr. David Cook and the Whitefield Institute kindly provided financial backing that substantially aided my period of research. Especially beneficial has been its termly seminar sessions, in the supportive environment of which I have been enabled to take further confidence in the value of my studies.

My parents-in-law, Rev. John and Margaret Carrick, deserve more than just a mention of thanks. They have invested a considerable amount of financial support and emotional energy into the four years of research and writing. Without them this study could not even have begun.

The context for my learning and questioning, has been provided by my parents. They had sacrificed much to bring me to the place where theological study became possible.

Coming to know Dr. Mike Higton has been a significant blessing. Through long conversations in 'The Eagle' I have become increasingly aware of the value of Christian hope and the personal encouragement that it brings to a life travelling in the darkness. Moreover, for the material of Hans Frei's thesis on Barth I am indebted to Chapter One of his thesis, *The Identity of Jesus Christ in the Church: An Exploration in the Theology of Hans Frei* (unpublished PhD: Cambridge, 1997).

I would also like to thank Sarah Lloyd of Ashgate, Professor W.P. Stephens, Professor David Fergusson, David Moseley, Norman and Sandra McKinney, and my former philosophy students in Cambridge, all of whom have variously contributed a great deal to facilitating and developing my research and/or bringing it to publication. Many others could be named, and have certainly not been forgotten, who have both provided conditions of support, and have frequently reminded me of what it means to live a human life before God.

My young son, Archie, has been a wonderful distraction from the recent pressures and strains that attend the manifold pursuits that I have been involved in.

Lastly, and most of all, I am grateful to my wife, Sandra, who has been limitlessly patient and supportive. Without her I would never have made it through these past few years. It is to her, Archie and the newest addition to the McDowell clan, Jonathan, that this book is dedicated.

Finally, I am grateful to T&T Clark, publisher and copyright holder, for permission to cite at length material from the *Church Dogmatics*, 14 part-volumes, 1958-81; to T&T Clark for permission to reuse the material from 'Learning Where to Place One's Hope: The Eschatological Significance of Election in Barth', *Scottish Journal of Theology* vol. 53 (2000); and to Oxford University Press for permission to reuse the material from 'Silenus' Wisdom and the "Crime of Being": The Problem of Hope in George Steiner's Tragic Vision', *Literature and Theology* vol. 14.4 (2000).

List of Abbreviations

Karl Barth

C	*Credo*
CD	*Church Dogmatics*
CL	*The Christian Life*
CPS	'The Christian's Place in Society'
ET	*Evangelical Theology: An Introduction*
FC	*The Faith of the Church*
FGG	*Fragments Grave and Gay*
FI	'Fate and Idea in Theology'
FQI	*Anselm: Fides Quaerens Intellectum*
GD	*The Göttingen Dogmatics*
HG	*The Humanity of God*
HGCL	*The Holy Ghost and the Christian Life*
KD	*Kirchliche Dogmatik*
R	'Revelation'
1Ro	*Der Römerbrief, 1919*
2Ro	*The Epistle to the Romans*, 6th edn.
RD	*The Resurrection of the Dead*
TC	*Theology and Church*
WGWM	*The Word of God and the Word of Man*

George Steiner

AT	'Absolute Tragedy'
DT	*The Death of Tragedy*
LS	*Language and Silence*
RP	*Real Presences*
TPS	'Tragedy, Pure and Simple'

KBDT	'Karl Barth's Doctrine of Time: Its Nature and Implications'
TW	*A Theology on its Way? Essays on Karl Barth*

Other Abbreviations

BT	Friedrich Nietzsche, *The Birth of Tragedy*
FCF	Karl Rahner, *Foundations of Christian Faith*
H	G.W.F. Hegel, *Hegel on Tragedy* [selections from *The Philosophy of Fine Art*]
JTS	*Journal of Theological Studies*
L	William Shakespeare, *King Lear*
OC	Sophocles, *Oedipus at Colonus*
OT	Sophocles, *Oedipus Tyrannus*
P	Aristotle, *Poetics*
SJT	*Scottish Journal of Theology*
SL	Philip J. Rosato, *The Spirit as Lord*
TG	G.C. Berkouwer, *The Triumph of Grace in the Theology of Karl Barth*
TH	Jürgen Moltmann, *Theology of Hope*
TI	Karl Rahner, *Theological Investigations*, 23 volumes
TKG	Wolfhart Pannenberg, *Theology and the Kingdom of God*

Introduction

Lapsing into an Incomplete Nihilism

In Nietzsche's narration of nihilism's origins, an acute contrast in attitudes is portrayed between the madman, who exclaims "I seek God! I seek God!", and the derisively facetious crowd.[1] Contrary to Jesus' cries from the cross (even if they express God-abandonment), this madman is devoid of any hope of being heard by God. For it is he alone who has grasped the significance of God's 'death' at humanity's hands. Thereby driven into the apprehensive insecurity of feeling set adrift with the cold night continually closing in, his terrified and anguished response becomes expressed by both his brief panic-stricken questions, and his apocalyptic allusions to the "sequence of breakdown, ruin, and cataclysm that is now impending" for "the whole of our European morality".[2]

Frequently, the West's late twentieth-century reflections on this "strange, frightening journey", embarking from a lostness, had entered the traumatic dark places of the possibility of human self-mutilation. Announced with unrestrained depth has been humanity's intensely self-destructive urge, drawing its catastrophic potency from the power of modern technology. An overwhelming pessimism can be the outcome for consciousness of "the dark silence of God's absence" [*LS*, 204]. As Bell argues, with reference to the macabre journeying of this past century's history, "the world ... holds absolutely no consolation for human beings".[3] Pre-eminent expression of this may be discovered in the existence of cultures that have been starved and beaten of all hope and imagination of the future. However, such bleakness cannot be endured easily, as Steiner argues in respect of "absolute tragedy" [*DT*, 9].

The culture of the "free play of *différance*" and the celebration of the "carnival" appears to be a laughing in the face of despair, the staving off of the anxiety of being adrift in a postmodern, post-death-of-God

---

[1] Friedrich Nietzsche (1974), *The Gay Science*, trans. Walter Kaufmann, Vintage Books, New York, 125.

[2] Ibid., 343; Brian D. Ingraffia (1995), *Postmodern Theory and Biblical Theology: Vanquishing God's Shadow*, Cambridge, 31.

[3] David F. Bell (1993), 'Introduction: Of Silence and Insouciance in Philosophy', in Clément Rosset, *Joyful Cruelty: Towards a Philosophy of the Real*, trans. David F. Bell, New York and Oxford, vii-xvi (viii).

world.[4] Beck's comment appears pertinent: "Where there is no escape, people ultimately no longer want to think about it" (hence the hedonistic escapism of 'drug-cultures').[5] Escape comes primarily through apathy or suicide. One needs some form of light to dispel this darkness, for in the dark the demons strike.

None of this admission of the precarious balancing over the precipice of nihilism is to claim with Bauckham that

> western society finds itself bereft of a story to live by, lacking
> a worldview which can give meaning and hope for the world
> and the future.[6]

Contemporary Western society is too diverse and complex to be summarily described by such a statement. Precisely where one aspect of this pluralism may be detected is in the prolongation of the life of not wanting to 'think the worst' that occurs with those who refuse to learn the lesson of Nietzsche's madman: i.e., that one needs to acknowledge the existence of the void. In certain quarters the song may still be heard that science and technology offer increasing possibilities for control (over self, society, etc.), particularly in relation to the future. Here Bauckham and Hart rightly do recognise that this 'myth'

> has so dominated and permeated the culture of modernity we
> cannot easily leave it behind.[7]

Fukuyama, for example, according to Lash,

> supposes there to be no thinkable alternative to an historicist
> understanding of history as a tale of 'progress, an 'evolution
> from primitive to modern'.[8]

---

[4] Jacques Derrida (1982), *Margins of Philosophy*, trans. Alan Bass, University of Chicago Press, 27; Kenneth Gergen (1991), *The Saturated Self: Dilemmas of Identity in Contemporary Life*, Basic Books, New York, 189.

[5] Ulrich Beck (1992), *Risk Society. Towards a New Modernity*, London, 37.

[6] Richard Bauckham, in Richard Bauckham and Trevor Hart (1999), 'Salvation and Creation: "All Things New"', in *The Scope of Salvation: Theatres of God's Drama. Lincoln Lectures in Theology 1998*, Lincoln Cathedral Publications, 40-54 (42).

[7] Bauckham and Trevor Hart (1999), *Hope Against Hope: Christian Eschatology in Contemporary Context*, Darton, Longman and Todd, London, 7.

[8] Nicholas Lash (1994), 'Beyond the End of History?' *Concilium* vol. 5, 47-56 (47), citing Francis Fukuyama (1989), 'The End of History?' *The National Interest* vol. 16, 18 and (1989-1990) 'A Reply to my Critics' *The National Interest* vol. 18, 23.

Similar forms of lighting the way into the future appear in apocalyptic-style predicting of our futures. Given the growing excitement that could have been detected in certain quarters over Christendom's dawning third Millennium and the subsequently heightened apocalyptic expectation, of the multiplication of these End-time 'prophecies' there is (and will be) no end.

Despite their contrary appearance, these optimisms and pessimisms share a common field of operation and are indeed fuelled by a similar facing of nihilistic potentialities (although thereafter they move in opposite directions). Both know and determine the shape of the future and thereby attempt to provide the end to history's unfinished narrative with an unwarranted certainty of future events. Pessimism observes that future as dwelling in darkness, while optimism sees only light.

Hoping Beyond Optimism and Pessimism

Some form of hope is necessary to human existence in order to open otherwise closed avenues towards the future, one that can resist the contemporary loss of certain imaginings of our futures. Hope actively struggles against despair's paralysing effects by imagining the possible.[9] One, for example, would not sow if there was absolutely no hope of a harvest. As such, hope functions to provide imaginative counter-factuals (the seeds are not a crop), which then creatively determine the nature of one's planned contribution to the constructing of the future (because they will hopefully yield, I shall sow them). And this, in turn, actively influences the shaping of things to come (the seed produces a harvest).

However, hope, if it is not to topple over into something illusory (the persistent expectation of a harvest from soil that is unfit for sowing), voicing thoughtless and inane platitudes ('don't worry, the crops *will* grow there'), or something more sinister (the murder of another for their produce or more fertile land), needs to be firmly taken out of the vicinity of optimism, and by virtue of their common field of operation, also of pessimism. Optimism, in its utopian and evolutionary forms, menacingly drives towards destructive illusion by trampling on memories of rupture and humanly inflicted de-humanisation, suffering and *hubris*, struggle and uncertainty.[10] This it does by not taking these disruptive stories seriously

---

[9] See W.F. Lynch (1965), *Images of Hope: Imagination as Healer of the Hopeless*, University of Notre Dame Press, 31f.

[10] See David Tracy (1994), *On Naming the Present: Reflections on God, Hermeneutics and Church*, SCM Press, London, 51.

as proper accounts of human limitations; marginalising sufferers' voices; or even reducing their impact through the banalities of generalising "platitudes of consolation and formulaic obsequies".[11]   It thereby condemns itself to repeat the horrors of its past in a continuous cycle. Hence, less than half a century after the 'liberation' of Auschwitz (even though mere physical liberation would not necessarily end the nightmares of the 'liberated'), the atrocities in the Balkans once again remind one of the actualisation of humanity's self-destructive tendencies in the most brutal fashion.

Hope, on the other hand, lives through trial, refuses any form of escape through the securities of uninvolvement in the messy business of human life and thought, and risks disappointment and necessary revision. Human limitations, in their finitude and fragility, not to mention *hubris*, are here taken seriously. In contrast to the predictively assertive nature of both optimism and pessimism, hope iconoclastically breaks open premature objectivised notions of the whole, and thereby retains a nescience and tentativeness, as well as an active creativity, in its knowing of the details of the future. "I was born somewhere", admits Ricoeur, and therefore, as Lash argues, "We do not live nor can we see, beyond the end of history".[12] Our particular temporal and spatial co-ordinates entail that speech can only be performed within the provisionality of situated perceiving (that we live, and speak, blinded by the darkness, in some sense) and continually risk hubristic error, particularly in its giving form to our creative journeying into the future.

And yet, as Chapter 1 discusses with regard to George Steiner's reflections on the nature of the tragic, that is a form of hope which is generally thought to be excluded by the theological imagination. The question being raised in this study is whether this is a legitimate reading of Barth's account of hope.

The Problem of Hope in Barth's Eschatology

It would appear banal to rehearse the cliché of 'Karl Barth, the greatest theologian of the twentieth century', and even church Father.[13]   The voluminous nature of the secondary literature on his theology certainly

---

[11] Alan E. Lewis (1987), 'The Burial of God: Rupture and Resumption as the Story of Salvation' *SJT* vol. 40, 335-362 (339).

[12] Paul Ricoeur (1986), *Fallible Man*, trans. Charles A. Kelbey, Fordham University Press, New York, 20; Lash, 1994, 49.

[13] So Barth is accoladed by T.F. Torrance (1990), *Karl Barth: Biblical and Evangelical Theologian*, T&T Clark, Edinburgh, 1.

supports this thought as being a truism. And yet, Barth's hope, and the eschatological soil in which it is germinated and is nourished, is a little treated element.[14]

    Certainly, the *CD* was never completed, with the final volume on Redemption remaining outstanding. Moreover, eschatology is located *last* in Barth's dogmatic scheme of Prolegomena and the Word of God (volume I), God (volume II), Creation (volume III), Reconciliation (IV), and eschatology (proposed volume V). Even volume IV.3, Barth's most eschatologically significant published part-volume, *completes* the theological reflections on the work of Christ. Has Barth here relegated eschatology to the final chapter, or appendix, that he had originally denied [*GD*, §35.Intro]? Marty and Peerman, for instance, explicitly include Barth within the scope of the claim that "eschatology was a postscript or minor motif in neo-orthodoxy".[15]

    However, five points can be raised against this paucity of substantial study of Barth's eschatology of hope. Firstly, eschatological themes play a significant part in Barth's creedal expositions [*C, DO*, and

---

[14] Both Joseph Bettis and John Colwell treat Barth's supposed *apokatastasis* [Bettis (1967), 'Is Karl Barth a Universalist?' *SJT* vol. 20, 423-426; Colwell (1992), 'The Contemporaneity of the Divine Decision: Reflections on Barth's Denial of "Universalism"', in *Universalism and the Doctrine of Hell. Papers Presented at the Fourth Edinburgh Conference on Christian Dogmatics*, ed. Nigel M. de S. Cameron, Paternoster Press, Carlisle, 139-160]. An earlier study by Colwell briefly treats the *parousia* and hope in relation to eternity [Colwell (1989), *Actuality and Provisionality: Eternity and Election in the Theology of Karl Barth*, Rutherford House Books, Edinburgh]. Keith Randall Schmitt discusses death and after-life [Schmitt (1985), *Death and After-Life in the Theologies of Karl Barth and John Hick*, Rodopi, Amsterdam]. John Thompson briefly outlines some eschatological themes in relation to christology and pneumatology [Thompson (1978), *Christ in Perspective in the Theology of Karl Barth*, T&T Clark, Edinburgh; (1991), *The Holy Spirit in the Theology of Karl Barth*, Pennsylvania]. Robert W. Jenson reads Barth's theology in the light of the 1960s' 'theologies of hope' [Jenson (1969), *God After God: The God of the Past and the God of the Future, Seen in the Work of Karl Barth*, Bobbs-Merrill, Indianapolis, New York]. John S. Reist, Jr., briefly discusses hope's christological character [Reist (1987), 'Commencement, Continuation, Consummation: Karl Barth's Theology of Hope' *Evangelical Quarterly* vol. 87, 195-214]. John Webster describes hope's practical nature [Webster (1994), '"Assured and Patient and Cheerful Expectation": Barth on Christian Hope as the Church's Task', *Toronto Journal of Theology* vol. 10, 35-52; (1991), 'Eschatology, Ontology and Human Action', *Toronto Journal of Theology* vol. 7, 4-18]. Two very good recent treatments, paralleling some of what has been done in this project, are Timothy Gorringe's (1999) 'Eschatology and Political Radicalism. The Example of Karl Barth and Jürgen Moltmann', in *God Will Be All in All: The Eschatology of Jürgen Moltmann*, ed. Richard Bauckham, T&T Clark, Edinburgh, 87-114; and (1999), *Karl Barth: Against Hegemony* Oxford University Press. See also, Gerhard Sauter (1999), 'Why is Karl Barth's Church Dogmatics Not a 'Theology of Hope'? Some Observations on Barth's Understanding of Eschatology', *SJT* vol. 52, 407-429.

[15] Martin E. Marty and Dean G. Peerman (1968), 'Christian Hope and Human Futures' in *New Theology 5*, eds. Martin E. Marty and Dean G. Peerman, Collier and Macmillan, London and New York, 7-18 (12).

However, five points can be raised against this paucity of substantial study of Barth's eschatology of hope. Firstly, eschatological themes play a significant part in Barth's creedal expositions [*C, DO,* and *FC*]. In second place, three of Barth's later letters (to Werner Rüegg, 1961; Jürgen Moltmann, 1964; and Tjarko Stadtland, 1967) explicitly deal with eschatological themes, and in particular with Barth's complaint against the 'theologies of hope'.[16] Thirdly, on one occasion in *CD* I.2 Barth reiterates the force of *2Ro*'s and *GD*'s emphasis on eschatology's universal importance [*CD*, I.2, 875].[17] Eschatology, then, cannot and must not be considered and treated merely as an appendix to the doctrine of atonement. Fourthly, Barth later mentioned

> how much about the desired sphere of eschatology may be gathered indirectly, and sometimes directly, from the earlier volumes [*CD*, IV.4, vii].[18]

Finally, eschatology and hope surface particularly powerfully in IV.3, no doubt paving the way for the intended exposition in V.

In other words, one needs to recognise the importance of Barth's interconnecting eschatology and other dogmatic loci, and therefore the crucial place of eschatology in his theology. So, in the *CL* he claims that

> Only in its [i.e., history's] threeness [of creation's prologue, history's main statement and eschatology's epilogue] is the totality the theme of the Christian message and the Christian faith [*CL*, 10].

Perhaps the primary reason for the commentators' neglect of eschatology and hope within Barth's *oeuvre* is to be sought instead in a reading to the effect that Barth comprehensively subsumed all time within the temporality of the present Eternal Now of revelation, so that time itself becomes frozen in the realisation of this revelational Moment. Chapter 2 discusses this, and its relevancy for Christian hope, in the context of the diverse, but overlapping, studies of Barth by Richard Roberts, Jürgen Moltmann, G.C. Berkouwer, and Philip Rosato.

The contention of this study, however, is not merely that neglect of Barth's eschatology is detrimental to an adequate grasp of his theological account, but that the readings by Roberts, *et al.*, are fundamentally flawed

---

[16] Barth (1981), *Karl Barth: Letters, 1961-1968* ed. and trans. Geoffrey W. Bromiley, T&T Clark, Edinburgh, 9, 174-176, 232-236 respectively.

[17] Cf. *2Ro*, 314; *GD*, §35.

[18] Cf., *CD*, I, 56f., 164f.; I.2, 875ff.

at this particular juncture. Much of what passes for Barth-scholarship fashions a 'straw man' who is helpless against critical assault, a figure whose apparently one-sided theological presentation actually bears little resemblance to the complex movements and counter-movements, recapitulations and contrasting themes of the symphonically-charged style of the *CD*'s composer.[19] The danger of pinning Barth's thoughts to any single mast is that when one turns around Barth will have slipped free.

It will be proposed that Barth's eschatology does not function to foreclose the future (whether that be thought's being foreclosed through prediction, or temporality's through a 'realised eschatology'). Barth's theology will be presented, then, as an attempt at an eschatological location of thought which generates consequent ethical engagement.

Firstly, Barth locates responsible Christian grammar, and its communal rules of discourse, within the tension of the promise and fulfilment of the divine Self-giving in its own spatiality and temporality. That is why in *GD* Barth claims that many theological errors have been the result of trying to achieve a "premature eschatology", of Christian hope being unable to wait and pretending instead to be already at its goal.[20] Consequently, Barth opens up time and space for the dimension of Christian hope, a hope that is grounded in, shaped by, and an anticipation of the presence of Jesus Christ having come, coming, and yet to come.

This, as will be indicated later, is a form of hope which is expressed as more fallible, fragile and hubristic than George Steiner's description of Christian hope's optimistic temperament would permit. In its concreteness it contrasts with, as Barth claims about the Gospel, "both the sweet sadness and the false optimism of mere reverie".[21] Moreover, Barth's account of hope functions to fully immerse and regulate one's engaging in critically transforming present actualities, rather than as enabling one to stand "above the [earthly] battle", as Reinhold Niebuhr incorrectly claims.[22] This is Christian hope's interrogative and transformative functioning.

---

[19] On the likening of Barth's theological style to his beloved Mozart, see George Hunsinger (1991), *How to Read Karl Barth: The Shape of His Theology*, Oxford University Press, 28. John Bowden simply refers to Barth's style as "symphonic" [Bowden (1971), *Karl Barth*, SCM Press, London, 24].

[20] Cited by Daniel L. Migliore (1991), 'Karl Barth's First Lectures', in *GD*, xv-lvii (lviiif.).

[21] Barth (1959), *Christmas*, trans. Bernhard Citron, Oliver and Boyd, Edinburgh and London, 12.

[22] Reinhold Niebuhr, cited in Joseph Bettis (1976), 'Political Theology and Social Ethics: The Socialist Humanism of Karl Barth', in *Karl Barth and Radical Politics*, ed. George Hunsinger, Westminster, Philadelphia, 159-179 (172).

Chapter 3 suggests that even in the pre-*GD* period Barth's eschatology is more complex than being a simple espousal of an eschatological-given. On the contrary, the eschatology of the period appears to move more in a futurist direction than certain critics recognise. Even the past, as well as the future, here plays an extensive role in Barth's early theology, providing a foundation and dynamism to a supposedly 'stilted' conception of time. The eschatological Future is that 'place' wherein the God, whose provisional presence is indicated by the sign of the empty shell crater or dried up canal structure, comes to his creation. Such themes may only prove to be a subcurrent within *2Ro* in particular, but they remain identifiable streams of thought nonetheless. Furthermore, serving as an influence on his later reflections on hope's interrogative mood, in these years this eschatological discourse specifically serves as an interrogation of life in the present.

Chapter 4, focusing on *GD* and *CD* I, traces the christological direction that the Göttingen Barth was moving in and its relevancy to his eschatology. It is this intensive christologically-centred theology that leads Balthasar to use the image of an "intellectual hourglass", so that "There is no other point of encounter between the top and bottom portions of the glass".[23] Hence, Barth's account of Christian hope was coming to have a codified focus in the person of Jesus Christ.

Moreover, although this christological eschatology lends weight to an increasing sense of eschatological actuality, the note of provisionality is heavily written into Barth's treatment of revelation. As Colwell argues, "An eschatological faith which focuses upon Jesus Christ as the *Eschatos* is determined by the Already as well as the Not Yet".[24] Christology now comes to play the role of eschatological critique that the *Novum* did in *2Ro*.[25]

Identifying the 'metanarrative' of Barth's eschatology of existence occurs in Chapter 5. Here Barth's christological reading of eschatological assertions is displayed in his discussion of election, creation and covenant (*CD*, II and III). Various alternative eschatologies are ruled out in order to clarify the nature and place of eschatology in relation to the divine election of Jesus Christ, the *Protos* and *Eschatos*.

Chapters 6 and 7, focusing on *CD*, IV.3 and IV.4 (incorporating also the fragments of IV.4 posthumously published as *CL*), draw these

---

[23] Hans Urs von Balthasar (1972), *The Theology of Karl Barth*, trans. John Drury, Anchor, New York, 157f.; cf. *CD*, I.2, 133.

[24] Colwell, 1989, 27.

[25] See Bruce L. McCormack (1995), *Karl Barth's Critically Realistic Dialectical Theology*, Clarendon Press, Oxford, 328.

themes together to present the rudiments of a form of hope that can move some distance toward answering Steiner's critique. Barth's eschatology, it is maintained in the penultimate chapter, postulates that the Absolute Future has come in Christ on our behalf (the actuality of the particular); and yet God provides 'room' for creaturely participation in that *Eschaton* (the provisionality of the many). The existentiality of 'hope' therein receives not only its impetus and its regulating activity, but also its fragility and nescience, as Chapter 7 highlights.

In conclusion, a weak point in Barth's writings is identified for this advocation of hope's fragility. That Barth occasionally does not appear to move far enough in this direction is a side-effect of his championing certain categories: pre-eminently a dialectic couched in triumphal terms. Certain corrective suggestions are made, particularly through Donald MacKinnon's reflections on the relation of tragic drama and the Gospel narratives.

Chapter 1

Silenus' Wisdom and the 'Crime of Being': George Steiner on the Untragic Nature of Christian Hope

Count no mortal happy till
he has passed the final limit of his life secure from pain
(Chorus in *Oedipus Tyrannus*, lines 1529f)

Introduction

'All's Well...'? Edgar's Untragic Theology

Given the play's tragic events there is a sense in which Edgar's extolling of the divine cosmic justice heightens the sense of tragedy and waste [*L*, V.iii.168]. Reverberating in one's memory, at this point, is the fatalistic admission of that other theist in *King Lear*, Edgar's father (Gloucester), that "the gods kill for their sport as wanton boys do flies" [*L*, IV.i.35-6]. What kind of justice uses and abuses human lives for divine pleasure? Such a question constitutes a harkening back to some of the Attic tragedies, with their catastrophic clashes with the gods. Significant, in this regard, is Euripides' *The Bacchae*, with its amoral presentation of the Dionysian hedonistic-style excess. Yet, what Edgar intends appears to be significantly different from this despairing recognition. His blaming his father's misfortunes on the latter's carnal sins, wherein Gloucester ironically bore the agent of his misfortune (Edmund), suggests that he precisely understands cosmic justice as the retribution of the gods on human sins.

The gods are just, and of our pleasant vices
Make instruments to plague us:
The dark and vicious place where thee [Edmund] he [Gloucester] got
Cost him his eyes [*L*, V.iii.168-171].

Bradley describes *L* as "the most terrible picture that Shakespeare painted of the world", and Hunter portrays it as a "final *nothing*, not only of death, but of a world emptied of meaningful content".[1] Certainly the kingdom could now be stronger with the deaths of Lear's two manipulative daughters (Goneril and Regan) and Edmund. But this is by no means a simple providential restoration of justice. What sin has Cordelia, in particular, committed? She appears to be an innocent, almost, entangled in the unfolding tragedy. At most she is a victim of her own lovingly honest silence to a father who indulges in the dishonest flattery from his other two ambitious daughters [see *L*, I.1.62-119]. Moreover, Gloucester pays the price of loyalty to his self-deposed king, and thereby suffers the wrath of these megalomaniacs. Indeed, albeit without any explicit revision of his theology, Edgar's emotions force him to conclude with a partial recognition of the loss [*L*, V.3.321f.].

It is difficult to adequately assess the significance of *L*'s pre-Christian setting. Is Edgar's theology a link between this pagan context and its *post-Christum* composition? Is tragedy the play's genre precisely *because* it is pre-Christian? Speaight, for example, suggests that the play indicates "the fallibility of pagan heavenly reliance".[2] Kent and Gloucester's pagan superstitiousness, for instance, quickly relapses into a despairing fatalism, followed eventually by stoical acceptance of fate;[3] and Edgar's aptitude for believing in divine providence strikes one as misplaced rather than as an indication of real Shakespearean hope in divine justice, as Cavell incorrectly imagines.[4] If this was the case, however, then little sense could be made of the Christian settings of the tragedies *Hamlet* and *Romeo and Juliet*, for example. Or do the tragic heroes 'fall' precisely because they lack Christian sensibilities and consciousnesses? Is there even a hint of Shakespearean agnosticism in the face of the barrage of 'evil'? So Edwards argues that Shakespeare's tragedies, and *L* in particular, "are full of religious anxiety and have little religious confidence".[5]

---

[1] A.C. Bradley (1957), *Shakespearean Tragedy*, London, 225; G.K. Hunter (1972), 'Introduction', in *L*, 7-55 (26).

[2] Robert Speaight, cited in Kenneth Muir (1986), *King Lear*, Penguin, London, 43.

[3] *L*, IV.i.36-7, V.ii.9-11.

[4] Stanley Cavell (1969), *Must We Mean What We Say? A Book of Essays*, Charles Scribner's Sons, New York, 309.

[5] Philip Edwards (1987), *Shakespeare: A Winter's Progress*, Oxford and New York, 158.

These questions raise the general problem of the relationship of Christian hope and the tragic vision, one on which it has become almost commonplace to draw a contrast, as an explication of the work on tragic drama by George Steiner will indicate.

The climax of Steiner's presentation of the tragic comes in the strong connection between his darkened Jewish consciousness and his bleak picture of existence, mediated through high Attic tragic drama, and to a great extent echoing the general philosophy of Arthur Schopenhauer. Hence, pervading his *oeuvre* is a vision of the 'tragic', an understanding of existence's destructive potentialities informing the events of 'tragic drama' that raises complex issues of living in a hostile environment; the very legitimacy of hope itself; and of theology's place in lighting our way through this darkness. For it is in this tragic sensibility that Steiner leaves his reader gasping for some form of hope - one that is not provided, and whose potential shape he explicitly denies to Christian theology.

However, Padel's statement that "Tragedy is the basis of Steiner's work" needs to be unpacked and qualified, however, lest it suggest that tragedy is the primary reference point for all of Steiner's work.[6]

As will be narrated later, hope does lighten the mood, arriving in the form of a faint echo of the early Nietzschean account - artistic creativity and the act of reception of the aesthetic, particularly that of the act of reading. Herein is suggested certain possible ways of presenting a hope capable of facing the tragic vision. Hence he does not follow the nihilistic advocating of aesthetic silence in Adorno's stark admission of "No poetry after Auschwitz".[7] Where Nietzsche's reflection particularly significantly recedes is in the fact that Steiner portrays this aesthetic and hermeneutic transcendence in theological colours. This sits uneasily alongside his presentation of the tragic vision, perhaps being an example of Steiner's own refusal of simple conceptual resolution [*RP*, 86]. However, without providing any resolution to the problem of the tragic, it may be argued that in one sense this discontinuity need not be quite so pronounced since more careful attention to the complexity of the tragic dramas themselves could render this antithesis, along with a more modest claim concerning the incompatibility between the tragic vision and Christian hope, too simple.

---

[6] Ruth Padel (1994), 'George Steiner and the Greekness of Tragedy', in *Reading George Steiner*, eds. Nathan A. Scott, Jr., and Ronald A. Sharp, The John Hopkins University Press, Baltimore and London, 99-133 (99).

[7] Cited in George Steiner (1984), 'Introduction', in *George Steiner: A Reader*, Penguin Books, 7-22 (14).

George Steiner: After Auschwitz ...! Divine Silence

In one way or another, questions concerning the tragic vision and Christian hope are not novel. Nietzsche had suggested a parallel between Christian belief and the Socratic-style optimism of the Enlightenment.[8] Marx had famously damned Christianity, in particular eschatology and its resultant hope, as ideological and 'other-worldly' escapism.[9] Moreover, D. Daiches Raphael had raised the issue of post-Hebraic religions' anti-tragic nature.[10]

Unlike the rhetorical violence and hyperbole of Nietzsche's anti-Christianity, however, Steiner's discussion appears to treat the tragic's relation to Christian hope from a literary perspective. There is here, therefore, no Nietzschean attempt to joyfully (albeit this is not a naïve joy) proclaim "the greatest recent event" of the death of God at humanity's hands; or to "vanquish God's shadow" through providing a Zarathustrian replacement which necessarily learns "the art of *this-worldly* comfort first".[11] Nevertheless, Steiner's writing, in which there is a fluidity of borders between the literary and the philosophical, does raise some important philosophical and theological questions. After all, he laments the paucity of philosophical approaches to tragedy, which are regarded as, "of course, of the essence" [*TPS*, 545n1].

The particularly interesting note in Steiner's reflections, however, is not primarily sounded in the admission of an incompatibility, which is almost a commonplace in late twentieth-century literary criticism. Although, on saying that, it is significant that he appears to soften the tone of this, even to the point of withdrawing it, in his tribute to Donald MacKinnon. In MacKinnon, Steiner discovers a voice in which Auschwitz puts in question "the resurrection itself".[12] The particularly important note can be heard rather in the fact that this philosophically informed literary critic is a Jew expressing moral indignancy over all versions of hope that cannot bear to look into the tragic, whatever sight one may see there. In other words, this philosophically informed literary critic's identity has been formed with the haunting death knells of Auschwitz and Belsen ringing in his ears. "We cannot pretend," he exclaims, "that Belsen is

---

[8] E.g., *BT*, 'Attempt at a Self-Criticism', in *BT*, 17-27 (23); 1974, 151.

[9] See, e.g., Karl Marx (1975), *Early Writings*, Penguin, 244.

[10] D. Daiches Raphael (1960), *The Paradox of Tragedy: The Mahlon Powell Lectures, 1959*, George Allen & Unwin Ltd., London, 37-68.

[11] Nietzsche, 1974, 343f.; 108; *BT*, 'Attempt', 26.

[12] George Steiner (1995), 'Tribute to Donald MacKinnon', *Theology* vol. 98, 2-9 (6).

irrelevant to the responsible life of the imagination"[*LS*, 22]. Almost in shock, Steiner recalls that

> Barbarism prevailed on the very ground of Christian humanism, of Renaissance culture and classic rationalism. We know that some of the men who devised and administered Auschwitz had been trained to read Shakespeare or Goethe, and continued to do so [*LS*, 23].

Without intending to conceive of bygone eras after the manner of Edenic golden ages, Steiner indicates that this particularly horrific recent story of human self-mutilation that pummels his imagination leaves its indelible mark by calling into question the whole humanist heritage of the most recent centuries, particularly this recently past one. Smashed are the liberal dreams of human progress through technological advance. After all, Steiner emphasises, as well as being incapable of making the "future less vulnerable to the inhuman"

> Science may have given tools and insane pretences of rationality to those who devise mass murder [*LS*, 25].

These statements are left without further elaboration or justification, as if the mere mention of twentieth-century history clearly supports Steiner's claims. Indeed, David Tracy argues that

> this interruption of the Holocaust is a frightening disclosure of the real history within which we have lived.[13]

Steiner's question of what it is that reduces human beings, particularly those who pride themselves on their rational, and aesthetic heritages to the status of beasts, poses itself as intractable [*LS*, 23]. And yet consciousness of it places an intolerable strain on late twentieth-century speech and culture. If Nietzsche's madman called into question the legitimacy of living as if God was not dead, Steiner calls into question procedures of avoidance of the carnage in the contemporary formation of human identity: "We come *after*, and that is the nerve of our condition" [*LS*, 22].

Particularly troublesome religious imagery and symbolism haunt his reflections on the human disaster that was the *Shoah*, and this from one conscious of his place as a *secular* Jew. Those dark days of the mid-

---

[13] David Tracy (1994), *On Naming the Present: Reflections in God, Hermeneutics, and Church*, SCM Press, London, 64; cf. 67f.

twentieth century raise the whole question of God in a manner that renders any attempt at a theodicy problematically facile. If, as Moltmann claims,

> The suffering of a single innocent child is an irrefutable rebuttal of the notion of the almighty and kindly God in heaven.

how much more six million Jewish people, among many others?[14] Expressed is Steiner's almost unutterable horror over a God who "suffers the gusts of murderous exasperation at the Jews".[15] He quickly changes this image, somewhat, as if this thought is too shocking to even entertain. While the dark mood remains, the divine exasperation at human self-mutilation becomes equally disturbingly depicted as producing the sigh of lethargy and increasing passivity. In a medieval Polish parable, recited in *DT*, God is depicted as being found by a Rabbi sitting in a dark corner in a small synagogue. On being questioned as to why he was there, God replied, "with a small voice: 'I am tired, Rabbi, I am tired unto death'" [*DT*, 353]. So it is "When God's back parts are towards man, [that] history is Belsen" [*LS*, 122].

Although Steiner does recognise the post-1989 light that has begun to shine over the end of the century, he is wary of attributing too much to it and claims that

> Kafka's stark finding that 'there is abundance of hope but none for us' may prove to be sober reportage [*NPS*, 134].

Correspondingly, he is painfully forced to conclude that

> To a degree which numbs understanding, this entire crucible of creation and of hope now lies in ash.[16]

In this image that expresses the darkness of history, alluding to the post-gas chamber incineration of the executed, hope can no longer be considered to be an option. How can one continue to hope after the day that hope died [*LS*, 196]?

---

[14] Jürgen Moltmann (1981), *The Trinity and the Kingdom of God: The Doctrine of God*, trans. Margaret Kohl, SCM Press, London, 47.

[15] *LS*, 121, based on a rereading of Exodus 4:24.

[16] 1984, 13; cf. *LS*, 196.

Hope and the will to action spring from the capacity of the human mind to forget, from the instinct for necessary oblivion [*LS*, 122].

It is this sensibility that fuels Steiner's appreciation of tragic drama since in the latter, read 'realistically' and 'mimetically', one encounters a tragic perspective on the nature being in the world. For here is one whose Jewish post-Auschwitz sensibilities and his reading of tragic drama interrogate the shortened memories of liberal optimism, and raise the problem of hope in a world whose memory is punctuated by humanly caused devastation. And yet Steiner's early paintings of hope characterise it in an optimistic vein, allowing it to stand, therefore, in stark contrast with his reading of tragic drama's tragic vision. It is only later, when hope is taken beyond the scope of all optimisms and pessimisms, that it is able to play a more important role in his imagination.

Into the Night of Terror: The Black Art of "Absolute Tragedy"

Defining the Complex?

Reflection on tragedy certainly is a risky business. Not only is this so in the sense of the *phobos* ('fear') invoked over the dramatic events that is the spectator's or reader's lot [*P*, 1452bff.], however, but also in the sense that the multifariousness of the different plays that constitute the category 'tragic drama' resist schematic specification. The literature contained within that generic expanse contains so many rhythmic and thematic variations that discovering a single melody appears to be impossible. For instance, Shakespearean tragedy is not a homogenous whole, and neither is Attic tragedy; moreover, there are great differences between these two periods. As Kaufmann recognises, "theories of tragedy always run the risk" of activating Procrustean tendencies to excise those elements which stubbornly refuse to fit.[17]

Nevertheless, although Vickers claims that because tragedies "are all unique, and we need no special key to appreciate them", and thereby definition becomes "notoriously difficult", he does discern a central core or thematic pulse.[18] One may, therefore, in Wittgensteinian mood, speak with MacKinnon of being able to "at best ... discern a family resemblance

---

[17] Walter Kaufmann (1969), *Tragedy and Philosophy*, Doubleday, New York, xivf.

[18] Brian J. Vickers (1973), *Towards Greek Tragedy. Drama, Myth, Society*, Longman, London and New York, 41, 52.

between them", provided one avoids "a blind indifference to the multiple complexity of those works which we class together as tragedies".[19]

Recognising this difficulty in defining tragedy, Steiner attempts, through several thematic parallels, to explicate this core [see *TPS*, 535]. Hence, during his autopsy on tragic drama's corpse, a distinct image of tragedy implicitly forms, one which serves to define the tragic corpus, and one in which the spectres of Schopenhauer and Nietzsche may be more than faintly discerned and in which the literary concern remains as to whether he is attentive enough to the complexities of tragic drama.[20] The pattern that Steiner weaves highlights tragic drama's fifth-century BCE Athenian background [*DT*, x], although here a loose thread hangs in Steiner's presumptive and rhetorical presentation of a homogeneity of the three Attic dramatists. Controversially and without explicit justification, he proceeds further to classify only a few of their extant plays as utterly unique "high tragedy", "absolute tragedy" or "tragedy in the radical sense".[21] These plays alone truly fulfil his explicitly unstated literary 'rules' of tragic drama [see *AT*, 131], albeit in *L* and *Timon of Athens* Steiner does admit, on one occasion, that the Shakespearean mould of tragicomedy is broken by the "dramatic ontology" of the "tragic vision".[22]

From a purely literary perspective, Steiner certainly appears to have Procrusteanly selected tragic dramas according to a pre-defined "tragic vision" of "absolute Tragedy", failing to acknowledge the *basic* nature of the Athenian *texts* themselves in canonic-categorisation. If, as Frye declares, *tragedy* is a description of an artistic form that dramatises "a certain kind of structure or mood" of human conflict and suffering, particularly where the disaster is sparked by the protagonist(s) own action(s), then it is only by analogy, but therefore really, that we can speak

---

[19] Donald M. MacKinnon (1969), *The Stripping of the Altars: The Gore Memorial Lecture Delivered on 5 November 1968 in Westminster Abbey, and Other Papers and Essays on Related Topics*, Collins, London, 42.

[20] See Kaufmann, 83, 234; Raymond Williams (1966), *Modern Tragedy*, Chatto and Windus, London, 57f.

[21] *DT*, x; xi; cf. *TPS*, 538; *AT*, 130. In doing this, however, Steiner is not alone [see, e.g., I.A. Richards (1924), *Principles of Literary Criticism*, Routledge & Kegan Paul, London, 247; Lionel Abel (1963), *Metatheatre: A New View of Dramatic Form*, Hill & Wang, New York, 5].

[22] *TPS*, 540; cf. *DT*, xiii. However, *AT*, 133 limits this only to *Timon*.

of tragedy generally in a non-dramatic context (perhaps a distinguishing of 'tragic drama' and 'tragedy' could indicate this difference).[23]

However, the reason for Steiner's doing this is because of his perception of the tragic ontology.

Absolutely Tragic! Schopenhauer's Shadow Over the Unhoused

While Myers claims that tragic drama is "two-sided always", according to Roochnik its overall mood is optimistic, "both illuminating and affirming of the value of human life".[24] By this he appears to intend the fact that through the unfolding of the tragic events the protagonist undergoes a process of learning and repenting of her tragic mistake while suffering nobly.   Lear, for example, arguably develops in stature through his struggles with his sanity on the heath. Reunion, albeit momentary, with the daughter he had foolishly estranged is his 'reward'.

For Steiner, on the contrary, the proper (philosophical?) core of "absolute tragedy" "is a terrible, stark insight into human life", one that is "almost [so] unendurable" to human sensibility and reason that it is infrequently "vigorously professed" [*DT*, 9; xiif.]. The performance of tragedy's *Leitmotiv* combines the cries of pain and sorrow which accompany any period of sustained sounding of the death knell. Its dark colour "entails a stringent nihilism" and "a stringently negative, despairing view of man's presence in the world" [*DT*, xii].

Two synoptical citations seminally encapsulate Steiner's account of this "annihilating terror" [*TPS*, 539]: that placed by Sophocles on the lips of Silenus, which similarly animates Nietzsche's *BT*: "it is best not to have been born", and second best, to die young;[25] and Gloucester's fatalistic expression: "the gods kill for their sport as wanton boys do flies" [*TPS*, 536]. These are reinforced further by Kafka's haunting *summa*, "there is abundance of hope, but none for us" [*TPS*, 536].

Here is an account in which human beings are presented as discovering themselves imprisoned within an inhospitably suffering and destabilising cosmos. With little to create laughter from the victims' perspective, human life is thereby rendered a terrifically tragic cosmic "practical joke", at humanity's expense of course, and "paradox".[26] In

---

[23] Northrop Frye (1966), *Anatomy of Criticism*, Atheneum, New York, 162; cf. J. Cheryl Exum (1992), *Tragedy and Biblical Narrative: Arrows of the Almighty*, Cambridge, 1.

[24] Henry A. Myers (1956), *Tragedy: A View of Life*, Ithaca, N.Y., 4; David A. Roochnik (1990), *The Tragedy of Reason. Toward a Platonic Conception of Logos*, Routledge, New York and London, xi.

[25] *TPS*, 536; *AT*, 129; cf. *BT*, 42.

[26] *AT*, 131; *DT*, 128.

such a universe humanity can exist only as *Unheimlichkeit*, "one who is thrust out of doors", as "unwanted in life" and "an unwelcome guest in the world" [*DT*, xiif.]. As with Schopenhauer, Steiner indicates a "daemonic negation" and "tragic rift, an irreducible core of inhumanity ... [which lies] in the mystery of things", something particularly perceivable in the Attic poets' admission of the cruelty of the malevolent gods [*DT*, xi, 16]. This negation operates blindly, but necessarily, as a cruel "*autre*" or "outside" at whose hands humanity, as unwitting "intruders on creation", suffers in the most complete and horrific manner in the ensuing conflict.[27]

During these "[pre-]destined" hostilities humanity's fate is portrayed in the most horrific of terms [*AT*, 129]: being blinded, mocked and ambushed, lawlessly tortured, chastised and humiliated, and therefore "destined to undergo unmerited, incomprehensible, arbitrary suffering and defeat" [*AT*, 129]. In such an existence, "non-existence or early extinction are urgent desirates". This is Silenus' wisdom [*TPS*, 536].

Here Steiner moves beyond the Nietzschean reading of tragedy by implying not merely that the world is not evolving toward an ultimate goal or redemption of present horrors, but rather existence *itself* is ultimately cruel [see *BT*, §7]. Nietzsche, on the other hand, even in the *BT*, a work in which the hand of Schopenhauer may be strongly felt, can invoke the image of an amoral child-god in capricious yet playful mood in her creative activity [*BT*, §24]. His later discussions, moreover, clearly implicate not so much existence's hostile nature toward human aspirations, as its utter indifference "beyond good and evil".[28]

Although Steiner's account of tragedy primarily portrays the tragic confrontation of humanity with the cruel inhuman *autre*, he does not completely fail to provide a suggestion of the relation of the tragic to the 'ethical' problem of human activity and responsibility, that which Vickers describes as integral to the tragic drama's plot.[29] In doing this Steiner implicitly distinguishes himself from Schopenhauer and Nietzsche since, as Houlgate declares, Nietzsche's Schopenhauerian and anti-Aristotelian portrayal of the tragic hero's inevitable destruction "by supra-personal cosmic forces" tends to shift questions of responsibility and blame onto a transcendental plane.[30] Steiner, however, announces that the heroic nature

---

[27] *DT*, 128; 1996, 129.

[28] See 'Attempt', *BT*, 22.

[29] Vickers 3, 52.

[30] Stephen Houlgate (1986), *Hegel, Nietzsche and the Criticism of Metaphysics*, Cambridge, 213. Is there a tendency towards ethical quietism in Nietzsche? [see 216ff.].

of the protagonist "does not make him innocent" of the unwitting creation of his *metabole* (reversal of fortune), and that personal activity and destiny are interconnected [*DT*, 9f.]. The enormity of this suffering, however, entails that this concordance is often difficult to make out, with there clearly being no poetic justice (e.g., Lear, Oedipus, and Cadmus in *The Bacchae*).[31]

The reason for this is that what generally appears to be treated almost banally as Aristotle's named tragic 'flaw' [*P*, 1452b] in some writers receives a much more radical and Schopenhaurian treatment in Steiner, therein traversing the thematic paths more of *kakia* (radical defect or wickedness) and 'original sin' than mere flaw.[32] So in speaking of the hero's 'sacrilege' (*Frevel*) in overstepping the limits of individual action, Steiner refers to a "fall of man" and locates tragedy in some fatality of over-reaching or self-mutilation *inescapable* from human *nature* [*DT*, xi]. Here, the newly born become inescapably entangled in a conflict beyond their control, so that even their own actions are generated by their mere existing. So, for example, Lear's rash moment of temper was no mere bolt out from the blue, as the passions of the succeeding scenes indicate.[33] After all, in his lamentations over this century's "carnival of bestiality" and the enduring scars of the *Shoah*, Steiner argues that the Jews have only "*committed the crime of being*", although he does elsewhere claim that the Jew brings humanity face to face with an unflattering and threatening Other [*TPS*, 134, 129].

Even apparently pure and innocent actions have consequences far beyond their horizon, as Cordelia discovered to her cost. Hence, the well-intended Oedipus, as an apparent plaything of the gods, could justly echo Lear's torment of being "a man more sinned against than sinning" [*L*, III.ii.59]. He had *unwittingly* both committed patricide in his act of self-defence against an ambushing stranger, and become involved in incest in marrying a woman who was later discovered to be his mother. And these ironically occurred because he had attempted to flee the prediction of these events in the first place.

Tragedy itself provides no answers to theodicy questions. Lear's occasional cries to the gods and citations of fate or the planetary motions, as if they were the actors in the piece, appear to issue as projections in a

---

[31] See *DT*, 9, 128, 222.

[32] On Schopenhauer's postulation of a cosmic "original sin", see Williams, 1966, 37.

[33] Martha Craven Nussbaum appears to under-acknowledge the fragility of goodness of *character*, in arguing that "the change should come not from deliberate wickedness, but from the pressure of *external* circumstances over which they have no control" [Nussbaum (1986), *Fragility and Goodness: Luck and Ethics in Greek Tragedy and Philosophy*, Cambridge, 382].

momentary escaping from admitting personal responsibility (a process that Lear later reverses). Anti-fate speeches are put into the mouths of those evil characters who appear to be mentally alert (e.g. Edmund), in contrast with the honest characters who are presented generally as being less than mentally capable (e.g., Kent and Gloucester). Therefore, exclusively attributing the action to a transcendent power, for example, as Georgopoulos does, is difficult to maintain, particularly in *L*.[34] And yet, especially in certain Greek tragedies, with their greater complexity than Elizabethan on the nature of the action's source, 'fate' does almost occasionally appear above the stage as another principal actor.[35] Nevertheless, one must bear in mind the fact that it is precisely in his attempt to escape his predicted destiny of patricide and *mater coniugium* that Oedipus tragically creates it for himself.[36] Moreover, where *The Bacchae* presents the divine destruction of the human this is understood to be the punishment for the human offence by Pentheus of the deity Dionysius, although the nature of Dionysius appears suggestively arbitrary. Nevertheless, Vickers probably goes too far in the opposite, Hegelian, direction to Georgopoulos when affirming that "Greek Tragedy is about people, and what they do to each other".[37] Vickers is on safer territory, however, when claiming that Aristotle's silence on the issue is more of an indicator "that the Greeks did not evaluate tragedy with these rigid concepts".[38]

Steiner's interpretation of the fall enables one to legitimately notice that the world is one in which the well-meaning and the innocent are implicated in this arbitrary suffering, as is the case with Cordelia. Following Aristotle's comments that the fall of someone "innocent" is merely shocking but not tragic, and that tragic drama displays the fall of a

---

[34] N. Georgopoulos, 'Tragic Action', in *Tragedy and Philosophy*, ed. N. Georgopoulos, Macmillan, London, 104-122 (107).

[35] So Eric Auerbach (1953), *Mimesis: The Representation of Reality in Western Literature*, trans. Willard R. Trask, Princeton University Press, 319. Cf. Paul Ricoeur (1992), *Oneself as Another*, trans. Kathleen Blamey, University of Chicago Press, Chicago and London, 241; H.D.F. Kitto (1956), *Form and Meaning in Drama*, Methuen, 174ff.

[36] Antigone speaks of Oedipus' "destiny", and the leading of the gods [*OC*, 251ff.]; and Oedipus himself makes a similar complaint on one occasion [*OC*, 964ff.], while on another enmeshes divine causality and his own responsibility [*OT*, 1329ff.].

[37] Vickers, 3; cf. *H*, 48, 67, 113, 123f., 236; Paolucci and Paolucci, xxiv; H. Lloyd-Jones (1971), *The Justice of Zeus*, University of California Press, 10.

[38] Vickers, 132; cf. E.R. Dodds (1973), *The Ancient Concept of Progress and Other Essays on Greek Literature and Belief*, Oxford, 70; Auerbach, 318.

great but flawed character, many commentators have softened the horror of her hanging through either textual amputation, in favour of engrafting a Hollywood-style ending (Holingshed, Spenser, Dr. Johnson and Nahum Tate), or a search for Cordelia's *hamartia*, thereby restoring some sense of 'poetic justice' [see *P*, 1452b.34ff.]. For example, Coleridge sought it in her pride, Muir in her obstinacy, and Cavell in her wilfulness and hardness.[39] Such an evasion from the tragic supports Steiner's claim of its unendurability. However, without any simple justification of Cordelia's behaviour, thereby making her into some model of perfection, it must be suggested that this slavish worship of Aristotle is unbecoming to *King Lear*, as well as a number of Greek tragedies. For example, in Sophocles' *Electra*, *Philoctetes* and *Oedipus at Colonius*, and Aeschylus' *The Eumenides*, the 'change' is from misfortune to good fortune. Sophocles' *Antigone* and Aeschylus' *The Libation Bearers* move from misfortune to even greater misfortune. Sophocles' *Ajax* and Aeschylus' *Prometheus* portray *pure* misfortune (however, Aeschylus' plays are more akin to trilogies, which portrayed immense changes from misfortune to good fortune). Therefore, Aristotle's is a sufficient observation only of Sophocles' *Oedipus the King* and *The Women of Trachis*, and Aeschylus' *Seven Against Thebes*, *Persians* and *Agamemnon*.

This nihilistic account is accentuated in Steiner's discourse about 'endings' within tragic drama. Tragedies climax in a catastrophe that cannot "resolved by rational innovation", and declare

> that the spheres of reason, order, and justice are terribly limited and that no progress in our science or technical resources will enlarge their relevance [*DT*, 291, 9].

Hence, he tenaciously contrasts the movements of tragedy and comedy (and even tragicomedy), with the former being a constant descent from prosperity to suffering and chaos [*DT*, 11f.]. In a not too dissimilar vein, Schopenhauer's own preference was for a *trauerspiel* ('mourning play') rather than *tragödie*, since the former "involves a steady, undeviating descent towards catastrophe, without the sudden twist which in its steadiness implies that the tragic issue arises not from accidental misfortune or exceptional design, but from the regular course of life".[40] So the

---

39 See Cavell, 290.

40 For a summary of Schopenhauer's pessimism, see Julian Young (1992), *Nietzsche's Philosophy of Art*, Cambridge, ch. 1; M.S. Silk and J.P. Stern (1981), *Nietzsche on Tragedy*, Cambridge, 326.

strong, very nearly decisive, counter-currents of repair, of human radiance, of public and communal restoration.

in *Hamlet* and *Macbeth* speak volumes for them as tragic-comedies, Steiner continues.[41] There can be no 'rationalistic' thought of a resolution of the tragic conflict through the restoration of eternal justice within the drama (e.g., *Antigone, OT*), as is so recognisable in Hegelian dialectic with its "vision of harmony" in the sense of the "resolution" required for the collision [*H*, 135, 113]. So, in a passage recapitulating the melody of his dialectic, Hegel, in direct contrast to the mood pervading Steiner's account, states that "action, reaction, and resolution are constituent elements" in the tragic action [*H*, 130]. Lear's elder sisters and their husbands, "only deserve the fate they get" "on account of their atrocious conduct" [*H*, 89].[42] This Hegelian "vision of an affirmative reconciliation", Galle regards as an example of the post-Enlightenment's optimistic disjunction of the tragic, and Hodgson takes to be Hegel's "forgetfulness" of evil.[43] Robert R. Williams' thesis of Hegel's recovery of "the suppressed tragic elements", as "a reconstruction and critical corrective to the [theological] tradition", is, then, a surprising swimming against the stream of Hegelian scholarship.[44] Likewise, Silk and Stern warn that Hegel's was no facile optimistic approach to tragedy, for progress is strenuous and uncomfortable.[45] However, the frequently posed question is whether Hegel fatalistically regards *Geist*'s suffering as a 'necessary' means of progression toward the grand goal.

---

[41] Steiner's overall argument is not significantly affected by Williams' recognition that the 'ending' denotes not merely the final scenes but may be played out much earlier, so that death may occur much earlier than the end, as in *Ajax* [1966, 58; cf., Kaufmann, 192]. Nevertheless, this may raise a question about Steiner's treatment of *Hamlet* and *Macbeth*, since their own currents of repair insufficiently mask the preceding tragedy.

[42] For a discussion of Hegel's conception of eternal justice and absolute rationality within tragic drama, see Houlgate, 205; A.C. Bradley (1962), 'Hegel's Theory of Tragedy', in *H*, 367-88 (378).

[43] Roland Galle (1993), 'The Disjunction of the Tragic: Hegel and Nietzsche', in Georgopoulos (ed.), 39-56 (40; cf. 48f.); Peter C. Hodgson (1985), 'Georg Wilhelm Friedrich Hegel', in *Nineteenth Century Religious Thought in the West, vol. I*, eds. Ninian Smart, John Clayton, Patrick Sherry, and Steven T. Katz, Cambridge, 81-121 (111).

[44] Robert R. Williams (1993), 'Hegelianism', in *Encyclopaedia of Modern Theology*, ed. A.E. McGrath, Oxford, 250-258 (251).

[45] Silk and Stern, 314.

Apart from the part played by the music, Steiner maintains that redemption is either too costly or too late. There is no "compensation" or adequate healing of wounds, only "irreparable" damage [*DT*, 128f., 8]. For example, Lear's joy in the 'dream scene', albeit pervaded with shame in the acquired recognition of his folly, is quickly shattered by subsequent events which are all the more "dark and comfortless" *because of* the hint of redemption that has preceded it [*L*, IV.7]. Moreover, although Steiner identifies a "liturgical-grace note" in *L*, it must be remembered that when the religious Edgar praises the restoration of order and divine justice he is trivialising the pronounced devastation and waste.[46] According to Steiner, only Aeschylus' *Oresteia* ends in an affirmation of unequivocal progress, and it is a very special case, although what that entails is not elaborated. Redemptive themes are also present within Aeschylus' *Eumenides* and Sophocles' *OC*. However, care in interpreting their significance is cautioned [*DT*, 7].

This account of tragic endings leads to the claim that

> Antigone is perfectly aware of what will happen to her, and in the wells of his stubborn heart Oedipus knows also [*DT*, 7].

If tragedies end in catastrophe, and the hero *knows* that this is to be her fate, is it heroic or merely foolish to live on? May not this very *knowledge* paralyse human activity? Steiner's discourse of the dignity and heroic nobility of the sufferer "in the very excesses of his suffering", of being hallowed "as he had passed through flame", in part echoes Nietzsche's *BT* and his later Zarathustrian vision, and avoids Schopenhauer's belief that "it is better to tear his heart away from life, to turn his willing away from it, not to love the world and life".[47] Nevertheless, this anti-ethical concern over pessimism remains.

However, is this not an example of Steiner's over-simplifying the complexities involved in tragic drama? Surely Lear at least does not and cannot, in his short-sightedness, foresee the consequences of his earlier folly (can any of the others?). Indeed, Lear even entertains the hopeful possibility of reimbursing his disavowed daughter in the "come let us away to prison" speech [*L*, V.iii.8]. There is still hope, while the story *has not ended for them*. Even the audience cannot anticipate at least Cordelia's death, given the critical reception of her hanging. Moreover, Oedipus' natural mother (Jocasta) specifically attempts to avoid the oracle's

---

[46] Citation from *AT*, 142; cf. *L*, V.iii.169.

[47] *DT*, 9; Schopenhauer, cited in Silk and Stern, 329.

prediction of tragedy by sending him away at birth; and Oedipus later flees from Corinth for the same reason.

Steiner's 'too-late' could occur only as a death-bed lament when the cup of possibility runs dry. Where that hope is fulfilled, even if limitedly, one certainly steps beyond the boundaries of tragedy into tragicomedy and melodrama. But even here the fulfilment does not provide an *adequate* compensation. Events have moved too far, as Exum argues with respect to a Job who may both never be able to trust God again and never "again feel secure in such a universe".[48] The restoration of Duncan's royal house in his son (Malcolm) bears the weight of remembrance and the scars incurred over both the loss of his father (Duncan) and of the adept military commander (Macbeth). How much of a loss for Scotland these are one can only conjecture.

The Dead shall not Rise in Christ

Steiner's immediate concern in *DT* is with the post-Racinian death of Attic tragedy. Nevertheless, from pressing his almost parenthetic comments on the relationship of tragic drama (dramatising *this* world) and Christian hope (apparently imagining *another* world), the doors swing wide open into the caverns of questions of Christian identity and practice in the face of the indications of the tragic.

Although Christianity is not explicitly implicated in the assassination of tragedy, its "anti-tragic" nature for Steiner provides unwelcome grounds for the genre's resurrection [see *DT*, 324], although Sutherland's reflections draw attention to the over-simplistic nature of Steiner's assertion that "There has been no specifically Christian mode of tragic drama even in the noontime of the faith" [*DT*, 331].[49] Taking this metaphor further, Kuhns argues that tragic drama has been *buried* under Christian influence, apart from a short-lived Elizabethan rebirth.[50] "Christianity is an anti-tragic vision of the world" [*DT*, 331].

---

[48] Exum, 13; cf. 8.

[49] Stewart Sutherland indicates that "in actual practice" Christianity has provided a post-Renaissance matrix out of which has come a prodigious amount of tragic expression in many of the arts [Sutherland (1990), 'Christianity and Tragedy', *Journal of Literature and Theology* vol. 4, 157-168 (157)].

[50] Richard Kuhns (1991), *Tragedy: Contradiction and Repression*, University of Chicago Press, Chicago and London, 5.

Consequently, the notion of a 'Christian *tragedy*', rather than a Christian *use* of tragedy (which, at best, would be 'tragicomedy'), is incoherent.

The central problem appears to be eschatological. The eschatology of the Christian story furnishes hope with an essential optimism, a sense of the eschatologically comic rather than the tragic. According to Steiner, the gospel's direction is not downward, as in tragedy, but rather toward a "happy ending" [*DT*, 332].

It is admitted that "within its [i.e., Christianity's] essential optimism" there are moments of error, anguish and defeat, what he names "episodic or partial Tragedy" [*DT*, 332]. For example, one could ask what use the promises of release from Egyptian bondage could have had for the murdered Hebrew slave of Exodus 2:11, or his family? "[T]here are moments of despair" and "cruel setbacks", and sorrow even over the death of a Christian. However, Steiner continues, it is crucial to note that these only temporarily and provisionally "occur during the ascent toward grace" [*DT*, 332]. Hence despair is a mortal sin [*DT*, 342].

For example, some of P.T. Forsyth's reflections on the use of tragedy for Christian theology support Steiner' contention here. He argues that tragic drama only raises the question of the problem of life, whereas the 'solution' lies in "the Divine *Commedia* on the scale of all existence", albeit tragically achieved in the overcoming of the tragic collision and of the definitive 'new creation'.[51]

This entails, Steiner continues, that, at best, the Christian story can only be properly depicted in tragic-comic terms, or as Raphael describes, as "salvational tragedy".[52] Even the cross itself cannot be read tragically, since in the resurrection death has been destroyed, and the thereby released protagonist is raised to the Father [*DT*, 331f.]. This stains the Christian story in the colours of *comedy*, furnishing the tale with a "happy ending" which is extended not only to Christ but to all who have faith in him [see *DT*, 31].

Here, Steiner is not raising the question as to the ontological status of the dark eschatological themes of Judgment and Hell, but is rather making the claim that Christian *hope* takes the form of an optimistically unqualified 'All shall be well'. It is this optimistic form of hope for an eschatological way out, a righting of the wrongs, a "compensating heaven", that resists the tragic [*DT*, 129]. However, by way of partial and tentative critique of Steiner's argument, could one not ask whether the pain of losing a loved one in an accident, for example, can ever become

---

[51] P.T. Forsyth (1917), *The Justification of God: Lectures for War-Time on a Christian Theodicy*, Latimer House Ltd., London, 76; cf. 30.

[52] Raphael, 82.

bearable, or the psychological trauma less prominent, because of one's belief in or knowledge that some form of compensation will be paid out later, even if that be a reunion with the beloved?

"Real Tragedy" in Steiner's account is the torment of the too-late and the uncomforted solitude, whereas, according to Steiner, there is never a too-late in Christianity [*DT*, 332]. In the latter, as also in romantic melodrama, the tension is already released.[53]

> Christianity offers to man an assurance of final certitude and repose in God. It leads the soul toward justice and resurrection ...

revealing original sin to be a "joyous error" (*felix culpa*) and promising a restoration "to a condition far more exalted than was Adam's innocence" [*DT*, 332].

Christian anti-tragedy is further supported by the Hebraic sense of, or assured hope for, divine cosmic justice, even if that justice be, as yet, absent to one's sight. Tragedy, Steiner declares, is alien to the Judaic sense of the world, since the latter is

> vehement in its conviction that the order of the universe and of man's estate is accessible to reason. The ways of the Lord are neither wanton nor absurd [*DT*, 4].

Job's story does not counter this observation, standing as it does on the fringes of Judaiac theology. Moreover, Job's later days are divinely blessed [Job, 42:12]. And so they should be, for he is a divine "parable of justice" [*DT*, 8], a sense of which is continued in the Christian tradition in the image of the divine vindication of Christ and his followers.[54] There is, therefore, a real sense in which Exum's reading of Job as tragic hero is not a *natural* rendering of the narrative as presented. The epilogue, whether a later addition or not, speaks overwhelmingly in compensatory and reconciliatory tones [Job, 42:7-17].

---

[53] See *DT*, 332; Karl Jaspers (1969), *Tragedy is Not Enough*, trans. Harald A.T. Reiche, Harry T. Moore, Karl W. Deutsch, Archon Books, 31, 38f.

[54] Raphael moves further than Steiner by adding that these beliefs in divine providence and justice entail the belief that the problem of innocent suffering must receive a solution, thereby undermining the agnostic or Manichaean sense of tragedy's religious questioning [73]. These theodicies quieten one's questioning and satisfy the intellect, or at least the emotions, in their illusion of intellectual certainty.

Hoping Through the Tragic

'Predictive' Eschatologies

Steiner has painted a terrifying portrait of the drama of existence, the central character of which bears the markings of humanity's demonic torturer. In such a barbaric world, it is unsurprising that forms of escape have been devised. Indeed, according to the early Nietzsche, without such illusions, to which we could add hope as the manner of taking one beyond despair, one would be resigned to a paralysing, despairing, life-denying, nausea [*BT*, 60, 110]. However, some forms of illusion merely appear as rather fragile prophylactics against pessimism's feared assaults. Others, more menacingly, deny life by refusing to face the tragic, and thereby become "dangerous illusions". Particularly can this be so when the illusion becomes an optimistic over-riding of the fragility and limitations of the human.

Nietzsche presents Christianity as just such a repressive form of life-denial, a nausea over this life that is dressed up as faith in another, better, life to come. In a broadly similar fashion Steiner has identified within Christianity a hope that cannot take the tragic tragically, but always possesses the optimistic resources to surmount tragedy's life-limiting. Recalling his post-Auschwitz sensibilities, Steiner's argument once again raises the Marxian question of the morality of any optimistic approach to life in the present that leaves that present's structures untouched.

One general type of eschatology that falls into this categorisation of an optimistic approach to the Ultimate Future, is that which could be termed 'predictive' eschatology. Such a perspective is broadly detectable within the eschatologies of late seventeenth and eighteenth-century federal (J. Cocceius) and early pietistic (G. Schrenk, G. Möller) theologies, and their generation of the contemporary eschatological millenarian debates.[55] Here, with a biblical outline of the course of the *series temporum*, the future becomes identifiably blue-printable for, and esoterically known by, the 'initiated'.[56] As Cocceius declared, *Prophetia est quasi rerum futurarum historia* (prophecy is, as it were, the history of future things), or

---

[55] See Robert G. Clouse (ed.) (1977), *The Meaning of the Millennium*, IVP, Downers Grove; Anthony A. Hoekema (1978), *The Bible and the Future*, Paternoster, Exeter, ch. 15. On Joachim de Fiore's trinitarian periodisation of universal history, see M. Reeves (1969), *The Influence of Prophecy in the Later Middle Ages. A Study in Joachimism*, Oxford; Jürgen Moltmann (1996), *The Coming of God: Christian Eschatology*, trans. Margaret Kohl, SCM Press, London, 143f.

[56] So, for example, Wayne Grudem (1994), *Systematic Theology: An Introduction to Biblical Doctrine*, IVP, Leicester, 1091.

as a contemporary writer has urged, "legitimate [prophetic] forecasts of the future that God has authorized".[57]   In this mood, elevated to central importance amongst biblical writings has frequently been the book which Luther had brushed aside, the *Revelation of John*, for it supposedly contains the prophecy of the End-time.[58]

Consequently, as Moltmann claims, this "Historical eschatology has de-fatalized the experience of history", in the sense that the dark corridors of the future have been lit and therefore their passageways displayed to full view.[59]   It optimistically (and docetically) leaps the boundaries of human epistemic limitations by seeing the outline of that which has not yet happened to history.   And yet it has, in some sense, *already occurred* for God, and is therefore subsequently revealed to Christian perception.[60]   Contingency is thereby ruled out of court by the fact that no matter what form human creativity takes it will inevitably (because God 'does not lie or make mistakes') follow the pattern of events laid down in scripture's eschatological predictions.   (It appears also that the human reception of an infallible revelation has been eschatologically adjusted, thereby allowing for the writers' perfection in the hearing and recording of it.)

Are these predictive-type eschatologies, whose hope for their good future is secure and infallible, theological versions of what Lash describes as the "flight into thought", or instances of a desire for "reassuringly

---

[57] J. Barton Payne (1973), *Encyclopaedia of Biblical Prophecy: The Complete Guide to their Scriptural Predictions and their Fulfilment*, Hodder and Stoughton, London, 9; cf. vi. Robert R. Grundy "reconsider[s] the chronology of the rapture" [Grundy (1973), *The Church and the Tribulation*, Zondervan Publishing House, Grand Rapids, Michigan, 9].

[58] On the issue of Revelation's predictive nature, see Christopher Rowland (1982), *The Open Heaven: A Study of Apocalyptic in Judaism and Early Christianity*, SPCK, London, 143f.; Leon Morris (1969), *The Revelation of St. John: An Introduction and Commentary*, IVP, Leicester, 45; Robert H. Mounce (1977), *The Book of Revelation*, Eerdmans, Grand Rapids, Michigan, 19f.

[59] Moltmann, 1996, 133f.

[60] On apocalyptic literature's determinism, see David C. Sim (1986), *Apocalyptic Eschatology in the Gospel of Matthew*, Cambridge University Press, 41f.; H.B. Swete (1909), *The Apocalypse of St. John*, 3rd ed., London, 2; Mounce, 20, 24; D.S. Russell (1992), *Divine Disclosure: An Introduction to Jewish Apocalyptic*, SCM Press, London, 90.   However, Christopher Rowland disputes the deterministic reading of *Revelation*, and instead argues that there is the demand for action [Rowland (1993), *Revelation*, Epworth Press, London, 21].

comprehensive explanations of the world"?[61] A statement of Carl Henry, for example, although not speaking explicitly of eschatology or hope, suggests that this critique has some weight:

> The choice for modern man is between Christianity and nihilism, between the logos of God and the ultimate meaningless of life and the world.[62]

The alternative to Christian hope for Henry, one imagines, is quite unthinkable.

Inconclusive Interrogations: Steiner's Place for Hope

In his writings on tragedy, Steiner does not ask or answer the question of how the human is able to continue living while simultaneously recognising the debilitating pounding that one takes in an eminently inhospitable universe.   One recalls Steiner's Silenus sounding lament on the advantageousness of both suicide and renunciation of child-bearing [*TPS*, 536].   The tragic may be "a religious-metaphysical" "*world-view*" which mimetically springs from "outrage" and "protests at the conditions of life".[63] But, as he further notes, absolute tragedy is unendurable for human sensibilities.   Does this entail that "suicide is the only serious philosophic question", the only available option, as Steiner cites Camus as asserting [*TPS*, 536]?

A markedly different sensibility is perceivable in his writings on hermeneutics, which moves beyond both the Schopenhauerian account and the nihilism of Adorno's stark prescription.   This sits uneasily with his presentation of the tragic vision, perhaps being an example of his own refusal of simple conceptual resolution.   His published studies are too thematically   sporadic,   occasionalistic,   and   interrogative   to   be systematically   contained,   a   further   link   to   Donald MacKinnon,   a theologian whose own occasionalism manifests

> the belief that any system cannot in the end do justice to the realm of irreducible fact.[64]

---

[61] Nicholas Lash (1989), 'Incarnation and Determinate Freedom', in *On Freedom*, ed. Leroy S. Rouner, University of Notre Dame Press, Notre Dame, Indiana, 15-29 (24).

[62] Carl F. Henry (1976), *God, Revelation and Authority, volume 1*, Waco, Texas, 41.

[63] *TPS*, 535f.; *DT*, 167f.

[64] Christopher Devanny (1997), 'Truth, Tragedy and Compassion: Some Reflections on the Theology of Donald MacKinnon', *New Blackfriars* vol. 75, 32-42 (32).

Without identically repeating the Nietzschean pattern of redemption through artistic performance, Steiner does insist that the process of creativity itself is transcendence.[65] As Neumann proclaims with reference to *RP*, "art becomes the mouthpiece of meaning, that which makes humankind feel at home in the world".[66] Indeed, Steiner later complains about the loss of the primary sense of creativity to the parasitic stress of contemporary academia and journalism on review and commentary, with its welcoming of "those who can domesticate, who can secularize the mystery and summons of creation" [*RP*, 39].

In contrast, in the mid-1960s Steiner presents artistic creativity as dangerously rivalling the divine creativity and speaks of there being at the frontiers of language a "certitude of ... divine meaning" and a proof of a "transcendent presence in the fabric of the world" [*LS*, 58]. So, in 1989's *RP*, Steiner likens aesthetic creativity to an *imitatio* of the "inaccessible first *fiat*" [*RP*, 201].

And yet his enigmatic theology of culture is qualified, and even bears testimony to a *mysterious* Being, or "metaphysical scandal" of the incommensurability of the categories God and humanity.[67] Here, in the late 1960s and early 1970s Steiner begins to consciously situate his thoughts between two positions: first, the logocentric sacramental portrayal of the "Word's [real] presence in the word";[68] and second, what 1989's study explicitly identifies as pertaining to a "deconstructive and postmodernist counter-theology of absence" that is characterised by the "broken contract" of the relation of linguistic expression and the referential sayability of the world [*RP*, 122; 51]:

> the withdrawal of words from any reference to an external
> world to which they are a response.[69]

---

[65] Similar to Nietzsche, Steiner even discovers aethestic superiority in music [*LS*, 64; 1989, 6].

[66] Gerhard Neumann (1994), 'George Steiner's *Real Presences*', in Scott and Sharp, 247-261 (256).

[67] *LS*, 159. Steiner expresses mystery and unnameability in the essays, 'Schoenberg's *Moses und Aron*' [ibid., 169-182] and 'The Great Tautology' [*NPS*, 348-360]. This entails that he denies any grounds for a natural theology [1984, 96; *NPS*, 387f.].

[68] Steiner (1975), *After Babel: Aspects of Language and Translation*, Oxford University Press, London and New York, 231.

[69] Graham Ward (1993), 'George Steiner and the Theology of Culture', *New Blackfriars* vol. 74, 98-105 (100). Contra many reductive readings of the philosophy and hermeneutics of deconstruction Tracy argues that it is best understood as "linguistic therapy", exposing

Avoiding this second is an interesting move since it shows how Steiner, despite his presentation of the tragic and his approval of Adorno's advocacy of silence in the face of the unspeakability of Auschwitz, is not content with cultural and hermeneutical nihilism.[70]

In partial agreement with this second identified approach, he prevents the provision of a "theological insurance or underwriting" when noting the density of divine absence, admits that disclosure is partial in a hiddenness-in-revealedness paradox of the semantic act [*RP*, 164], and recognises that artistic creativity may be "eroded or possibly falsified by human transcription".[71]   Language, after all, is not only used to communicate "But to conceal, to leave unspoken".[72] Steiner is acutely sensitive to the difficulties involved in any act of translation, whether that be the translation of other grammars into one's own, or the act of interpreting the discourse of an other speaking from within one's own grammatical frame.   The Adamic linguistic divine presence was lost through the "fall" that was Babel's confusion and there then developed a "pluralistic framework" of "mutually incomprehensible tongues".[73] To a great extent human being is now estranged from the speech of her fellow human in the Babelic multifariousness of linguistic discourse. The need to translate is an indication of humanity's exile from herself. In this diversity "linguistic differences and the profoundly exasperating inability of human beings to understand each other have bred hatred and reciprocal contempt".[74]

Moreover, Steiner emphasises the "undecidability of unbounded sign-systems", with their weave of incommensurable connotation even in the formalisations of literature, and the excess of the signified beyond the signifier [*RP*, 61]. There are always further layers to be excavated, deeper shafts to be sunk into the manifold strata of inception in the archaeology of sense and meaning, without sterile punctuation through the "undecidability of unbounded sign-systems", as if figuration and representation can arrest hermeneutical openness in final closure [*RP*, 61].

Nevertheless, although meaning cannot be totally grasped, he asserts in contrast to the deconstructive indeterminacies of tracings, the

---

certain illusions [Tracy (1987), *Plurality and Ambiguity: Hermeneutics, Religion, Hope*, SCM Press, London, 60]. Similarly, Steiner explains deconstruction as being a significant unmasking of the pretensions and self-delusions of linguistic and epistemological claims to innocence and immediacy [cf. *RP*, chapter 2, §7].

[70] This is so even as early as his 1961 essay 'The Retreat from the Word' [*LS*, 31-56].

[71] Steiner, 'Introduction', in 1984, 7-22 (8); 1984, 85.

[72] 1975, 46.

[73] Ibid., 49.

[74] Ibid., 59.

artistic products "have in them the live vestiges of transcendent intrusion", an "edge of presence".[75]   In 1979 Steiner introduces discourse about reading

> *as if* ... the singular presence of the life of meaning in the text and work of art was a 'real presence'.[76]

What is presented here is a *moral*, rather than theoretical or empirical, way or leap beyond hermeneutic nihilism, an approach that is as "liberating as ... [it is] does not engage finality. It does not confront in immediacy the nihilistic supposition" [*NPS*, 33]. Descartes is cited as an example of this approach since he

> postulates the *sine qua non* that God will not systematically confuse or falsify our perception and understanding of the world, that He will not arbitrarily alter the rules of rationality (as these govern nature and as these are accessible to rational deduction and application) [ibid.].

Steiner continues,

> Without some such fundamental presupposition in regard to the existence of sense and of value, there can be no responsible response, no answering answerability to either the act of speech or text. Without some axiomatic leap towards a postulate of *meaningfulness*, there can be no striving towards intelligibility or value-judgement however provisional (and note the part of 'vision' in the provisional) [*RP*, 34].

It is in this context that a Pascalian sounding notion of a "wager on transcendence" that might be "wholly erroneous" is expressed, responding tentatively to Steiner's own admission that

> *On its own terms and planes of argument,* ... the challenge of deconstruction does seem to be irrefutable.[77]

---

[75] 1984, 85; *RP*, 229.
[76] 'Critic/Reader' in 1984, 67-98 (85).
[77] *RP*, 132; 4. Ward argues for Steiner's using this from 1979. However, although the notion is implicit in the language of the *as if*, the actual term does not appear in 'Critic/Reader'.

The idea of reciprocal encounter with the other (Other?) in the hermeneutic act is thereafter depicted through the language of faith, trust, risk and hope, or that of Kantian regulative ideals, since it is the *as if* of the "presence[s] of a realness" operative in the text. It is this wager that grounds the somewhat bold and controversial claim that "There is language, there is art, because there is 'the other'" [*RP*, 137].

> This instauration of trust, this entrance of man into the city of
> man, is that between word and world. Only in the light of that
> confiding can there be a history of meaning which is, by exact
> counterpart, a meaning of history [*RP*, 89].

Interpretation is encounter with the meaningful and authentic, but such things cannot be verified or legislated for. Steiner is well aware of the plural forms involved as consequences of the act of reading, and the provisionality, fragileness and risk that thereby ensues for any hermeneutics (and similarly for the act of translation since translation can never be accomplished but must nevertheless be pursued). Reading is a "never fully to be realized ideal of all interpretation and valuation" [*NPS*, 39].

A fruitful analogy for what Steiner is doing here could be found in Jürgen Habermas' 'ideal speech situation'. This situation is usually a counter-factual that serves to provide regulation and critique of all conversations, and a content and shape to all our strivings for authentic conversation. It does this by providing a vision of what communication could and should be, a goal to aim at. Tracy argues that although "we never find ourselves in the ideal speech situation", the "regulative model is useful for sorting out the ambiguities of all actual communication".[78]

Language of 'meaning' becomes appropriate when the reader learns new ways of seeing and reciprocally encountering the textual 'other' in an welcoming openness that transcends oneself and embraces that which is other.[79] Indeed, this answerability to the text, depending in some sense on presence-in-absence, is necessary for an ethical reading inseparable from the aesthetic, an inseparability that deconstruction has severed [*RP*, 101]. As Fuchs argues, "The texts must translate us before we can

---

[78] Tracy, 1987, 26.
[79] *RP*, 8; 141; *NPS*, 17.

translate them".[80] In this vulnerable encounter with the other, one's self-possession is undermined by our entertaining the stranger, a hermeneutical process for which there can be no closure. The risk is that the entertained "guest may turn despotic or venomous", and yet the gamble of *cortesia* in the communicative act is worth making [*RP*, 156].

> The reader opens himself to the autonomous being of the text. The dialectic of encounter and of vulnerability (the text can bring drastic hurt) is one in which the ontological core of the text, its presentness of inward being, both reveals and makes itself hidden.

This journeying, reminding us of our visitors' visas in existence, leads Steiner into a rich depiction of the eschatological significance of temporality which opens up the space for human hope in creative process. In *RP*, Steiner's reflections on the necessary place of hope in human life thereby suggest that his darkly painted view of existence is, or has to be for the sake of human survival, fundamentally incomplete, although, on saying that tragedy is hopeless, however, one must remind Steiner of the distinction between the recognition of this by the spectators and the retained hopeful agency of the dramas' characters. Language, as the future tense implies and expresses, knows no conceptual or projective finality, according to Steiner.

> Inside grammar, future tenses, optatives, conditionals are the formal articulation of the conceptual and imaginative phenomenality of the unbounded. What logic and grammatology define as the 'counter-factual' tells of a capacity absolutely central and specific to man. ... There is in reach of human speech an infinity of willed and dreamt supposition [*RP*, 135].

Life, and we must add even tragedies themselves, contains forms of human joy and creativity in ways that cannot be specified in advance or legislated for.[81] Creative and unlimited possibilities are open. Of course,

---

[80] Ernst Fuchs (1971), 'The Hermeneutical Problem', in *The Future of Our Religious Past*, ed. J.M. Robinson, London, 277.

[81] *RP*, 56. Steiner does at least hint, in *DT*, about the existence of "a fusion of grief and joy, of lament over the fall of man and rejoicing in the resurrection of his spirit" [*DT*, 9f.].

by way of qualification, one must point out that the merely futural is not necessarily the stuff of hope. After all, the thoughts of the future can be the places of dark and fearful imaginings, and even certain possibilities dreamt by some can bring destruction to the humanness of others. Nevertheless, bearing this qualification in mind, Steiner's point is that the future can be the inspirer of hope, expressed in the language of the counter-factual, but also he relates hope with discourse about the necessary tentativeness involved in trust, risk and the inherent fragility of these acts.

Subsequently, he metaphorically draws on the temporality of the Easter weekend, partially reflecting the *triduum mortis* of von Balthasar's *Mysterium Paschale*, in order to present the temporality of human hope.[82] Friday is portrayed as the day of solitude, failure and pain. And, indeed, Steiner would do well to recognise that it is a day of death, that boundary-limit of humanness and all forms of creativity. Sunday, by contrast, is a day of liberation, resurrection and justice, the 'resolution' of all our Good Fridays, although MacKinnon's writings indicate that the sense of 'resolution' should be theologically qualified so as not to exclude, reverse or undermine the prior consciousness of rupture.[83] It is "The lineaments of that Sunday [that] carry the name of hope", that provide propulsion to all our creative imaginings [*RP*, 232].

> But ours is the long day's journey of the Saturday. Between suffering, aloneness, unutterable waste on the one hand and the dreaming of liberation, of rebirth on the other. In the face of the torture of a child, of the death of love which is Friday, even the greatest art and poetry are almost helpless. In the Utopia of the Sunday, the aesthetic will, presumably, no longer have logic or necessity. ... [Artistic creations] have arisen out of waiting which is that of man. Without them, how could we be patient? [*RP*, 232].[84]

Steiner here uses this theme in a specific way, by way of reflection on *humanity's* perspective and vision of temporal and eschatological

---

Even Nietzsche regards art as a "metaphysical supplement of the reality of nature", a "transfiguring mirror" which transforms the imagination [*BT*, §24; also §21].

[82] *RP*, 231ff. Cf. Hans Urs von Balthasar (1990), *Mysterium Paschale: The Mystery of Easter*, trans. Aidan Nichols, T&T Clark, Edinburgh.

[83] See MacKinnon, *Borderlands of Theology and Other Essays*, eds. George W. Roberts and Donovan E. Smucker, Lutterworth Press, London, 102f.

[84] Ward fails to notice that the darkness belong to Friday, and not Saturday, when claiming that "even though the emphasis is on 'journeying', and the paradox leaves us not unparalysed, Steiner can only speak of emptiness, rupture, tragedy and waste 'in the *name* of hope'" [Ward, 1993, 'George Steiner', 104f.].

possibilities after the original Easter. Of course, one must note that for Jesus, Easter Saturday was not a day of journeying. Rather, Friday had ceased his life movements. Saturday was his day of death and hell, the day of the coldness and silence of a body beginning its decay in the grave. It is for this reason that Sunday's events can only be portrayed through language of miracle, eschatological *novum*, the unexpected.

But Steiner does not delineate his sources of his hopefulness, or examine or describe its genealogy. He admits that his wager is "itself in need of a clear foundation", and it is here that theological questions cannot be so easily bypassed if hope is not to succumb to self-induced delusion [*NPS*, 35]. Indeed, Steiner' eclectic use of religious images and theological themes suggest a *purely* regulative ideal, implying a non-realistic picture of God. Hence Ward is right to indicate that Steiner's "work emphasizes that such an appeal to the theological can only question".[85] Consequently, it is difficult to imagine that Steiner intends the referent of his theological language realistically. In an essay of 1985 he does admit to borrowing "vital currency, vital investments and contracts of trust from the bank or treasurehouse of theology" [*NPS*, 36]. While Scott complains that this leaves Steiner's theology at the level of "sheer assertion" without justification, it is possible to suggest that theological language functions as part of Steiner's eclecticism, and even haunts his discourse without the capacity of becoming enfleshed.[86] Consequently, Ward's speaking of the irony of Steiner's theological stance may be more appropriate to the character of theological discourse within the Steinerian *oeuvre*.[87] This corresponds to Carroll's observation that at times in Steiner's as yet unpublished Gifford lectures of 1990, "the term *God* carried no more freight than does an allusion to *transcendence*".[88] It must be remembered, as Carroll recognises further, that Steiner is a secular Jew.

Steiner's reflections centre on providing a hermeneutics beyond deconstructive nihilism and the presence of the Logos in meaning. As a consequence, 'hope's' character is developed, and it is here that his work serves to critique certain Christian versions of hope.

Steiner himself speaks of the possibility of art's "interrogation" of life, since it functions, in an important sense, as "a sharply political

---

[85] Ward, 1993, 'George Steiner', 105.

[86] Nathan A. Scott, Jr. (1994), 'Steiner on Interpretation', in Scott and Sharp, 1-13 (11).

[87] Ward (1994), 'Heidegger in Steiner', in Scott and Sharp, 180-204 (200).

[88] Robert P. Carroll (1994), 'Toward a Grammar of Creation: On Steiner the Theologian', in Scott and Sharp, 262-274 (266).

gesture, a value-statement of the most evident ethical import", and in so doing "It purposes change".[89] In the perspective of hope's refusing to shy away from an appropriately defined tragic vision, one is enabled to utilise tragic sensibilities in order to interrogate all easy optimisms that refuse to taste the bitterness of rupture. Here, tragedies, in identifying and presenting certain dramatic instances of the tragic vision, can perform the critically interrogative function by asking us just what day we imagine today is.[90] They present themselves as "a kind of perpetual moral wakefulness", asking about the complexity of motives, the wisdom in decisions, the characters we develop, and the importance of external factors in shaping events, to name a few features of our narrative identities.[91] Highlighted, herein, by Nussbaum is the "fragility of goodness" and the risky delicacy of human self-control and movement toward all forms of possession (be they psychological, economic, political, intellectual, etc.), and hence "our vulnerability to evil".[92] In other words, human limitations in a not hospitable world. Kekes claims that in such a world "[t]he best we can do is to plan our lives so as to minimize their [i.e., the conditions that create tragedies] influence", assuming, of course, that we can adequately identify them all.[93]

They do not answer any philosophical or theological questions, for instance those that Steiner's reflections on tragic drama are prone to solve about the ultimate condition of the universe in an Archimedian perspective denied by his hermeneutics [cf. *RP*, 61]. The very multiplicity and diversity of the dramas themselves speak of the problem of transcripting tragic experience into theory, and thereby disrupt easy coherences of thinking about the whole of reality. Instead they raise questions in acute fashion, particularly over any created securities of meaning and value. Tragedies can teach, then, less by didactic or conceptual means, but, as Ricoeur argues, by "more closely resembling a conversion of the manner

---

[89] *RP*, 143, 144, 143. This approach stands in marked contrast to that of Nietzsche's *BT*, in which both the Dionysian music and the cathartic *Stimmung* (mood/atmosphere) virtually appear to bury plot and character, for the purpose of the spectatorial affirmation of life [see *BT*, §7; 'Attempt', 26].

[90] See Steiner, *DT*, xi, 5; 1996, 130, 136. "In essence, Tragedy is a questioning and an enacted testing of theodicy. It ministers to radical doubts and protests in a radical confrontation with the non- and inhuman" [*NPS*, 137].

[91] Elizabeth Wyschogrod (1994), 'The Mind of a Critical Moralist: Steiner as Jew', in Scott, Jr., and Sharp, 151-179 (151).

[92] Kekes, 5. Cf. Michael Trapp (1996), 'Tragedy and the Possibility of Moral Reasoning: Response to Foley', in *Tragedy and the Tragic: Greek Theatre and Beyond*, ed. M.S. Silk, Clarendon Press, Oxford, 74-84 (81); John D. Barbour (1983), 'Tragedy and Ethical Reflection', *Journal of Religion* vol. 63, 1-25.

[93] Kekes, 26.

of looking" through destabilising interrogating which therein reorients action.[94]   As such they profoundly critique Christian hope's mood of discourse, reminding it of its long Saturday in which the hope for Sunday's dawning regulates and shapes its fragile agency for the sake of the humanisation and de-demonisation of the world.[95]   Changing the image from Saturday to the Garden of Gethsemane, Lash argues, that

> the darkness of Gethsemane remains the place of Christian hope, the context of all attempts at conversation, all 'anticipations' in history of God's still future kingdom.[96]

Therefore,

> In the light of Easter we are given the possibility and hence have the duty, even in Gethsemane, of keeping conversation [ethically defined] alive.[97]

The senses in which Christian hope can incorporate the tragic vision, and what that Christian taking of the tragic tragically could look like, will be discussed in the following chapters with reference to Barth.

---

[94] Ricoeur, 1992, 245ff.

[95] This is not so much a case of promoting what Larry Bouchard describes as a theology aware of its own blindness, but rather a theology that gropes its way in the dark, stumbling certainly and yet fragilely enacting the drama of redemption [Bouchard (1989), *Tragic Method and Tragic Theology: Evil in Contemporary Drama and Religious Thought*, Pennsylvania State University Press].

[96] Lash (1991), 'Conversation in Gethsemane', in Werner G. Jeanrond and Jennifer L. Rike (eds.), *Pluralism and Truth: David Tracy and the Hermeneutics of Religion*, Crossroad Publishing Co., New York, 51-61 (59).

[97] Ibid., 52.

Chapter 2

Escaping Contingency: Barth's Eschatological Actuality

Introduction

It was asserted earlier that 'hope' is a rarely discussed theme in the secondary literature on Barth. Rather than merely decry such paucity of study on this theme, however, it is important that one notices that this lack makes some sense when certain wide-ranging censures of Barth are borne in mind, which, despite their diversity, overlap to the effect that Barth in some sense forecloses the future. The particular form of that foreclosure differs, however, particularly between the accounts of Roberts and Moltmann and that of Berkouwer, for example. Nevertheless, what type of future can there be if Barth either advances its immediate presence in the event of revelation (Roberts and Moltmann), or prematurely knows temporality's outcome (Berkouwer)? Barth's eschatology would thereby either formally permit no time for any future fulfilment, given its concentration on the revelational present (Roberts' logic); or materially require that the eschatological Future constitutes a 'noetic' or epistemic fulfilment of that which is already 'ontically' true of our being in the present (Berkouwer, Rosato).

By way of expressing the concerns that these readings entail for Barth's account of hope, this chapter focuses firstly on Richard Roberts' reading of Barth, supported by that of Jürgen Moltmann; secondly, on the account provided by G.C. Berkouwer; and finally, on the evaluation of Barth's pneumatology by Philip Rosato. The theme that pervades all of these studies is that Barth tends to subsume all reality and contingency within a christological matrix, so that they lose their existence. Apparently damningly, numerous critics use the term 'christomonism' to name this flaw.[1]

Moreover, frequently flowing from this account comes the further complaint that Barth prevents 'room' for human life and agency, and

---

[1] For example, Paul Knitter (1971), 'Christomonism in Karl Barth's Evaluation of the Non-Christian Religions', *Neue Zeitschrift für Systematische Theologie und Religionsphilosophie* vol. 13, 99-121 (99).

denies the impact of evil's existence, therein particularly preventing any space for human rejection.[2]

Richard Roberts: Barth's Temporal Vacuum

In Roberts, one discovers an uncompromising critic who encapsulates much that especially English-speaking critics, albeit deriving from several continental theologians' assessments, have claimed about Barth's theology. Although his concern pre-eminently lies in the specific area of theological methodology, the questions asked of Barth are eschatologically significant, particularly in relation to hope's temporality; the seclusion of theology, and therefore also eschatology, from the public arena; and a flight from the intricate complexities of the development of and contingent nature of human life and thought.

The context of Roberts' critique is his desire to promote a *theologia viatorum*, in other words, a theology engaged in a repentant and kenotic thinking within the terrain of the contemporary human condition and public discourse [*TW*, xv]. Such an approach, however, he finds distinctly lacking in Barth's *CD*, although he discovers in the *Römerbrief*, and its *Sitz im Leben* in the "first postmodernity" precisely its rudiments.[3]

Barth, Roberts observes, derives his view of 'reality' from neither metaphysics nor, more importantly for Roberts, the social sciences. Rather, following his encounter with Anselm's *Proslogion*, he develops it from God's Self-positing in Christ. The 'noetic necessity', which Barth had discovered in Anselm, understands the nature of theological truth as self-posited and self-authenticated. Faith, therefore, essentially becomes the obedient exploration of the given.[4] This in itself, according to Roberts, is a

---

[2] On the former, see, e.g., Sheila Daveney, cited in John Webster (1995), *Barth's Ethics of Reconciliation*, Cambridge, 7. On Barth's 'denial' of evil see, e.g., Gustaf Wingren (1958), *Theology in Conflict: Nygren, Barth, Bultmann*, trans. Eric H. Wahlstrom, Oliver and Boyd, Edinburgh and London, 25, 38, 112, 117; Scott R. Rodin (1997), *Evil and Theodicy in the Theology of Karl Barth*, Peter Lang, 221f., 223-233.

[3] *TW*, 196ff.; cf. Graham Ward (1995), *Barth, Derrida and the Language of Theology*, Cambridge, 8, 103.

[4] See *FQI*, 45f.; *CD*, I.1, 11.

> gigantic celestial tautology, the *circulus veritatis Dei*. God is
> known by God alone; he is the objective reality of such
> knowledge in his Word and its subjective possibility in the
> Holy Spirit; real knowledge is therefore acknowledgement
> [*IR*, 165].

Following on the heels of Kant's segregation of philosophical and theological activity into their own discrete spheres, and Hegel's subsequent Idealist leap over those epistemic boundaries, Barth's post-*Römerbrief* isolation of theology leads to the "dangerously close collusion between his voice and that of God". Entailed is a "totalitarian" method that "demands conformity and submission rather than critical investigation", a problem also detected by Pannenberg [*TW*, xv].[5] This, Roberts argues, constitutes a repression of human freedom and all forms of contingency.

Roberts admits, however, that Barth does not wholly intend to imply this since he is concerned with the revelation that is historical in its occurrence and grounded in the man Jesus Christ. Only if knowledge of God appears as a presuppositionless piece of reasoning, with no point of anchorage in the world, could it be classed as "something of an intellectual monstrosity, an ontological and epistemological exclusiveness, even a quasi-gnostic *afflatus*" [*KBDT*, 144f.].

> [T]he comprehensive universality of the category of time
> means that the reality of revelation must be temporal if it is to
> be a reality accessible to humanity [*IR*, 165].

Hence, Barth attempts to re-temporalise the eschatological 'Moment' of *2Ro*, structuring it through the concrete historical life of Jesus of Nazareth and, above all, in his forty days after Easter [*IR*, 175]. *2Ro*'s 'Now-Moment', without temporal before or after, undergoes a temporal extension and is experienced as the fulfilment, rather than negation, of time.

Although this lessens the danger of unreality, Roberts proceeds, it does not wholly banish it. As Prenter claims, summarising Bonhoeffer's critique of Barth's actualism,

---

[5] Wolfhart Pannenberg (1985), *Anthropology in Theological Perspective*, trans. Matthew J. O'Connell, The Westminster Press, Philadelphia, 16; cf. Richard Crigg (1990), *Theology as a Way of Thinking*, Scholars Press, Atlanta, Georgia, 39-48. For a critique of Pannenberg, here, see Paul D. Molnar (1995), 'Some Problems with Pannenberg's Solution to Barth's "Faith Subjectivism"', *SJT* vol. 48, 315-339.

> In an actualistic concept of revelation there is no room for a
> *being* of the revealed or the revealer in the world.[6]

So when Roberts declares that Barth's mature work exhibits a "logology" (influenced by Hegel's theme of synthesis), one precisely imagines that Barth falls foul of that esotericism he intends to avoid [*IR*, 168].

It is in the *CD*'s pervasive time-eternity conceptuality that Roberts locates the problem. Through language of inclusion, Barth states that 'God's time' in Christ is the prototypical basis of time, the original source from which temporal reality, or 'real time', will flow. However, temporality is undermined by conceiving of its source in eternity along Boethian lines: as simultaneity and therefore transcendent of temporal connotations, simultaneously possessing endlessness in a *totum simul*. Thus, although Barth comes to perceive the shortcomings of his negative presentation of *2Ro*'s dialectic of time and eternity, he nevertheless fails to retrieve revelation from this temporal vacuum. Subsequently, this

> temporal vacuum of the eternal 'Now' moment ... become[s]
> the [*CD*'s] vehicle of the time of revelation itself [*KBDT*, 88].

This actualistic non-temporality of revelation's *nunc stans* is secured through his conception of Christ's "contingent contemporaneousness" (*kontingente Gleichzeitigkeit*), the very concept, Roberts argues, which makes Barth's doctrine of time thoroughly ambiguous [*CD*, I.1, 149]. For although Barth is at pains to posit the contingency of the basis of revelation, this is not achieved upon the basis of what are normally considered historical acts. As a divine act, revelation is temporally transcendent and vacuous on the basis of its "contingent contemporaneity". This is a "temporal togetherness" which sets it apart from time as the condition of contingency and historicity in any normally accepted sense. And this, Roberts continues, would be "a temporal docetism" [*IR*, 177].

> The ontological dogma of the Incarnation loses its roots in
> the shared and public reality of the world in which we live; it

---

[6] Regin Prenter (1967), 'Dietrich Bonhoeffer and Karl Barth's Positivism of Revelation', in *World Come of Age: A Symposium on Dietrich Bonhoeffer*, ed. Ronald Gregor Smith, Collins, London, 93-130 (106).

hovers above us like a cathedral resting upon a cloud [*KBDT*, 145].

Particularly noted is the problematic treatment of the temporal character of the 'Resurrection-time'. That Barth attempted to place it within our time is clear [*CD*, III.2, 463]. But he immediately retracts this through a "relapse back once again into the language of 'inclusion'" [*IR*, 178]. Hence the resurrection becomes a freeing from temporal enclosure, and consequently there can be no *substantial* coinherence of Christ's resurrected time of revelation with ours.

Barth's tendency here is further encapsulated in his discussion of election, for herein the fulcrum is shifted from incarnate history to eternal decision. It is not time *per se*, upon which Barth's theological attention is concentrated, but eternity as the temporal *plenum* from which time takes its reality. So Barth argues that election is something that

> happened *to* and not *in* their human nature and its possibilities, *to* and not *in* their human history and its development [*CD*, II.2, 321].

However here, Roberts argues, "the area of divine antecedence and that of temporal consequence ... becomes blurred and ambiguous" [*KBDT*, 119].

What is emerging from these broad brushstrokes is a portrait of one who utterly failed to theologically engage with what Roberts calls "our commonplace reality". Barth has "become the entextualised, but no longer context-bound mouth of 'God'", and therein has provided theology with its own 'breathing-space' in protected isolation from public scrutiny [*TW*, 175]. In a similar vein, Webb speaks of a Barthian lapse into the Protestant scholasticism of a stable authorial voice, an over-confident logocentrism, authoritarian position, and closed system, a criticism somewhat further echoing Jülicher's suggestion of the arrogant "spiritual enthusiasm" of the Barth of *2Ro* [*2Ro*, 20].[7]

In eschatological terms, a failure to engage with this range of contextual spaces could result in failure to incorporate all manner of human hopes for the contingent future into Christian hope, and/or to forsake participation in transformatory practice in the present. As Roberts argues, Barth's theology is nothing "short of [a] total alienation and lack of personal authenticity" [*KBDT*, 145].

---

[7] Stephen H. Webb (1991), *Refiguring Theology: The Rhetoric of Karl Barth*, State University of New York Press, 153. See even the otherwise sympathetic von Balthasar, 1972, 29.

Furthermore, Barth's eschatological frame becomes the "realised eschatology" of the non-temporal revelatory event, as Roberts describes it, or a "transcendental eschatology", as Moltmann names it.[8] In this the Eternal presents himself immediately in the event of revelation, overwhelming time, and therefore emptying temporality of any mediating significance. Eschatology and hope consequently lose their future directedness in this de-temporalising of revelation or "epiphany of the eternal present" [*TH*, 57]. Therefore, Moltmann asserts,

> Anyone who hears the thunderous word of the eternal God in
> the moment loses interest in the future.[9]

Barth's eschatology is aligned here to that of Bultmann, with Moltmann arguing that the latter's eschatology similarly leads to the logical conclusion that

> faith would itself be the practical end of history and the
> believer would himself already be perfected. There would be
> nothing more that still awaits him, and nothing more towards
> which he is on his way in the world in the body and in history
> [*TH*, 67f.].[10]

While one needs to be fair to Bultmann by recognising that the 'future' does not wholly disappear from his thought,[11] nevertheless, one could further legitimately maintain that this detracts little from the overwhelming sense of a dehistoricisation of eschatology in his existentialist rendering of eschatological themes.

---

[8] *KBDT*, 98; *TH*, 45.

[9] Moltmann, 1996, 14.

[10] The difference between the two theological giants, however, lies not in their eschatological structure, but rather in their interpretation of the content of Herrmann's 'self' [*TH*, 52; cf. 1996, 19].

[11] See Rudolf Bultmann (1961), 'Man Between the Times According to the New Testament', in *Existence and Faith. Shorter Writings of Rudolf Bultmann*, trans. Schubert Ogden, London, 300f.

G.C. Berkouwer: Barth's Triumph of Electing Grace

'Triumph'

Leaving aside the problematic procedure of isolating any *Konstruktionsprinzip* or singular map to guide wanderings in the Barthian labyrinth, in his influential account of Barth's theology, Berkouwer detects a central theme: *The Triumph of Grace* in a "triumphant Christianity" [*TG*, 74].

Triumphal language pervades *2Ro* and beyond, no doubt reflecting Barth's grasp of certain scriptural patterns through the medium of the elder Blumhardt's image, *"Jesus ist Sieger"*.[12] So in Berkouwer's reading the *CD*'s theology is characterised by an overwhelming christologically grounded optimism that can only be expressed in the exultant terms of 'triumph' and 'victory'. Indeed, Berkouwer cites Barth to the effect that the Christian message is a protest against "all pessimism, tragedy and skepticism" [*TG*, 170]. It takes its "triumphant and joyful character" from the outcome of the conflict between Christ and sin, revealed in the resurrection, rather than "from a vague and superficially optimistic attitude to life" [*TG*, 212]. So Berkouwer claims that

> The triumph to which he gives expression bears, rather, a
> concrete Name: Jesus Christ as very God and very man. In
> Him the Sovereign and merciful action of God is revealed.
> Jesus Christ is *the* Conqueror and in *Him* the entirety of
> triumph consists and finds its basis [*TG*, 212].

Because of this event, as Zahrnt indicates, Barth is given the confidence that it will also conquer in the future, and drive from the field everything that seeks to resist it.[13]

With this motif intact, Barth rejects any form of soteriological immanentism, in the sense of 'mythological' connections between God and humanity grounded in, necessitated by, or achieved by, any contingent being. The German *Kriegstheologie* of the First World War, the *Kulturtheologie* of Liberal relationalism, the *analogia entis* and Brunner's *Offenbarungsmächtigkeit*, are all implicated in such a crime of anthropocentrically founding God-talk. Thus the *Christus Victor* motif permits Barth to express his conviction of the 'properly' structured asymmetry of the God-human relations: that

---

[12] *KD*, IV.3.1, 188/*CD*, IV.3.1, 165.

[13] Heinz Zahrnt (1969), *The Question of God: Protestant Theology in the Twentieth Century*, trans. R. A. Wilson, Collins, London, 56.

Reconciliation in the sense of the Christian confession and the message of the Christian community is God's active and superior Yes to man [*CD*, IV.3.1, 3].

Christ, for Barth – as his treatments of christology, virgin birth, resurrection, etc., indicate – was not the most perfectly realised human form of the God-conscious spirit. In other words, Christ was not an expression of the creature's inherent 'capacity' for God-realisation, God-consciousness, and so on. The act of reconciliation

is actual in the *free act of grace* for which God determines Himself and upon which He resolves in Jesus Christ [*CD*, IV.3.1, 166, my emphasis].

Moreover, Barth utilises such language to exclude any thoughts of a static and dualistic relationship between God and

the surrounding world of darkness. · It is certainly not dualistic. We do not have the equilibrium of opposing forces, as though darkness had the claim and power finally to maintain itself against light, as though its antithesis, opposition and challenge to light, its restricting of it, rested on an eternal and lasting order [*CD*, IV.3.1, 168].

Such a concern characterises Barth's treatment of the dialectic in *2Ro*, and is present in Barth's later discourse of the "dynamic teleology" of history [*CD*, IV.3.1, 168].

Nevertheless, such triumphal discourse can all too easily, if unqualified, lend weight to the development of a 'predictive' model of eschatology, since the character of the future is confidently predicated from the knowledge of this past-event. The real future is imaginatively conceived with certainty before its manifestation, and its shape is thereafter blueprinted. Barth would certainly not here be following the lines of the seventeenth-century Federal theologians or of millennialist groups by mapping the exact form of *future history*. Nevertheless, 'victory' talk in Barth, when read in a framework suggesting that all that is theologically significant has already happened, leads down a similar path with respect to one's knowing of the *ultimate outcome* of the future. This is precisely the road that Berkouwer implies that Barth is unwittingly travelling on in relation to the question of *apokatastasis*.

Election and the Apokatastasis

Barth explicitly rejects *apokatastasis* as presumptuous on three grounds. Firstly, it is based on a conjunction of an optimistic estimate of humanity with the postulate of the infinite potentiality of the divine being [*CD*, II.2, 295], a broad type of approach that appears more recently in Hick's evolutionary hypothesis: humanity will come to freely choose God, albeit with a certain degree of divine input in aiding this process.[14] Secondly, it imposes a "right or necessity" on God's election and calling [*CD*, II.2, 417f.]. And thirdly, a point not often recognised by critics, Barth refuses to speculate as to the exact form of the future [*C*, 171]. If he maintains a *hope* that the circle of election and calling will be finally and comprehensively enlarged, it is because he believes in the superabundant divine love and grace expressed in Christ [*DC*, II.2, 418].

Nevertheless, it is argued by Berkouwer and Zahrnt in particular, following Brunner's lead, that in spite of his denial the logic of Barth's model of election leads clearly and necessarily to the door of a christologically conceived *apokatastasis* [*TG*, 116].[15] Therefore, his refusal to open this door is, it is argued, due to a failure to take his own theological model seriously, whereas Gunton, on the other hand, expresses the opinion that although Barth does occasionally appear to run in this direction, on other occasions he appears to be moving in another.[16] However, missing this supposed *implicitness* involved in detecting *apokatastasis* in Barth, leads Aung to unsophisticatedly and simplistically claim that "Barth's theological conception of universal salvation is ... open to criticism".[17]

Much of Berkouwer's discussion (and also that of Brunner, Zahrnt and Gunton) pivots on the supposed accomplishment of the victorious election in a remote eternal 'past', a reading that differs significantly from Roberts' detection of a Barthian eternal present-centredness.[18] Humanity, in effect, stands as a spectator of the divine drama of salvation, accomplished on its behalf in this past. The problem, Berkouwer for example argues, lies in Barth's "wholly *objective* conception of the

---

[14] See John Hick (1976), *Death and Eternal Life*, Collins, London, 242f., 251f.

[15] Zahrnt, 107; Emil Brunner (1949), *Dogmatics Volume I: The Christian Doctrine of God*, trans. Olive Wyon, Lutterworth Press, London, 348.

[16] Colin E. Gunton (1978), *Becoming and Being: The Doctrine of God in Charles Hartshorne and Karl Barth*, Oxford, 164.

[17] Salai Hla Aung (1998), *The Doctrine of Creation in the Theology of Barth, Moltmann and Pannenberg: Creation in Theological, Ecological and Philosophical-Scientific Perspective*, Roderer Verlag, Regensburg, 77.

[18] Brunner, 1949, 347; Zahrnt, 197, 112f.

triumph of grace", a conception that has its roots undoubtedly in "the decisive place which election occupies in Barth's dogmatics" as the election of all to salvation [*TG*, 179, 52]. As Barth maintains in IV.3, with reference to 1 Tim. 2:3f., in Christ is accomplished God's will of the salvation of all [*CD*, IV.3.1, 4]. In other words, the difficulty is understood to be the nature of the theme of Christ's vicarious work.

Standing parallel to this is the account provided of Barth's treatment of reprobation. Berkouwer correctly recognises that for Barth predestination is double, as with the older Reformed definitions [*TG*, 107]. However, this is the eternal rejection of a particular human being, which takes place on behalf of, and in the place of, others. Accordingly, Brunner cites what he takes to be a suggestive statement of Barth to the effect that "the only person who is really 'rejected' is His own Son".[19] After all, Barth claims that

> Because Jesus Christ takes [the rejected man's place], He takes from him the right and possibility of his own independent being and gives him His own being. He cannot *be rejected* anymore [*CD*, II.2, 453].

So Berkouwer asks,

> If it be of the essence of the triumph to be revealed over against godlessness and resistance to grace, and if the *real* reprobation consists in the rejection of Christ in contrast to the rejection of others, is it possible to escape drawing the conclusion of the apokatastasis doctrine? If the great decision has been made, if the universal tide has turned, if the great change has taken place through the radical substitution of Christ, then the asking of the apokatastasis question is not illegitimate but is warranted by the simple fact of taking Barth seriously [*TG*, 112].

This is why, Berkouwer argues, Barth reduces the difference between the elect and the rejected to a merely "subjective" difference while "objectively" they are alike under the lordship of God's grace [see *CD*, II.2, 346f.]. "Thus", Zahrnt claims, "in the ultimate sense Barth cannot take unbelief seriously" since grace is *always* the conquest of the

---

[19] *KD* II.2, 350 [*CD*, II.2, 353], cited in Brunner, 1949, 348.

darkness.[20] Barth's refusal to see the story of the outcome of Judas as one of divine rejection is perceived to be a prominent example of this, so that Ford, for instance, can claim that

> The drive behind the distortion of the story is clearly the desire to enclose all rejection in Jesus' death and so see it all overcome in his resurrection.[21]

Accordingly, Berkouwer advances, God in his grace has made the life of reprobation "an objective impossibility" for human beings. The unbeliever attempts, albeit unsuccessfully and ultimately powerlessly, to undo this eternal divine decision [*CD*, II.2, 319ff.]. There is a reverberation of the echo of that curse which struck Christ, but only the reverberation of an already eliminated curse [*CD*, II.2, 352].

It is for this reason that Berkouwer claims that Barth has no place, logically speaking, for genuine evil, as he feels the language of the "impossible possibility" of sin indicates (although he does recognise Barth's *intention* to accord it genuine status).

> Barth does not regard our actual liberation from the power of chaos as a matter for the *future* [*KD* III.3, 420]. The liberation has been accomplished and the power of evil is now no more than a dangerous *appearance* [ibid., 425]. This chaos has been *objectively* eliminated. We do not yet see this, but this is only because of the blindness of our eyes. This chaos has only *apparent* power and therefore it is not dangerous [*TG*, 237].

Similarly, Zahrnt's focus on eternity regards this *eternal* victory as entailing that there can be no serious or significant struggle of God against evil in history, what Reinhold Niebuhr describes as the

> offering a crown without the cross, a triumph without a battle, and a faith which ignores the confusion of human existential life instead of transforming it.[22]

---

[20] Zahrnt, 110.

[21] David F. Ford (1981), *Barth and God's Story   Biblical Narrative and the Theological Method of Karl Barth in the Church*, Peter Lang, New York, 92. Cf. *CD*, II.2, 458-506.

[22] Niebuhr, cited in Zahrnt, 121; cf. 115f.

Even though one lives one's life in the midst of threatening powers of evil, one has assurance on the basis of God's electing love in Christ that God's final purpose *cannot* be overcome [*KD*, III.3, 417ff.].

The price paid by this soteriological objectivism, or perhaps Hegelian-type synthesis as Hendry identifies as being regulatively active in Barth's work, is described as a "*monistic* conception of the works of God" [*TG*, 249].[23] By this, Berkouwer implies that Barth undermines creaturely subjectivity and activity. The consequence is obvious, Brunner argues of Barth,

> that the real decision only takes place [or better, has taken place,] in the objective sphere, and not in the subjective sphere. Thus: the decision has been made in Jesus Christ - for all men. Whether they know it or not, believe it or not, is not so important. The main point is that they are saved. They are like people who seem to be perishing in a stormy sea. But in reality they are not in a sea where one can drown, but in shallow water, where it is impossible to drown. Only they do not know it. ... [I]t is no longer possible to be lost. ... If the decision of faith is not deadly serious either; everything has already been decided beforehand.[24]

Zahrnt believes that this accounts for Barth's apparently one-sided exposition of the Gospel's identity without its development of

> the question of how the gospel can be preached in the contemporary situation of mankind and appropriated by man.[25]

In this, he even regards Barth's theology as "harmful", and in explicit support of the earlier critique by Bonhoeffer of Barth's *Offenbarungpositivisimus*, and paralleling Roberts' discussion, he adds that

---

[23] George S. Hendry (1966), 'On Barth, the Philosopher', in John Hick ed., *Faith and the Philosophers*, St. Martin's Press, New York, 210-218 (215).

[24] Brunner, 1949, 351; cf. David F. Wells (1978), *The Search For Salvation*, Inter Varsity Press, Leicester, 61.

[25] Zahrnt, 69.

> Barth's theology is [esoterically] lacking in a relationship to
> the concrete existence of man and the actual development of
> the world.[26]

Leaving aside the problematic language of eternity as temporally 'before' history, Brunner indicates that he conceives of 'faith' as in some sense salvific, or, as he says, "deadly serious". Barth's, and also Berkouwer's, understanding of election and divine and human freedoms denies that possibility, however, so that the latter can accuse Brunner of advocating Arminianism [*TG*, 264]. And yet, even when this divergence between Barth and Brunner is recognised and the subsequent language of the complaint is modified, the charge remains that Barth has *settled* and *foreclosed* the actuality of salvation in the Christ-event. If that is so, then reconciliation and redemption have already happened to humanity 'over its head', or "automatically", as Zahrnt argues.[27] An appeal to Barth's ethics in response, cannot solve the problem, although it could undermine those criticisms that claim that Barth has no theological place for humanity.[28] Barth's ethics could, at most, according to this reading, be adduced to be the ethics of creatures who have absolutely no formal potentialities of disobedience, a *non potest peccare* rather than a *potest non peccare* (how, then, could the actuality of sin be accounted for?). And, at least it could be claimed that here is an instance of Barth's self-contradiction. What then becomes of the future?

Philip Rosato: Barth's 'Noetic' Future

It has been suggested that Roberts' reading creates difficulties for any conception of an eschatological future in Barth. Berkouwer's account entertains that there *is* a future, an eschatological fulfilment; however, its form is controversial, as one can perceive from Rosato's critique of Barth's pneumatology.

---

[26] Ibid., 92, 117.

[27] Ibid., 118.

[28] A number of commentators suggest that Barth threatens humanity's existence and agency. So, e.g., R.E. Willis (1971), *The Ethics of Karl Barth*, E.J. Brill, Leiden, 433; Klaas Runia (1982), 'Karl Barth's Christology', in *Christ the Lord: Studies in Christology Presented to Donald Guthrie*, ed. Harold H. Rowdon, IVP, Leicester, 299-310 (308); A.E. McGrath (1986), *The Making of Modern German Christology. From the Enlightenment to Pannenberg*, Oxford, 105f. For a brief critique of this position, see Webster, 1995, 'Introduction'.

Rosato's complaint is not so much that of a Colwell or a Berkhof who perceive in Barth a theologically-weakening "pneumatological reticence" or "neglect".[29] Rather, for Rosato, Barth's presentation of eschatological provisionality is conceptually irredeemable, or better, tends towards a realised eschatology because of his christologically defined pneumatological model that undergirds it.[30] So, to Jenson's puzzle, "You Wonder Where the Spirit Went" in Barth, Rosato's thoughts would add a link to 'You wonder where the future went'. And this is a problem that is displayed in Barth's concept of *'noetic'* eschatological provisionality. What for Alan Torrance is Barth's "preoccupation with [a] revelation" model and a "strongly epistemic drive" is, for Rosato, a suppression of contingency, novelty and openness to the future, in favour of an orientation to the past and its future noetic unveiling.[31]

Because of what Rosato names Barth's "Logos Christology", nothing salvifically and redemptively new can occur since all has already happened in Christ's history [*SL*, 158]. In a similar manner to Moltmann, Rosato laments that subsequently Barth's "*eschaton* is uniformly [and statically] present at each moment" [*SL*, 167]. Consequently, "the Spirit's creative and redemptive functions are considerably eclipsed" since he does not *add* anything to Christ's work, or "foster a totally new turn in history as such".[32] The Spirit can bring no new saving event(s) that is (are) different from that already ontologically achieved in Christ in the past.

Paralleling Berkouwer's thesis that the triumph of grace is "*eternal in God*" but merely "*revealed* in history" [*TG*, 260], Rosato declares that the Spirit's role is "rather formalistically" presented as *noetic* [*SL*, 161]. Eschatologically speaking, he does "no more than noetically realize this achievement" of Christ's already having "redeemed mankind ontically" [*SL*, 164]. This future will constitute the Spirit's

---

[29] Colwell, 1989, 305; Hendrikus Berkhof, cited in Horton Davies (1992), *The Vigilant God: Providence in the Thought of Augustine, Aquinas, Calvin and Barth*, Peter Lang, New York, 141. In contrast, however, see Robert E. Cushman (1981), *Faith Seeking Understanding: Essays Theological and Critical*, Duke University Press, Durham, N. Carolina, 156.

[30] *SL*, 27; cf. 138; Robert W. Jenson (1993), 'You Wonder Where the Spirit Went', *Pro Ecclesia* vol. 2, 296-305.

[31] See Alan Torrance (1996), *Persons in Communion: An Essay on Trinitarian Description and Human Participation, With Special Reference to Volume One of Karl Barth's* Church Dogmatics, T&T Clark, Edinburgh, 302. If pressed further, this critique could support the type of undervaluation of Barth's ethics that Webster so vehemently complains about.

[32] *SL*, 158, 167.

> reaffirm[ing] on a universal scale the fully effective salvific
> work of the divine Ontic, Jesus Christ [*SL*, 161].

While Rosato does admit to hearing a note of soteriological provisionality in *CD*, IV.3, he attributes to Barth a failure to consistently apply this insight [*SL*, 208n31]. Consequently, his account concentrates on the idea that humanity, through the Spirit, will come to know what *has been* true for it in Christ's work but is not yet universally recognised. This is the divine Ontic's (Christ's) being "confirmed by individual men through the Holy Spirit, the divine Noetic" [*SL*, 124]. The Christian/non-Christian differentiation therefore centres on noetic recognition, i.e., insight into the theological truth of their existence.[33] In this sense, then, Bettis is incorrect to claim that

> The work of Christ is not some ontological reorganisation or
> historical reorientation which men are called on to
> acknowledge.[34]

It is argued by Rosato, therefore that "the Spirit" protologically "directs man back in time and does not encourage him forward to the completion of the cosmos".[35] This last statement is misleading to the effect that Rosato accords precisely such a completion to Barth, but one which has occurred in the past, however. Nevertheless, his point remains that eschatology in Barth has already been realised in Christ but is yet to be fully and universally revealed as such. Gunton similarly expresses this perspective:

> the history of God with man is telescoped, for the future is
> not understood eschatologically as the era when there will
> take place new triune events, but seen to be merely the
> vehicle of the repetition of the timeless past.[36]

So irredeemable does Rosato find Barth's pneumatology, and subsequent eschatology, that his consequent "improvisations" on Barth's theology appear less as corrections and more as alternatives antithetical to many of Barth's theological concerns. For instance, although he does postulate the pneumatological operation as a 'complement' to the

---

[33] See *CD*, IV.3.1, 338f., 345f.

[34] Bettis, 1967, 434.

[35] *SL*, 140; cf. *CD*, IV.3.1, 10. Similarly, Jenson, 1993, 302f.; Colwell, 1989, 312; Gunton, 1978, 163, 183. Gunton, however, does admit that Barth is "ambiguous" [1978, 165].

[36] Gunton, 1978, 183.

christological, Rosato complains of Barth's depriving the Spirit "of an independent contribution to the process of salvation and the arrival of the *eschaton*" [*SL*, 158, 163]. This drives Rosato's 'modern' sounding desire to 'rectify' the apparently "scant attention" that Barth gives to human freedom and reason, and thereby re-open the way for human "mediation" and "co-operation" in the creation of the soteriological and eschatological future.[37] A more creative role is here attributed to human beings, in the construction of the apparently open future, than Barth is willing to allow.

> [M]an's own search for a just future ... [is] indicative of the manifold salvific encounters of God and man which occur in the Church and beyond it [*SL*, 159].

Conclusion

Both of the main roads here trodden, those of Roberts-Moltmann and Berkouwer-Rosato, suggest that Barth's eschatology would find it impossible to generate a hope which could take seriously the problematic raised in the previous chapter, about Christian hope's optimistic character. In Berkouwer's and Rosato's theses, Barth's eschatology unwittingly predicts the universalist nature of redemption. In that of Roberts, and to an extent also Moltmann, Barth's eschatological optimism would take a somewhat different form. The Future eschatological has already arrived in the event of revelation. Consequently, there is no 'time', to adopt Roberts' focus on temporality, for hope if that hope is perceived as the anticipation of an as yet awaited eschatological Future. Significantly, Barth's would then be a hope that cannot take the tragic tragically, since the divine becomes an immediately given present in the eschatological Moment of revelation, and human history would therein be absorbed by the divine activity in Christ. There is, then, no place for tragic contingencies.

The following chapters address these readings by suggesting that they are mistaken in a number of respects. Firstly, they fail to appreciate the significance of the fact that the eschatological Future bears the *name* of One who has come, is coming, and will come. Talk of the presence of the Future, therefore, does not mean that the eschatological Future is being emptied of significance, or time; it refers instead to *Christ's* personal presence.

---

[37] *SL*, 137, 159f., 164, 168.

Secondly, these critics fail to appreciate the nature of Barth's christologically conceived actuality, and therefore also his presentation of provisionality. The former is understood as christologically particular (i.e., redemption has come in Christ *alone*), and as such remains an eschatological concept (i.e., future *for us*). Hence Barth's thought accords to humanity a *time for hope*. As he recognises in 1930, in a paper entitled 'Promise, Time, and Fulfilment',

> Without having time it would be impossible to have promise, and without a promise it would be unbearable to have time.[38]

He continues by complaining of

> Those who are responsible for the Christian proclamation [who] still talk of fulfilment as if with the coming of Christ the promise had ceased to be promise, as if there were no more time and no more expectation. The promise fulfilled is supposed to mean: what the promise only promised, is now here; and mankind, or at least certain people, Christians, possess and enjoy it ... [that] there is now given to mankind, or rather to certain people, an island, as it were a piece of timeless present or a piece of eternity.[39]

Thirdly, both Barth's *noetic Future* and his revelation-model are misconstrued by these critics. The Future is *more than* mere informational impartation about the Christ-event, since it involves one's coming to *be* that which Christ has redeemed one for.

Fourthly, these critics do not discuss the practical and ethical *function* of Barth's eschatology. Barth does not intend to speak prematurely about the details of the content of the Future, but rather grounds Christian hope's practice 'realistically' in Christ; shapes hope's direction by what hope knows of Christ as *Eschatos*; and sustains its confidence and provides its momentum during hope's critically interrogative and transformative performance for society's humanisation, in the time of eschatological provisionality.

Finally, particularly in Chapter 7 will it be argued that Barth's resultant account of hope, as a human activity grounded in one's knowledge of God in Christ, operates in a much more fragile and risk-laden manner than the readings of the aforementioned critics imply.

---

[38] Barth, 1959, *Christmas*, 35.
[39] Ibid., 36.

Herein is a hope which suggests that it may have the resources to 'take the tragic tragically'.

Chapter 3

Barth's Developing Eschatology (1909-1924)

Introduction: Eschatological Time-Telling

From sundials to the pinpoint accuracy of contemporary timepieces, the days' recurring rhythms can be regulated. Timetables are subsequently created and lives rigorously scheduled in order to squeeze the greatest degree of productiveness out of every existing moment.

Theological time-telling is an immensely more complex skill, however, and yet central to the business of Christian living. It is located within a greater whole than in the mere awareness of the repetitive regularity of the sun's movements, for example: that of a particular story of a life lived before God, a non-identically repetitious human response of obedience, and an eschatological consummation. And yet within life's framework, without either the passing which befits the use of hindsight, or a God's-eye perspective, the process of "interpreting time", as Lash remarks, "is always darkly difficult".[1]

This study aims to indicate that, contrary to the claims of the critics discussed earlier, Barth does not de-temporalise eschatology. The context of Barth's eschatology is re-read, with the suggestion being made that these critics oversimplify, and indeed one-sidedly misread, a much more complex dialectic. Conversely, theological temporality is eschatologically structured, something which is particularly, albeit not exclusively, evident in *CD*, IV.3. It is *a time between* Easter and the Consummation, a provisional time of the 'Not Yet', albeit over this flies the flag of the christological 'Already'. In other words, a proper understanding of this temporality of eschatological provisionality, or penultimacy, is crucial to one's grasping of Barth's account of creation and redemption. And it is through this that Barth both opens time for the existential dimension of Christian hope, and not only gives the form but also determines the content of that hope.

---

[1] Nicholas Lash (1990), 'Friday, Saturday, Sunday', *New Blackfriars* vol. 71, 109-119 (111).

This chapter briefly scans the development, context, and function of Barth's eschatology from his liberal period to the dawn of the *GD*.[2] Included are the early Göttingen lectures (*RD*) since they materially resemble much in *2Ro*. *GD*, on the other hand, because of its affinities with *CD* I, will be treated in the following chapter.

The first section contends that Barth's Liberal understanding of revelation tends to bypass the contingent and presents itself in terms of eschatological immediacy, therein engendering a de-eschatologising of the revelation-event (i.e., over-concentration on its *presence* rather than its *future* coming). As Barth becomes involved in the political and social struggles in his Safenwil parish his writings come to reflect more on the theory-practice relation, and therein eschatological discourse comes to firmly inhabit the context of these struggles. Here Gollwitzer argues that

> In reality the entire direction of Barth's thought leads to *praxis*: to faith as the praxis-determining element, not to faith as the enabling of dogmatic utterance – the latter is only a stage on the way to praxis.[3]

Although this somewhat echoes a later statement of Barth's to the effect that "we have to do with a theory which is to be understood only with its origin and goal in practice" [*CD*, IV.3.1, 79], a question may be asked over Gollwitzer's use of language depicting dogmatics as "only a stage", implying, as it does, something less in the theology-ethics relation than Barth seems to have intended. Moreover, he also simplistically suggests that Barth retains "a vestige of the idealist faith in the power of ideas, namely, that on the basis of right theology, the right praxis will be created".[4] Nevertheless, Gollwitzer has suggested that ethics, and political agency as a substantial practical outworking of that ethics, is cardinal to Barth's theological development and endeavours. Indeed, going further than Gollwitzer, Gorringe reads Barth

---

[2] However, this tracing of Barth's development will not follow von Balthasar's identification of *clearly locatable* critical 'turns' or moments of radical Barthian conversion, especially since there is considerable thematic overlap between the suggested periods [von Balthasar, 1972, 76f.; in contrast, see McCormack, 1995, ix].

[3] Helmut Gollwitzer (1976), 'Kingdom of God and Socialism in the Theology of Karl Barth', in *Karl Barth and Radical Politics*, ed. and trans. George Hunsinger, Westminster, Philadelphia, 77-120 (97).

[4] Ibid., 111.

'prophetically' rather than 'systematically', as a theologian
who is above all concerned with the way in which God's
Word shapes history, rather than in setting out an account of
the divine essence.[5]

Perhaps the word 'merely' should be added to the clause "rather
than in [merely] setting out ..." since theology and ethics/politics are
integrated in Barth, and since Gorringe himself continues by denying that
he intends anything reductive by his thesis as if "Barth's doctrine *emerged*
purely as a response to contemporary needs".[6]

The second section maintains that Barth's relative 'break' from
Liberalism, relative because Barth had learned and continued to carry with
him much from his interactions with Schleiermacher and Herrmann in
particular,[7] occurs because he feels that the divine sovereignty is
undermined in Liberal thinking. This, however, is not exclusively, or even
primarily, a theoretical move on Barth's part, but develops out of his
ethical concern to do justice to the nature of the relationship between
divine and human agencies. Thus, while T.F. Torrance claims that Barth's
theological motivation takes seriously people's concrete reality and actual
daily relation to God, one would need to add that this entails that Barth
necessarily takes seriously one's concrete relations to others also.[8]

What one perceives in the earlier period(s) of Barth's writing,
something that never disappears, is that eschatological discourse is rooted
within his ethical concerns and comes to serve as an interrogation of all
thinking and living, including that of Religious Socialism, since its
regulative horizon remains *futural* (rather than immediately present, unlike
in his 'Liberal period'). As Gorringe argues about an important influence
on the Barth of the time,

> It was the radical edge which his eschatological faith gave
> him which ensured that Christoph Blumhardt's involvement
> with Social Democracy was never as unambiguous as that of
> Ragaz. He was concerned to change the present, to find
> anticipations of the kingdom of God here on earth, but the
> critical power of the coming kingdom made easy

---

[5] Gorringe, *Karl Barth*, 8.
[6] Ibid., 9.
[7] See Gary Dorrien (2000), *The Barthian Revolt in Modern Theology: Theology Without Weapons*, Westminster John Knox Press, Louisville.
[8] T.F. Torrance (1962), *Karl Barth: An Introduction to His Early Theology, 1910-1931*, SCM Press, London, 31.

identifications   with   existing   political   programmes impossible.[9]

No form of escape from life and thought's contingencies is here encouraged, whether that be through unwarranted future-prediction, circumventing of the temporality of hope, or ignoring practical engagement with the sources of human alienation's sources.

What is often missed by critics, and will be explored in the third main section, is the fact that despite emphasising the divine-human *diastasis* (distance) and eschatological *krisis* (judgment) during this period, Barth also meagrely suggests that this eschatological horizon casts its shadow over thinking and living in the present.   Hence, a modest exhortation for positive human activity in humanising the present is tentatively provided.

Beginnings: Barth's Liberal Relationalism (Geneva 1909-1911)

Barth's extant written work suggests that prior to his encounter with socialism in Safenwil he had not too deeply reflected on eschatological issues.   The title of a 1909 essay, '*Moderne Theologie und Reichsgottesarbeit*' ('Modern Theology and Work for the Kingdom of God'), suggests a link with Ritschlianism's optimistic appraisal of the human constructing of the kingdom.[10] This claim is strengthened by the fact that Barth concentrates on the individual's *Gotteserlebnis* (experience of God).[11] The connection of theology and ethics, which the essay was attempting to achieve, was done under the auspices of a Pietistic-type *Gotteserlebnis* in a manner more akin to Ritschl's ethics than Harnack's inwardness.[12] As Fisher argues when discussing Barth's early attempts at *Kulturtheologie*:

---

[9] Gorringe, 'Eschatology', 92f. Cf. John Webster (1998), *Barth's Moral Theology: Human Action in Barth's Thought*, T&T Clark, Edinburgh, 19.

[10] On Ritschl's progressivistic optimism, see James Richmond (1978), *Ritschl: An Appreciation*, Collins, London, 259f.

[11] See Simon Fisher (1988), *Revelatory Positivism? Barth's Earliest Theology and the Marburg School*, Oxford, 272.

[12] See Albrecht Ritschl (1902), *The Christian Doctrine of Justification and Reconciliation*, trans. H.R. Mackintosh and A.B. Macaulay, 2nd ed., T&T Clark, Edinburgh, 13, 282; David L. Mueller (1969), *An Introduction to the Theology of Albrecht Ritschl*, Philadelphia, 160f.;

> That reality and culture might need to be changed, and
> changed, perhaps, through revolutionary struggle, is a
> thought that never seems to have crossed Barth's mind.[13]

Barth's Schleiermachian-style stress on the immediacy of self-authenticating revelation (*Offenbarung*), or what Frei calls Schleiermacherian "relationalism", learned from his Marburg teacher Wilhelm Herrmann (1846-1922), was not intended to promote a theological non-realism.[14]   As early as 1909 Barth attempts to avoid wholly subjectivising religious experience in a Neo-Kantian constructivist fashion.[15] Without recourse to a propositional understanding of revelation, Barth endeavours to do this by allocating the genesis of *Gotteserlebnis* and religious *Bewußtsein* (consciousness) to the objective reality of God, the Object's being *gegeben*.[16] He further speaks of the efficacy (*Wirksamkeit*) of the divine-human relation as deriving from the miracle of faith, thereby stressing the divine, gracious, and miraculous activity of God in initiating conversion.   The Barth even of 1912 presumes that faith and intuition "may *not* be *presupposed* as given along with the general concept of man".[17] So, in describing the personal relation (*persönliche Beziehung*) of Barth's early theology, Frei can speak of it as "critically realistic", and consequently Webb's seeing this theological realism as occurring post-*2Ro* may be perceived as being inaccurate.[18]

Barth therefore defines *Denken* as a *Nachdenken*, as he would famously also later, i.e. a reflection upon that which is given. But at this stage this Barth argued that the 'Object' was *immediately* given in human consciousness.   In fact, even in 1916, when coming to seriously concentrate on drawing a contrast between the will of the Wholly Other and our will and desires, Barth could still speak of the certainties of conscience [*WGWM*, 9-27].

Adolf von Harnack (1904), *What is Christianity?*, trans. T.B. Saunders, 3rd ed., Putnam, New York, 53.

[13] Fisher, 239.

[14] Hans Frei (1956), *The Doctrine of Revelation in the Thought of Karl Barth, 1909-1922: The Nature of Barth's Break with Liberalism*, unpublished Ph.D. thesis, University of Yale, 27, 33.

[15] See McCormack, 1995, 44.

[16] See Karl Barth (1912), 'Der christliche Glaube und die Geschichte', *Schweizerische Theologische Zeitschrift*, 1-18, 49-72 (53), cited in Fisher, 227.   On Schleiermacher's realism, see McCormack (1998), 'Revelation and History in Transfoundationalist Perspective: Karl Barth's Theological Epistemology in Conversation with a Schleiermachian Tradition', *Journal of Religion* vol. 78, 18-37 (21f.).

[17] Barth, cited in Fisher, 228.

[18] Ibid., 246, 281; Webb, 153.

Here Barth is following the rudiments of Schleiermacher's placing of conceptualisation (*Reflexion*) in second place so that doctrine becomes understood simply as the result of an attempt to set forth the content of the religious affections in speech. The contents of the secondary process of theological reflection are, as Frei argues,

> mediate and in principle distinct from ... the nature of the experience upon which they report. Furthermore, they are reliable only insofar as they are reports of the actual state of Christian consciousness.[19]

For Barth, then, as with Herrmann but in contrast to Troeltsch and his historical method, faith is primarily not a matter of assenting to some external historical facts, but is rather an experiential assent to an inward epiphany of divine grace in the hidden depths of individual experience, something which is self-authenticating and therefore unprovable apart from faith. It is an

> experience of God, unmediated consciousness of the presence and reality of the trans-human, trans-worldly and therefore simply superior power of life.[20]

However, although the individual's *Gotteserlebnis* transcends human rational and cognitive capacities, Barth does not relax his realist emphasis with reference to the immediacy of encounter and the individual's absolute security and certainty of experience. Nevertheless, he does further appropriate Schleiermacher's conception of the disintegrating influence of cognition and reflection on the original perception.[21]

Nonetheless, any attribution of the name 'God' to the 'object' of that supposed experience appears to be arbitrary given the very abstract nature of Barth's discussion of the Christian *Bewußtsein*. Fisher argues that he could not resolve the problem of how an essentially private and individual experience could be construed as possessing universal validity (*Allgemeingültigkeit*) for all Christians, and provides no criteria for

---

[19] Frei, 1956, 242.

[20] Barth, 1912, cited in Gorringe, 1999, 27.

[21] See Barth, 1912, cited in McCormack, 1995, 75.

recognising this experience as a *persönliche Beziehung* with the divine.[22] Barth's extreme actualism of the revelational *event* almost entirely usurps reflections on divine being and presence, and thereby makes it impossible for any discourse to speak about God's being or activity.[23] Moreover, in this exclusively actualistic stress on the immediacy of experience, Fisher argues, "Time was swallowed up in 'history', eschatology in religious experience".[24] This appears as an eschatology of the 'Moment', something which characterises much of the language of *2Ro*.

Whereas Barth would later locate the cognitive content of the encounter christologically, he, at this time, could speak of christology only in terms of Jesus' God-consciousness, echoing Herrmann's stress on the inner life of Jesus that is knowable only to faith.[25] This suggests a theology ultimately christo-morphic in character, with the symbol, image or *Bild* of Christ receiving the status of a cipher or conceptual stimulator, origin (*Ursprung*) and goal (*Zweck*), of personal *Gotteserlebnis*. Our consciousness is "somehow historically conditioned" and grounded "through the *personality of Jesus*", as contemporaneously mediated by the gospel narratives and the lives of his earliest witnesses in particular.[26] We, to put it crudely, internalise Christ as Barth indicates when he insists that "the Christ outside us is the Christ within, efficacious history is effected faith".[27] Consequently, Fisher argues that "Had the vocabulary of existentialism been available to Barth, no doubt he would have used it".[28]

The crucial question that could be asked of Barth is whether the relatedness of the individual to God could be portrayed non-christologically? Although Barth claims that true objectivity is found in the Christ who gives himself to be known in the depths of the human soul, his Christ tends to follow the general lines Ritschl's human exemplar or "archetype of moral personality".[29] And Barth's relationalism, stressing divine contemporaneity and actualism in revelation, implies that the divine-human togetherness has always been available, historically

---

[22] Fisher, 178, 280.

[23] See Ernst Troeltsch on Herrmann's "agnostic theory of religious knowledge" [Troeltsch (1977), 'Half a Century of Theology: A Review', in *Ernst Troeltsch: Writings on Theology and Religion*, ed. Robert Morgan and Michael Pye, John Knox Press, Atlanta, 58].

[24] Fisher, 235. Cf. Frei, 1956, 38.

[25] See Barth (1982), *Karl Barth-Rudolf Bultmann Letters, 1922-1966*, ed. Bernd Jaspert, trans. Geoffrey W. Bromiley, T&T Clark, Edinburgh, 153.

[26] Barth, 1912, cited in McCormack, 1995, 76.

[27] Barth, cited in Frei, 1956, 72.

[28] Fisher, 232.

[29] H.R. Mackintosh (1937), *Types of Modern Theology: Schleiermacher to Barth*, Nisbet, London, 162.

unmediated, to individuals as a permanent possibility. Though Barth constantly reiterates that religion is not a human work but an unmerited divine gift, God is nevertheless indissolubly bound in the relational nexus to the individual who accepts or 'undergoes' the experience of revelation.[30]

It is only later that Barth both perceives these problems and, learning particularly from both Feuerbach and his own experiences of 1914, comes to perceive a danger in this non-cognitivist-style revelational scheme. As the events of 1914 come to instruct him, such a idealist-constructivist approach to doctrine, and a stress on revelational immediacy, is open to ideological manipulation. German Protestantism then begins to appear as an ideological underpinning of, and being reciprocally paraded by, nineteenth-century nationalism, a *Vaterland*-religion devoted to the praises of the German God that provided a certain sacred justification for particular visions of cultural and national life and identity. As Fisher indicates, Barth's later criticism of Schleiermacher

> implied that Schleiermacher (and his [Barth's] own early theology) could not effectively speak either about God or his revelation in Christ because theologies of culture such as these projected onto God fanciful anthropological and ideological concerns, as well as their own humanist preoccupations. Their deity, in other words, was simply the prevailing *Kulturbewußtein* writ large.[31]

As such, God's sovereignty and freedom to be what he is *an und für sich selbst* had become endangered in a type of creaturely hegemony over the Creator, and God's self-revelation was apparently so intermingled with a revelation in the human self and its culture, that the two became indistinct. Fisher continues:

> God was a prisoner of his power to save, with his revelation binding him to believers in an a-temporal and eternal relationship of effector and effected. He was no longer free to have mercy on whom he will, to have compassion on whom he will, ... [or] free to ... judge.[32]

---

[30] See Fisher, 205; Frei, 1956, 49, 117, 456.

[31] Ibid., 277.

[32] Ibid., 297f.

Consequent to this theological assessment, therefore, came Barth's critique of the religious and cultural status quo by way of his general aversion to religiously inspired and supported ideologies.

Historically speaking, this 'break' only appears pronounced from 1916's address '*Die Gerechtigkeit Gottes*' (The Righteousness of God), and this theme of divine sovereignty became the central one of the 1921 edition of *Römerbrief.* This disillusionment with his Liberal theological background evolved primarily through an increasing critique of theology, culture and ethics from the perspective of religious socialism.

Progressing: Eschatology in Religious-Socialistic Perspective (Safenwil, 1911-1915)

In 1972, Marquardt controversially advanced that Barth's theology may be wholly genealogically accounted for by referring to his radical socialist politics.[33]   Although, on the one hand, he had moved too far in anthropologically reducing Barth's theology to his socialist politics, on the other, he had identified a vital element in Barth's theological development. For it was through this encounter with Religious Socialism that the seeds of revolt against his liberal education were sown.   Moreover, even in the *CD* Barth could speak fondly of socialism when criticising Leonhard Ragaz (1868-1945).   Socialism, Barth asserts, is a prophetic call for the church to be herself, to pursue her own proper task [*CD* I.1, 82].

This reading of Barth exposes the illusion of the picture of a thinker isolated from social and political concerns, as a later letter to T.A. Gill makes clear wherein Barth declares

> My thinking, writing and speaking developed from reacting to people, events and circumstances with which I was involved, with their questions and riddles. ... I was, did and said it when the time had come.[34]

Illusory, therefore, is Torrance's docetic-Barth, the man who almost unimpededly hears the Word of God in its direct and immediate

---

[33]   Friedrich-Wilhelm Marquardt (1972), *Theologie und Sozialismus.   Das Beispiel Karl Barths*, Kaiser, München.   Cf. George Hunsinger (1976), 'Conclusion: Toward a Radical Barth', in Hunsinger, 181-233 (186); Eberhard Jüngel (1986), *Karl Barth: A Theological Legacy*, trans. Garrett E. Paul, Westminster Press, Philadelphia, 101f.

[34]   Barth, letter to T.A. Gill, 10 August 1957, cited in Gorringe, *Karl Barth*, 16.   Cf. Barth, *Briefwechsel Karl Barth-Eduard Thurneysen, 1913-1921*, vol. I, 30, cited in Martin Kitchen (1991), 'Karl Barth and the Weimar Republic', *Downside Review* vol. 109, 183-201 (186).

fullness. Torrance speaks as if Barth, prior to 1911, was not wholly indebted to and influenced by his Liberal heritage. Secondly, Torrance argues that Barth's post-1914 theological redirection burst "out of this sermon preparation and the fulfilment of encounter between the Word of God and modern theology".[35] Thirdly, Torrance misleadingly refers to Barth's relation to Kutter and Ragaz only three times, all of which are characterised by a negative appraisal.[36]

On the contrary, as Hunsinger for example rightly argues, Barth wants precisely

> to work out a viable theological solution to the problem of
> theory and praxis - including political praxis.

so that Barth's theology "retained an intrinsic relationship to society and politics".[37] This perspective portrays a theologian deeply involved in the practical issues of living, and engaged in transformative 'praxis' for the sake of the humanisation of the human.

What is particularly important to note is the fact that this was not merely the case at an early stage in Barth's career, with Barth turning from political engagement to biblical theology, as Scholder, for example, believes.[38] Of course, in *Theologische Existenz Heute*, published in 1933, Barth declares that he intends "to carry on theology ... as if nothing had happened", and insists that

> The one thing that must not happen to us who are theological
> professors, is our abandoning our job through becoming
> zealous for some cause we think to be good.[39]

These statements need to be carefully read in context, however. In this pamphlet Barth is specifically pleading for the church to be true to its foundation in Jesus Christ, and to be obedient to him as its leader. This existence was being imperilled, Barth felt, by certain contemporary

---

[35] Torrance, 1962, 35. For a critique, see Hunsinger, 1976, 224.
[36] See ibid., 31, 37, 40.
[37] Hunsinger, 1976, 191.
[38] Klaus Scholder (1989), *The Churches and the Third Reich*, I: *1918-1934*, trans. John Bowden, SCM Press, London, 45.
[39] Barth (1933), *Theological Existence To-Day! A Plea for Theological Freedom*, trans. R. Birch Hoyle, Hodder and Stoughton, London, 9 and 11.

ecclesial alliances with the National Socialist State and its pattern of leadership, and these churches were thus listening "to the voice of a stranger".[40] In deliberate contrast to the rule of 'German Christians' that instructs the church to be "'the Church of the German people,' that is to say 'of Christians of the Aryan race'", he declares that

> If the German Evangelical Church excludes Jewish-Christians, or treats them as of a lower grade, she ceases to be a Christian Church.[41]

Given this, the original statements cited may be seen to pertain not to a necessary division of church and State in any Lutheran fashion, but rather to Barth's objections to the manner in which the *particular* relations between the German churches and *this particular government* were proceeding. When in 1938 Barth expresses that the state's power, belonging ultimately to God, is neutral as regards Truth in that it can go either way because of the non-neutrality of its members, he has already decided that the National Socialists were failing to fulfil the churches' proper function and the latter were going the 'demonic way'.[42] Instead, the church should preach the Gospel "*in* the Third Reich, but not *under* it, nor in its spirit", and the State should return to its proper function of granting the Gospel and the church a free course, a rather minimalist conception to which Barth later adds that "The essence of the State is ... the establishment of justice (*Recht*)" through its power.[43] By contrast, the fascist state, Barth declares, had lost its right to exist and thereafter "cannot be condoned by the Christian .... Fascism is pure *potentia*".[44] That is why, despite his own reservations about the Swiss government, "to protect Switzerland from National Socialism" Barth feels it necessary "to join the army and guard a bridge over the River Rhine".

Moreover, in a later response to Brunner's accusation that he had become passively unconcerned with the political problems, Barth claims that he had not advocated such passivity in 1933.[45] On the contrary, as a statement made in 1939 explains, "Wherever there is theological talk, it is

---

[40] Ibid., 27.

[41] Ibid., 49, 52.

[42] See Barth (1939), *Church and State*, trans. G. Ronald Howe, SCM Press, London, 15.

[43] Barth (1969), *How I Changed My Mind*, ed. and trans. John Godsey, St. Andrew Press, Edinburgh, 164; Barth (1963), *Karl Barth's Table Talk*, ed. John D. Godsey, Oliver and Boyd, Edinburgh and London, 75.

[44] Barth, 1963, 81.

[45] See Barth (1954), *Against the Stream: Shorter Post-War Writings*, ed. Ronald Gregor Smith, Philosophical Library, New York, 106-18.

always implicitly or explicitly political talk also".[46]   Hence, recently, Gorringe's contextual reading of Barth's theology argues that

> the great theme of his theology, from start to finish, is that the reality of God, and faith as response to that reality, is not a prop for the infirm, an opiate for the masses, nor an optional extra in the culture of contentment, but an essential aspect of human liberation, that without which human liberation cannot be achieved.

Therefore,

> Not just in 1933, though critically then, Barth believed that a Church obedient to the Word *made a difference*.[47]

Given Marx's famous critique of Christianity on eschatological perspective, it is somewhat ironic, and at the same time highly significant, that Barth's praxis finds its focus in eschatology, the details of which Marquardt pays too little attention to, albeit he does mention that the drive of praxis is released "out of expectation of the future".[48]   It is here that Barth seeks to discover the former's ground, and thus to develop his theology of practical engagement.

In a 1911 lecture in which Barth implicitly criticises Harnack's *What is Christianity?* a more politically and socially inclusive view of God's sovereignty emerges.   McCormack suggests this to be by virtue of Barth's having come to an appreciation of the Religious Socialist movement through Calvin's idea of a city of God on earth, and Werner Sombart's *Sozialismus und Sociale Bewegung* (although Barth's Ritschlian-sounding theology of 1909 could also partially account for it).[49] In fact, Barth had already positively cited Ragaz in a talk of January 1906, and had there declared that the social question was part of the human problem to which Jesus had responded.   However, too much significance

---

[46] Cited in Eberhard Busch (1976), *Karl Barth: His Life from Letters and Autobiographical Texts*, trans. John Bowden, SCM Press, London, 240.

[47] Gorringe, *Karl Barth*, ixf., 22.

[48] Marquardt, 167, cited in Hunsinger, 1976, 187.

[49] McCormack, 1995, 80.   Hunsinger incorrectly implies, however, that it was only here that Barth began his ascent to theological realism [1976, 198].   It is true, nevertheless, that Barth's realism was becoming more pronounced through the provision of an external goal for the ethics of hope.

cannot be attached to this speech since here Barth indicated not only how unable he was to offer any kind of generally positive appraisal of the socialist movement or how to address the social crises of the time, but also how he appeared to regard the socialists as something of a threat and denied that the kingdom of God can be brought in this way. Herrmann's 'praxis', after all, centred on the individual, and his own politics were conservative.[50] Misleading, then, is Jüngel's claim that Barth had already learned from Herrmann that theology is eminently concerned with reality, with 'real life', and that theology is therefore a "theory of praxis".[51]

In laying the eschatological foundations for *2Ro*'s critical ecclesiology by declaring that the church had *apostasised* from Christ in its spiritualistic neglect of social concerns, Barth is also coming to identify the necessity of ecclesial social engagement in his lecture of 1911. Some explicitly socialistic statements are distinctly made here, an unsurprising fact given that it is around this time that he is being "touched for the first time by the real problematic of life".[52]

In good Herrmannian fashion, Barth here argues that in Jesus a "spiritual power ... [has] entered history", bringing with it a new way of life and attitude.[53] However, in contrast to his Marburg teacher, he describes this socialistically, demonstrating that Jesus' desires were identical with those of the socialists. Particularly is this so in terms of the abolition of self-seeking through the possession of private property in favour of service to the common good, and the shaping of individualistically-centred persons into comrades, through social awareness and active concern.

Admitted is the idea that the Pietistic individualism of inwardness rests finally upon a false disjunction between spirit and matter. And this contradicts Jesus' life and teaching, in which there is only one world, and that is the kingdom of God. God's is a kingdom in which, albeit internalised within oneself as Harnack had argued, "must obtain dominion over the external - over actual life".[54] "The heavenly Father's love and justice come to rule over all things external and earthly."

Barth's thinking, at this stage, therefore, is coming to produce a powerful critique of existing society, founded upon the knowledge of the *totaliter aliter* of *Gotteserkenntnis* through Jesus. This claim of the

---

[50] See McCormack, 1995, 80f.

[51] Jüngel, 1986, 94.

[52] Barth, 1986, 154. Barth's involvement in the trade union movement is well documented [e.g., Torrance, 1962, 36; McCormack, 1995, 85f.].

[53] Barth (1976), 'Jesus Christ and the Movement for Social Justice (1911)', in Hunsinger, 19-43 (20).

[54] Ibid., 27.

"wholly otherness" of God is made here, and would become articulated consistently in *2Ro*, with reference to the moral chasm which separates God and humanity, of the prophetic message of "Either-Or!", and of a criticism of religion as a façade that conceals great unbelief. A sermon preached on March 9, 1913 pushes this further in the direction of a revolution being produced by the coming of the kingdom, albeit this does not refer to an armed insurrection but rather to the ethical striving of the converted. Human acts using coercive force are fundamentally flawed and unrighteous, and yet even if Christians ought not to participate in revolutions this does not mean for Barth that God would not be at work in and through them, expressing his displeasure at contemporary society and affairs.[55]

Barth is clearly not a Marxist. With Ragaz, he places enormous stress on the necessity of first creating new people in order to create a new and just order.[56] Nevertheless, Barth is moving toward wholescale critique of contemporaneity through arguing that the 'house' in which people live - the entire network of social, commercial, and political relationships - would have to be torn down and rebuilt from the ground up.

In this perspective Christian hope is perceived as making a person an alien in, and unable to make peace with, a world governed by sinful relationships as it presently is.[57] To take God seriously in the political realm necessarily means the refusal to acquiesce in existing possibilities, but to place revolutionary unrest in the service of the longing for something better than anything offered by this world.

Two weeks later, in another sermon (March 23), Barth suggests that he has moved to the view that because God alone can bring the eschatological renewal, human attainments - even those of the socialists - ought never to be identified with the kingdom. Here, Barth preaches that the outcome of the war between the kingdoms of God and evil was decided in principle in Jesus' crucifixion, although it has yet to be consummated for us.[58] Moreover, on December 23 of that year, Barth declares that all human action can only be transitory, and no more than a parable of the kingdom. Similarly, a lecture on 'Religion and Socialism' of 1915 claims

---

[55] Barth, cited in McCormack, 1995, 101f.

[56] Barth, 1976, 28.

[57] Barth, '"Die Hilfe" 1913', cited in Hunsinger, 1976, 199.

[58] See McCormack, 1995, 96.

that socialism is not itself the kingdom but a reflection or signpost of it.[59] No doubt Barth was learning from Herrmann Kutter (1863-1931) who had in 1910 asserted the gospel to be a critique of *all* ideologies and had thereafter refused strict association with any particular party.

Nevertheless, McCormack warns that the simplicity of the distinction between the divine and human agencies is deceptive in that it is never simple in practice.[60] It is clear, Barth believes, that God carries out his work through forces and powers resident in human history so that humans must be open to, and work for, the coming of the kingdom. The kingdom is spoken of not as a second world to be laid alongside this one, but as this world made new, and that, in some sense, by human action. Contextualising this entails recognising Kutter's religious interpretation of socialism as a kind of secular "parable of the Kingdom", and Ragaz's similar sounding belief "that the church must take a position toward socialism as a preliminary manifestation of the Kingdom of God".[61] This was grasped further as a demonstration in deeds as well as in words, of a vision of a new world that not only bears clear witness to that kingdom which Jesus had proclaimed, *but also was involved in God's very struggle against the false gods of this world.* Kutter termed this the "hammer of God" calling the churches to repentance, renouncing the dead God of the bourgeois classes, and renewing faith in scripture's living God.

Hence, despite Barth's partial limiting of human agency, there is evidence that in 1913 Barth has not renounced 1911's robust and unqualified words of social relationalism, that "Jesus *is* the social movement, and the social movement *is* Jesus in the present", and his celebration of the Religious Socialist movement as

> not only the greatest and most urgent word of God to the present, but also in particular a quite direct continuation of the spiritual power which ... entered into history and life with Jesus.[62]

Such an accolade, however, strikes Gollwitzer, and would similarly strike Barth later, as sounding

---

[59] See Gorringe, *Karl Barth*, 32.

[60] McCormack, 1995, 101.

[61] Herrmann Kutter (1904), *Sie Müssen! Ein offenes Wort an die christliche Gesellschaft*, Herrmann Walther Verlagsbuchandlung, Berlin, cited in McCormack, 1995, 83f.; Ragaz, cited in Jüngel, 1986, 30.

[62] Barth, 1911, 19, 20.

too much like a naïve attempt to legitimate one's own decision through a venerable historical example, or even more like an attempt to anchor one's own attitude in something absolute.[63]

Barth's only qualification of this comes through identifying God's will with what the socialists *want* rather than with what they do.[64] Even when the socialists capitulate by supporting the war, becoming a "new disappointment" for Barth, the politically *social* and *communitarian* element in this socialist vision remains true in Barth's view so that, regardless of what particular socialists did, this vision would bear significant witness to the New Testament image of the kingdom. For that reason, even subsequent to his disappointment over the Socialist Democratic Party's 'failure' in August 1914, Barth could join the Swiss Socialist Party in 1915 (26 January).

Consequently, McCormack correctly argues that in this period we do not have a critique of liberalism from any external vantage-point, but rather one from within its own house.[65] The pre-war Barth has not completely given up hope in a progress of the human race, albeit this is not an intrinsically inevitable evolution but rather a development inspired by the activity of God in Christ. And, even though Barth preaches about a move "towards an abyss" and stresses "that we are standing in a crisis like a sick man", he remains convinced that this crisis could be alleviated.[66] In fact, he speaks at times of socialism's *unstoppable* march. But by 1913 he has become conscious of the possibility, perhaps even probability, that progress might only be made by fits and starts, through "catastrophes and violent storms" - i.e., God's grace coming only through his *judgment*.[67] Such storms could well serve to awaken the people of God to the need of the hour, to the desire to obey God and establish justice.

Methodologically, then, Barth is here still indebted to Herrmann. But it is notable that he has departed from his teachers on the significant material question of the nature of God's kingdom, and signs are being shown of deviations in other areas as well, particularly in relation to divine

---

[63] Gollwitzer, 86.

[64] Barth, 1911, 21.

[65] McCormack, 1995, 86, 91.

[66] Barth, sermon, 9 Mar. 1913, cited in Ibid., 1995, 103.

[67] Ibid., 102.

judgment and human sin.[68] In this the role of the religious socialists is important, as Barth later declares with respect to the significance of the influence of Kutter on his theological development. Although this does not yet entail a break, it does help prepare the ground for it so that the war is not solely responsible for Barth's 'break' with Liberalism but serves rather as the catalyst for it.[69] This 'conversion', then, is therefore not a sudden occurrence but has already been developing.

Krisis: Doing, or Rather Un-Doing, Theology from Within a Shell-Crater (1915-1924)

During the immediate years after the commencement of European military hostilities, the prevailing cultural and religious crises served to impel and nourish Barth's theological journeying. His developing dialectical *Ansatzpunkt* (starting-point) entextualises this sense of crisis, recognition of which immediately undermines Torrance's implication of a Barth hovering over any cultural instantiation as purely hearer of the Word, one that ultimately leads him out of the recesses of a liberal 'embourgeoisment' of theology.[70] The latter's style of doing theology is, Barth comes to admit, one that has flattened the eschatological horizon into contemporary experience of God, thereby undermining any possibility of imagining a critically concrete transcendence of the conditions of social existence. Moreover, it has also weakly succumbed to external political pressures with its *Kriegstheologie*. God simply cannot be "drawn into the matter in this way".[71] Barth comes to the conclusion that the problem with this type of theology is, as he argues against Schleiermacher in 1922, "that one can *not* speak of God simply by speaking of man in a loud voice" [*WGWM*, 196]. At least by 1920, he has learned to take seriously Feuerbach's questioning of theology's reduction to anthropology, and becomes a critic of ideology - the absolutising of concepts or ideas through which sense is made of the world – in favour of a theology rooted in the concrete.

---

[68] See McCormack, 1995, 93, 95.

[69] See David Klemm (1987), 'Toward a Rhetoric of Postmodern Theology: Through Barth and Heidegger', *Journal of the American Academy of Religion* vol. 55, 443-469 (445).

[70] See Torrance, 1962, 35.

[71] Barth's letter to Martin Rade, 31 August 1914, cited in McCormack, 1995, 112. Gorringe cites a letter of Barth written during the Weimar period, complaining that the German professors were "masters at finding ingenious, ethical, and Christian bases for brutalities" [Gorringe, *Karl Barth*, 77].

Consequently, although the statement needs to be handled with care lest it depreciate Barth's 'realistic'-type intentions in his so-called 'liberal period', Frei declares that Barth turns to

> a stringent Realism, in which God, his reality and nature are to be understood as being the independent ground of all relation of God with creatures.[72]

Barth's pre-eminent post-1915 affirmation becomes God's sovereignty, a regulative concept that Barth feels is imperilled in German nationalism's *Kriegstheologie*.[73] This is particularly expressed in the tautological, "The World remains world. But God is God", serving, in Jüngel's words,

> to emphasize the radical difference between the divine essence, the Godness of God, and all ungodly essences.[74]

Eschatology becomes central to the expression of these theological concerns, since, as he argues in 1924, the "Last *things*, as such, are not *last* things" in the sense of being relegated to theological appendices, or being primarily concerned with depicting figures and events of the remote future [*RD*, 108]. The horizon of the End, rather, casts its shadow across the whole of theological awareness, and therefore,

> If Christianity be not altogether thoroughgoing eschatology, there remains in it no relationship whatever with Christ [*2Ro*, 314].

It is in eschatology that Barth expresses both the divine *krisis* over the condition of all that exists, and the positive reconstituting of this

---

[72] Hans Frei (1957), 'Niebuhr's Theological Background', in *Faith and Ethics: The Theology of H. Richard Niebuhr*, ed. Paul Ramsey, Harper and Row, New York, 9-64 (42).

[73] Jüngel argues that this sovereignty theme arose from a desire to obey the commandment, 'Thou shalt not take the Lord's name in vain' [Jüngel, 1986, 59]. However, it would be more accurate to portray this concern as consequent upon the more positive first commandment [see *RD*, 40].

[74] Barth, Nov. 1915, cited in McCormack, 129; Jüngel, *Barth-Studien*, cited in Werner Jeanrond (1988), 'Karl Barth's Hermeneutics', in *Reckoning With Barth: Essays in Commemoration of the Centenary of Karl Barth's Birth*, ed. Nigel Biggar, Mowbray, London & Oxford, 80-97 (89).

existence in line with that End, which is God. Kitchen, then, is incorrect to assume that Barth's *krisis* theology is radically detached from culture and social action.[75] As Barth argues in the late 1930s,

> It is the hope of the new age, which is dawning in power, that separates the Church from the State, that is, from the States of this age and world.[76]

The negative connotations of this statement need to be counterbalanced by Barth's affirmation also of a positive relation between them. As argued earlier, Barth is not intending to promote a two kingdoms antithesis between church and state, although he does maintain a "legitimate, relative *independence*" between them, but rather is drawing attention to the critical edge that Christian hope provides, and which indeed later set him at odds with the contemporary Nazi government.[77]

However, in this earlier period, it is true, the sound of the shells of his negative thematics tends to drown out the reconstructive, so that in 1914 Barth could declare that "This is a *Gotteszeit* as never before".[78] However, this is primarily because he feels the need to explosively annihilate all false theologies in order to ground God's relationship to humanity in God alone apart from all human efforts.[79] Hence the basic tonality of Barth's writings in this period, increasingly and consistently comes to exhibit a vigorous prophetic iconoclasm, and this deriving from the recognition of what Tracy calls Christianity's "dangerous memory" of Christ's Passion and Resurrection.[80] That is why Barth characterises it as a kind of marginal note and "corrective", a "pinch of spice" in the food of the theologians of the time, an image that could also characterise Barth's other writings of the period 1916-1921 [*WGWM*, 98].[81]

---

[75] Kitchen, 199. Webb misses the eschatological sculpting of this "root metaphor" of *krisis* to exhibit the shape of the divine sovereignty and consequently to describe the nature of the shadow that this casts over temporal affairs [Webb, 52].

[76] Barth, 1939, 39.

[77] Ibid., 1939, 29.

[78] Barth, sermon, 23 August 1914, cited in McCormack, 1995, 115.

[79] *2Ro*'s explosive nature was aptly observed by Karl Adam (1926), 'Die Theologie der Krisis', *Hochland* vol. 23, II, 276f., cited in John McConnachie (1931), *The Significance of Karl Barth*, London, 43.

[80] David Tracy (1990), 'On Naming the Present', *Concilium* 1990/1, SCM Press, London, 66-85 (76).

[81] Hence Barth is able to declare that, despite the differences between the two editions of the *Römerbrief* (believing the second to be a substantially radical revision of the first), an "identity of subject-matter as well as of the theme ..., guarantees a definite continuity between the old and the new" [*2Ro*, 2].

Nevertheless, it is also true that Barth has not yet come to locate theological discourse in a positively coherentist christological idiom that can incorporate eschatology within itself (as he did particularly in *CD* II.2 on election), and thereby to properly discover the healing and transformative message of the Gospel. Therefore, while Barth does not neglect to indicate that *2Ro* is in some sense about Jesus, this is a Jesus whose cross and resurrection primarily bear witness to the hidden God who is the world's *krisis*.

Further, the concern remains that the overall impression, particularly of *2Ro*, is one of a pessimistic rupturing of all forms of human culture and theological discourse and practice. Stressed is the actualistically coloured eschatological *krisis* that results from the divine assault on all human attempts to pass through the divide to the divine, and on every attempted human synthesis with the divine thoughts and acts. This proves to be the final sounding of the death-knell to Barth's earlier optimism over Religious Socialism. Not only is it, as Gorringe declares, "ultimately reductive and lacks the depth to do the job required of it", but it is itself part of the idolatrous human abrogation of the divine action into its own.[82]

From the reviews of *1Ro*, the heightened sense of cultural crisis, and a reading of Kierkegaard, Overbeck and Dostoyevsky, Barth comes to reapply this *krisis* metaphor in a more consistent way in the second edition. Admitting this is not to say with Frei and Hunsinger that the second edition constitutes a substantial 'break' from its predecessor.[83] God's strangeness to his creatures is present in *1Ro* also. What is decisive is the shift in explanatory model: from one of 'organic-growth' (or 'process', according to Beintker) eschatology to a radically futurist eschatology.[84] Barth comes to understand *1Ro*'s model as implying "a continuous connection between God's being and our own" [*2Ro*, 279]. McCormack, however, convincingly argues that this is to misconstrue Barth's intentions in *1Ro*.[85] Moreover, Gorringe argues that Barth's use of the contrast between organic growth and mechanical change is that between divine action and human-made change, with us being drawn into the former by Christ's

---

[82] Gorringe, *Karl Barth*, 10.

[83] Hunsinger, 1976, 210f.; Frei, 1956, 497.

[84] So McCormack, 1995, 208; cf. Michael Beintker (1985), 'Der Römerbrief von 1919', in *Verkündigung und Forschung: Beihefte zu 'Evangelische Theologie'*, ed. G. Sauter 2, 24.

[85] McCormack, 1995, 153.

resurrection.[86]   Hence Barth argues that "the fulfilment it [i.e., Christianity] expects is not ... the goal or result of a development or a gradual 'ascent of man' but the discovery of a new creation or the substance of a new knowledge".[87]

Highlighted is the "gulf" between the world and the *"deus absconditus"* who, being totally unlike the creature, is "too high for us and too far beyond our understanding" and grasp.[88] According to Barth, God is the Unknown and, humanly speaking, unknowable; the humanly impossible; the *nicht-geben* and *unanschaulich* (unintuitable) [*2Ro*, 35]. He is "utterly distinct from men", the *totaliter aliter* from all that exists [*2Ro*, 28].   In order to express this creaturely "unbridgeable chasm", *diastasis*, and separation between finite and infinite, Barth famously utilises Kierkegaard's phrase of *den 'unendlichen qualitativen Unterscheid'* ('infinite qualitative distinction') [*RD*, 87].

Barth's giving glory to God is not intended to be some kind of pious vault over the aporia created both by God's transcendence and Calvin's theme of *finitum non capax infiniti* [*2Ro*, 212].   He recognises both human obligation and tragic inability to think and speak of God [*WGWM*, 186].   Thus, his eschatologically dialectical discourse traces how the mystery of the transcendent Word's ineradicable otherness and strangeness evades the domestication of a presence in the direct saying of human words (as if the signifiers were the *res* rather than the signs), and how this evasion prevents theological foreclosure [*2Ro*, 38].   All thought and speech is thereby placed under a strict eschatological reservation:

> There can be no completed work. All human achievements
> are no more than Prolegomena; and this is especially the case
> in theology [*2Ro*, 3].

It is for this reason that Barth, when speaking of the divine communication, utilises metaphors strongly suggestive of divine absence: of a tangent touching a circle without touching it [*2Ro*, 30]; a void resulting from the impact of the collision of grace with this world; a crater resulting from an explosion [*2Ro*, 29]; an empty canal devoid of water; and a sign-post which points away from itself to another destination [*2Ro*, 88]. Grace leaves its mark on this world by accomplishing a negative work, but yet does not leave behind any positive trace that humanity could then manipulate or claim for itself by becoming a part of the world. There is no humanly immediate grasp upon the Word, but rather a fissuring of all

---

[86] Gorringe, 'Eschatology', 93; cf. *1Ro*, 9, 21.

[87] *1Ro*, 505-7, cited in Gorringe, ibid, 94.

[88] *2Ro*, 80,40, 42, 46.

referential meta-language of theologies of presence, as in relationalism. God never becomes an object but always remains the Subject of our knowing of him. Barth's is a dynamic and actualistic conception of God, as the image suggests of a bird in flight, whose energy cannot be captured in the momentary presentation of an artist, suggests [*2Ro*, 184].

In this context *2Ro* critiques theology, religion, church (as the particular cradle of religion), and culture, more generally spreading the net in comparision with *1Ro*'s specifically named Liberalism-Pietism, Idealism and Religious Socialism. Similarly, the earlier of the two editions maintains that movements for pacifism and social democracy do not represent the kingdom of God "but the old human kingdom in a new guise".[89]

Precisely what religion and the church attempt to do, in tragic obliviousness to their true situation, is domesticate revelation and bring about the kingdom of God. Religion, Barth argues in *2Ro*, is the most dangerous enemy that humanity can have, apart from God, since it all too easily lulls one into a false sense of security and into the complacent belief that one has done all that needs to be done for the sake of her justification. In its "criminal arrogance" it produces, thereafter, "comfortable illusions about the knowledge of God and union with him" [*2Ro*, 37]. This is, however, a sign of both religion's and the church's "veritable *Gotteskrankheit*" [*2Ro*, 332] and its Tower of Babel [*WGWM*, 19f.].

Religious Socialism is located within this category in the Tambach lecture of 1919, for here, although already prepared for in the first edition of *Der Römerbrief*, he announces the placing of "a religious halo over society's acting" as a betrayal of both Christ and society, and, therefore, as an unsuccessful attempt to mend an old garment with new patches [*CPS*, 279]. This theme continues into *2Ro* with talk of the tragic nature of human revolutions, those movements that forget that they are not Christ and cannot, consequently, arm themselves with God's measurement [*2Ro*, 480ff.]. Underneath the façade of righteousness the human will remains unchanged and therefore unrighteous.

God has judged religion, society, and humanity, and the ideologies that both give rise to and derive out of them, and found them wanting, corrupt and sinful [*2Ro*, 390].[90] Nothing escapes the rupture of divine

---

[89] *1Ro*, 42, cited in Gorringe, *Karl Barth*, 44.

[90] Underlying Barth's radically powerful return to Reformation conceptions of sin are particularly St. Paul, Kierkegaard, Luther, J. Müller, and Dostoyevsky, and Kähler's doctrine of the irrational and surd-like element in sin. Torrance argues that Barth's theology

judgment and condemnation. This theme finds particular expression in *2Ro* through explication of the central significance of the cross of Christ, a theme that theologically corresponds to Barth's vehement rejection of the Liberal 'lives of Jesus' movement [*2Ro*, 159]. The cross is perceived as the supreme and unique event of the meeting between a holy God and sinful humanity, in which all the subtle attempts of human self-deification and self-aggrandisement are interrupted and exposed as idolatrous.[91] In fact, Barth proclaims, it was the church that crucified Christ [*2Ro*, 389].

It is at this point that any attempts to capture the Word in human words are emphatically declared to be illusory. In this context Barth rhetorically names religion's 'god' as the "No-God", the 'god' that Feuerbach criticises in his projection-theory of religion. Closely resembling aspects of Nietzsche's thought, Barth claims that this god, or idol, is created by humanity out of boredom because it lacks the courage to despair. What may then be perceived is the fact that this is a 'god' under human control, our companion with whom we are co-partners, and even our possessed object [*2Ro*, 47]. In fact, we desire to be God's patrons or advisers. The result is, and here Barth again echoes Feuerbach, that in worshipping God we are really worshipping ourselves [*2Ro*, 44].

This explosion of all human pretensions is so severe and all-embracing that *2Ro*'s text itself stands within the fall-out. Barth does not seek any assured heights from which to safely observe the *krisis*, but rather admits, in a moment of tragic irony, that there can be no abandonment of either religion or the church as if one had a superior vantage-point from which to criticise them, one which has not itself been applied to the *krisis*, in an implicit response to Ragaz's belief that "the church was impossible".[92] The best that Barth can claim for theology is a daring use of indirect communication through "broken" discourse and a "speaking in parables", not only a good strategy for avoiding idolatry but also a reflection of the indirectness of God's speech itself [*2Ro*, 221].

Roberts understands Barth's procedure here as an example of a radical and deconstructive change of the ontology of the subject, or an inspired and affirmed self (*1Ro*), to an endangered subject threatened with eschatological annihilation (*2Ro*), although this implies that Roberts

---

theology is here derived from the standpoint of Christ's cross and resurrection, and not from any personal misanthropic tendencies [see Torrance, 1962, 65].

[91] A similar treatment of the cross pervades Jürgen Moltmann's (1974) *The Crucified God: The Cross as the Foundation and Criticism of Christian Theology*, trans. R.A. Wilson and J. Bowden, SCM Press, London, 68ff., 212.

[92] Gorringe, *Karl Barth*, 62.

underestimates *1Ro*'s preparation for a theology under *krisis* [*TW*, 191f.].[93] Similarly, Webb claims that *2Ro* is an ironic piece of rhetoric which playfully dissolves itself without making any substantial theological or metaphysical claims.[94] The goal of this "rhetorical strategy", Ward claims, is to indefinitely hold open a space beyond human language for the eschatological appearance of a God who, here and now, is absent.[95] As such, it verges on "sheer agnosticism", Ward continues, and even "atheism", Zahrnt asserts.[96] Therefore, when Barth does hyperbolically refer to God's otherness, for example, Webb perceives the trope of irony as a qualification which prevents him "from taking his own hyperbole literally".[97] Webb is thereby prompted to proclaim that Jülicher misjudged *2Ro*'s mood when he accused the self-deceived Barth of an illegitimate attempt to escape the logic of his own epistemic restrictions through an esoteric perspective (and thus capitulated to a different but nevertheless real ideology) [*2Ro*, 10, 20].

However, not only does Barth emphasise the world's godlessness but the divine 'No' to the world stands firmly on the road to the divine 'Yes' of grace, so that through the screaming of the 'No' the melodious theme of the 'Yes' may still be audible. This is because, even at this stage in Barth's reflections, the world is the Creator's creature [*2Ro*, 247].

Secondly, the eschatological model with which Barth operates is one of *exitus* through sin and *reditus* through God's faithfulness and grace in Christ. Therefore, although Barth can argue that God is "pure negation", this is stated with reference to the world as fallen [*2Ro*, 141]. Subsequently, Barth adds that God wills to be both known and loved [*2Ro*, 305], a comment that raises serious questions over the legitimacy of Jenson's reading that *2Ro*'s concept of 'God', consequent on its being developed through a *via negativa*, is contentless, purely formal, and lacking all the features of a personal life.[98] In *2Ro* Barth speaks, for

---

[93] Webb and Ward both argue that Barth shares this problematic with Derrida [Webb, 68; Ward, 1995, 247]. Nevertheless, whereas for Derrida, theology is part of the quest for referentiality in language, for Barth it is precisely *God himself* – eschatologically conceived – who secures language's fracture.

[94] Webb, 98.

[95] Ward, 1995, 247.

[96] Ibid., 92; Zahrnt, 25.

[97] Webb, 115. However, Barth's theological realism is perceivable throughout this period [e.g. *CPS*, 277].

[98] Jenson, 1969, 30. Cf. Hunsinger, 1976, 216.

instance, of God's freedom [92]; goodness [80]; justice [107]; graciousness [102f.]; free decision and pleasure for creation [121ff.]; love [139]; wrath [42ff.]; faithfulness to his promise to his creation [93ff.]; and patience with that creation [96]. The most that one can claim is that although these things are present *in nuce*, Barth's later christological and trinitarian concentration necessitates a more sustained analysis of God *in sich*.

Similarly Barth argues that religion arises as the result of the experience of grace in revelation and only becomes 'evil' in seeking to preserve itself, to become something positive for itself, and to captively locate revelation in the craters. Although it does this only frailly, its justification belongs only in its witness, i.e. its proper function is to be like a sign-post that points beyond itself [see *2Ro*, 37].

Barth even regards his use of the Kierkegaardian theme of the 'infinite qualitative distinction' as having a positive as well as a negative function [*2Ro*, 10]. By speaking also of *des Qualitativen Unterscheids* (the qualitative distinction) between God and the world [*2Ro*, 39, 276, 330f.] and *jene qualifizierte Distanz* (the qualitative distance) between people and the final Omega, Barth is, Lowe claims, altering the Kierkegaardian language in order to avoid suggesting any *ontological opposition*.[99] However, somewhat contrary to the haste with which Lowe draws certain conclusions from this point, Barth does actually uncompromisingly declare that

> If I have a system, it is limited to a recognition of what
> Kierkegaard called the 'infinite qualitative distinction'
> between time and eternity [*2Ro*, 10].

Moreover, he frequently uses the full Kierkegaardian formula in his *2Ro* commentary.[100] Nevertheless, placing this distinction in the context of Barth's intentions to subvert human religiosity, one must agree with Lowe that there is no *necessary* (i.e., ontological) *opposition* in *2Ro* between infinite and finite as if Barth is deriding the finite for merely existing. Lowe draws attention to the fact that Barth frequently couples *Aufhebung* with *Begründung* (dissolved and established).[101] What appears in Lowe's account, then, is the fact that Barth is at pains to fashion a vocabulary of simple difference, eschewing the rhetoric of opposition. Therefore, Lowe concludes, Barth's is a moral dualism of a "righteous God

---

[99] Walter Lowe (1988), 'Barth as a Critic of Dualism: Re-Reading the *Römerbrief*', *SJT* vol. 41, 377-395 (382).

[100] *2Ro*, 40, 202, 355, 356.

[101] See *2Ro*, 30, 36, 38, 46, 51.

versus sinful humanity. This, it can be advanced, is quite distinct from a dualism of a *metaphysical* or ontological bent".[102]

Barth's universe of discourse, here, necessarily clears the debris (*Aufräumungsarbeit*) that remains after the explosive recognition of the divine-human discontinuity, in order that grace may re-function. So Barth argues:

> Only when the all-embracing contrast between God and men
> is perceived can there emerge the knowledge of God, a new
> communion with Him, and a new worship [*2Ro*, 80].

Although his emphasis in this period falls upon the fact that "The kingdom of men is, without exception, never the Kingdom of God", Barth can nevertheless emphatically hope for the advent of God's kingdom.[103] The *final* word is not judgment (or its correlates), but forgiveness [*2Ro*, 174]. So while Zahrnt can rightly cite Barth to the effect that "We are more deeply committed to negation than to affirmation, to criticism and protest than to naïveté, to longing for the future than to participation in the present", he is wrong to press this too far when he claims that "crisis threatens to become an independent theme".[104]

It is inadequate, therefore, to read Barth's eschatology as a purely negatively critical mode of discourse and a mere cipher for the repudiation of all that is finite, serving therein to codify the divine-human *diastasis*. Webb's rhetorical strategy and Roberts' dualistic ontology, with their consequent devaluing of time by eternity, promote just such a misleading suggestion.[105] Instead, "the two Blumhardts," Jüngel declares, "had opened Barth's eyes to see that the impossible becomes possible".[106] Humanly impossible certainly, but possible with God. That is why Barth describes faith paradoxically as the "impossible possibility" [*2Ro*, 123]. Faith is that which humanity cannot achieve but which comes

---

[102] Lowe, 394.
[103] *2Ro*, 138; citation from 56.
[104] Zahrnt, 31.
[105] To Ward's claim that Barth's theology of language follows a 'Nestorian' pattern (implying divine-human opposition), McCormack, albeit over-polemically, directs one to the basic *Alexandrian* structure of Barth's christology [McCormack (1996), 'Article Review: Graham Ward's *Barth, Derrida and the Language of Theology*', *SJT* vol. 49, 97-109; Ward, 52].
[106] Jüngel, 1986, 66.

eschatologically and miraculously [*2Ro*, 59f.]. Utilising Kierkegaardian imagery, it is described as being, from a human perspective, a hazardous gamble, a risk, and a leap [*2Ro*, 98f., 149].

A similar concern generates, and subsequently infuses, discourse about the 'Moment' of the revelational event with no before and after: i.e. it has no temporal extension that can be claimed as belonging to time's potentialities [*2Ro*, 137]. Thus, although paradoxes are used to describe this in-breaking and resultant faith, Barth does not *intend* to either undermine the reality of the encounter or wholly assert divine absence. Rather, such paradoxes serve to indicate God's absence to human striving, but his, particularly futural, presence through grace.

The same may be claimed for Barth's use of the time-eternity dialectic. If this image is pressed the incarnation would tend to become temporally vacant, and therefore revelation's in-breaking would lose touch with temporal reality altogether, as Roberts indicates.[107] McCormack convincingly claims, however, that Barth does not intend this consequence because of the designed metaphoricity and paradoxicality of his time-eternity discourse.

> What we are seeing here is Barth's use of the time-eternity dialectic to drive home the point once and for all that revelation is *in* history, but it is not *of* history.[108]

This frequently misunderstood dialectic usefully negates all human possibilities of domesticating the divine and bears witness to a theological state of affairs, since eternity cannot become time without ceasing to be eternity, whereas eternity can encounter time. So the structural similarity between time-eternity and *CD* I's dialectic of revelation's veiling-unveiling, makes the former a profitable, albeit limited, tool for bearing witness to the latter, as McCormack argues.[109]

Therefore, the possibility of righteousness before God (which comes from him) and the kingdom of God (God's unceasing universal rule) are interpreted as the inconceivable divine in-breaking, the Unknown into the known context of reality, the impossible possibility of the coming of the new world. Society "is not forsaken of God", for although there is no 'way' from 'here to there' there is from there to here [*CPS*, 275].

---

[107] The often cited instance of this is Barth's application of the eternal simultaneity of all times to the eschaton of revelation, through which Barth apparently became adverse to historical issues [e.g., *TG*, 31; Jenson, 14].

[108] McCormack, 1995, 252; cf. *CPS*, 288.

[109] Ibid., 265.

This encounter rests upon the presupposition of God's speaking "perpendicularly from above" in Jesus Christ [*CPS*, 283]. Barth, according to Mueller, had no intention here of positing a final separation between God and humanity, but rather stressed their union in Christ's particularity.[110] Hence, Jesus is spoken of in eschatological terms. He alone, as the 'Last Things', inaugurates the new covenant of God and restores the broken relationship of human union with God [*2Ro*, 417]. As such, he is the "altogether new, the decisive factor and turning-point in man's consideration of God" [*2Ro*, 36]. It is he who is the true and only "Christian" in society, the "new man", the Second Adam, and therefore "the true humanity on earth".[111] In a passage which anticipates Barth's later strongly accented soteriological vicariety theme, Barth even declares that

> Through His presence in the world and in our life we have been dissolved as men and established in God. By directing our eyes to Him our advance is stopped and we are set in motion [*2Ro*, 30].[112]

The process of articulating theology from within a christological matrix, so pronounced later in *CD*, is therefore beginning to be developed at this relatively early stage in Barth's theology. Indeed, although Barth has not yet adequately reflected upon the ground of our knowledge within God in himself, as he would later, his doctrine of revelation is already *functionally* trinitarian.[113] Hence, he can declare that

> The years AD 1-30 are the era of revelation and disclosure; the era which ... sets forth the new and strange divine definition of all time [*2Ro*, 29].

---

[110] David L. Mueller (1990), *Foundation of Karl Barth's Doctrine of Reconciliation: Jesus Christ Crucified and Risen*, The Edwin Mellen Press, Lewiston, Queenston, Lampeter, 11. Cf. Torrance, 1962, 51.

[111] *CPS*, 273, 2Ro, 273, 133.

[112] See *2Ro*, 182, 201, 205, on soteriological vicariety.

[113] True knowledge is participatory personal knowledge (*Erkenntnis*) which can *only be given by God himself*, distinguishable from a merely external *Kennetnis* (as can be acquired through the Law) [*1Ro*, 65]. Herein, Barth's theology is becoming a thorough-going *ein Denken von Gott aus* [*1Ro*, 71].

Even though Barth immediately qualifies this 'historical' sense of revelation by arguing that God "makes every epoch a potential field of revelation and disclosure", he still strongly links this disclosure to Christ in his universality [*2Ro*, 29].

Subsequently, Barth prevents the eschatological ramblings of one speculating, while also providing his eschatological assertions with a definite content that refuses to be divorced from the trinitarian context that he is coming to articulate.

Furthermore, it is important to note Barth's reticence in articulating the details of hope's content for the future. He declares that on the other side of death is life,

of which we can know nothing at all, which we can only comprehend as the life of *God* Himself, without having in our hands anything more than an empty conception thereof - apart from the fullness that God alone gives and His revelation in the resurrection [*RD*, 22f.].

He even argues that the last things can only be described *via negativa* [*RD*, 91]. The *eschaton* is, through Christ, partially conceivable since he *is* that "End of history" and kingdom of God, and in his resurrection God's rule has broken into this world [*2Ro*, 29]. Hence, Barth adopts various biblical images to tentatively express his 'vision' of the *future* sovereign rule of God that will take place at Christ's *parousia*, and in which he will be all in all.[114] For example, he speaks of the fulfilment of God's promises of the creation of a new heaven and earth [*CPS*, 323], a new age in which death as the last enemy and our limitation is finally destroyed [*CPS*, 324], when we shall see God face to face [*RD*, 76, 85], and no longer through the glass darkly [*RD*, 85]. Through God's great transformation and recreation of human life, love shall never cease [*RD*, 92f.]. Moreover, Barth encapsulates the discontinuity and continuity between our present and future in God in the metaphor of the 'resurrection of the dead'. This necessitates that the kingdom is not to be conceived of as lying within finite potentialities as, perhaps, "a higher continuation of this life" [*RD*, 180], as in the immortality of the soul [*RD*, 206f.; 216]. And yet, this contradicts any ultimate dualism [*RD*, 203]. Secondly, it expresses a hope "for the physical side of life".[115] Jüngel, therefore, claims that Barth learned from the Blumhardts (but also from Religious Socialism) that he could "love the world and still be completely true to God".

---

[114] *2Ro*, 153; *RD*, 71, 92f., 111, 176.
[115] Jüngel, 1986, 66f.

This christological mediation for eschatological reflection does not, however, lead Barth to suppose that all has already been given and realised in him by us, as Roberts and Moltmann imply. For Barth, a new day has certainly dawned in Christ, and the kingdom of God is now at hand.[116] Nevertheless, this is qualified by declaring that Paul countered the Corinthian claim that what had happened in Christ was

> something finished and satisfying in itself. In reality it is only a beginning, in fact only an indication [*RD*, 177].

Given the continuing conflict of Christ with "the powers warring against God", he is in the process of coming "to deliver the Kingdom to the Father" [*RD*, 177].

> The Christian monism of the Corinthians, who regarded the Kingdom of God as already established, is a pious godlessness [*RD*, 177].

Barth's intention is to prevent realisation in and with and under the conditions of time, for our present 'time' is associated with fallenness [*2Ro*, 301]. That is why Barth later clarifies himself by drawing a distinction between 'fallen time' and 'God's time for us' in *CD* I.1.

It is through a 'futurist-style' eschatology, with reference to our fulfilment, that Barth grounds warnings of not confusing our present with the eschatologically new [*RD*, 211]. Since the *Eschaton* is beyond the boundary of death (itself an event in time) it remains future for those within temporality. The *futurum resurrectionis* is yet to fulfilled [*2Ro*, 180, 196]. It is the prominence of this theme that accounts for why Barth's focus is less on our *reception* of 'eternity' (which Moltmann understands in temporal terms) than upon the 'crater' or *sign* that the revelational encounter leaves in its wake. Hence the theme of hope's waiting is prominent in *2Ro*, as also is the 'not yet' and the promise of redemption [e.g., *2Ro*, 102f.]. The Christian, for Barth, becomes "watchman" expecting the coming of the new world [*2Ro*, 41]. She "is a pilgrim on the road of God", moving in the event of the Spirit [*2Ro*, 33, 273].

However, Barth's particular dialectical model threatens this essential eschatological nescience at one fundamental point. Although the words are not shouted in 1921 as loudly as in 1919, Barth's hope remains,

---

[116] *1Ro*, 86; *CPS*, 319.

against his own desire to place hope beyond optimism and pessimism [*2Ro*, 309], an "immense optimism" sustained by the fact that the *last triumphant word* must belong to God and not to evil and sin.[117] Barth's dialectic, what Beintker categorises in the "supplementary type" rather than in an oppositional or paradoxical one associated with Barth's *2Ro* by Marsh, is a modification of the Hegelian dialectic of thesis, antithesis and synthesis.[118] Barth replaces the Hegelian synthesis with the dissolution of the antithesis (sin and evil) by the stronger thesis (God's sovereignty). An initial situation of simple opposition (God and sin) thus gives way to reconciliation (evil's final destruction and God's universal lordship in eternity's swallowing-up of time) [*2Ro*, 285]. Hence, images of 'victory', 'triumph', and the Blumhardtian "Jesus Victor", are pervasive by way of repelling the danger of a synthesis between God and evil/sin made possible by a 'complementary' type of dialectic [*2Ro*, 29, 301]. As argued in the previous chapter, if left unqualified these metaphors can break free from their pastoral context of providing hope with confidence, and imply a more logical 'predictive-style' eschatology.

Thus, although Barth does not intend to trivialise suffering by positing a compensating heaven, a concern remains that he has dangerously generalised evil out of existence by denying its tragic effects [*2Ro*, 302]. Roberts' claim that Barth's actualism does not permit revelation to become fully incarnated in our contingent reality appears to be warranted here. Barth has not adequately rooted revelation within the complexities of the historical life of Jesus of Nazareth since his christology is stripped to the barest bones of cross and resurrection. Despite his intentions to the contrary, to displace revelational immediacy, Barth appears to be struggling. His triumphal dialectic enables him, therein, to (or rather, appear to) speak with an unlimited confidence in the future.

One area in which Barth's eschatology actually directs particular forms of engagement in, with and for the world is discovered in the fact that during, and subsequent to, his pastorate in Safenwil Barth's eschatology has been recognisably significant for the character of Christian behaviour. His is not a 'vision' of the future in the sense of a static image or idea generative of contemplation.

> The Christian hope first deserves its name when with *one* stroke it makes materialism *and* idealism impossible [*TC*, 232, n.1].

---

[117] Citation from Torrance, 1962, 65.

[118] Michael Beintker, cited in McCormack, 1995, 163; cf. Charles Marsh (1997), 'Dietrich Bonhoeffer', in *The Modern Theologians*, ed. David Ford, 2nd ed., Blackwells, Oxford, 37-51 (39).

At first, his arguments appear to conservatively promote an anti-revolutionary perspective, with respect to human activity. Indeed, Marquardt complains that in *2Ro* Barth has taken an anti-revolutionary turn, in comparison with *1Ro*'s critique of legitimism and also, one must add, his promotion of a "revolutionary" assessment of the heavenly-earthly state contrast.[119] The revolutionary, according to Barth, in a Promethean vein attempts to abrogate to herself the divine right which results in a tragically unsuccessful attempt to overcome evil with evil [*2Ro*, 507]. By contrast, the *'real'* Revolution is solely God's eschatological action in Christ [*2Ro*, 481]. Barth, after all, was writing in the shadow of immense disappointment over the direction that the Russian revolution took.

Moreover, Barth appears to advocate political complacency through the combination of his suspicion of the state and what he names Christian "not-doing". For when the contradiction between divine and human agency is drawn in such radical terms, there appears to be not only no room for the relative continuity supposedly present in religious socialist principles and the nebulous dreams of Liberalism, but also for any ethical and political activity whatsoever.

Accordingly, Reinhold Niebuhr, for example, asserts that Barth's eschatology appears to isolate the Christian hope from the public realm of politics. Barth regards the political terrain from "an eschatological aeroplane", soaring at such a "very high altitude" so that his theology becomes "too transcendent to offer any guidance for the discriminating choices that political responsibility challenges us to".[120] It is a form of "religious absolutism which begins by making conscience sensitive to all human weakness", "ends in complacency toward social injustice", and "disavows political responsibility in principle".[121] To this, West adds that Barth's political complacency is reinforced by his "neglect [of] his responsibility for that difficult empirical analysis of real human relations".[122] Any specifically concrete practical interest, therefore, that Barth took had little essential connection with his theological scheme.

On the contrary, however, Barth refuses to reduce Christianity to the private and interior sphere. As he had learned from his time in

---

[119] Marquardt, 1972, 142.

[120] Reinhold Niebuhr (1959), *Essays in Applied Christianity* (Meridian Living Age Books, 186, 184. Cf. Charles West (1958), *Communism and the Theologians*, SCM Press, London, 211, 222.

[121] Ibid., 184, 187.

[122] West, 313f.

Safenwil, the Gospel "demands" that the created world, albeit subsequently fallen, be loved.[123] For Barth, as mentioned earlier, the resurrection was a "bodily, corporeal, personal" event [e.g., *CPS*, 287]. Secondly, *2Ro* lays greater stress on criticising the principle of revolution than the principle of legitimation because Barth feels that the revolutionary is closer to the truth than the reactionary.

These observations take on greater significance when it is also recognised that the indicative of the divine activity contains a necessary imperative for human activity, and subsequently neither permits one to remain a spectator of God's action, nor encourages any form of escapism from one's responsibility.[124] In other words, the divine revolution causes a certain 'overspill' into the concrete daily life, actions and general affairs of human beings.

Certainly, Barth does not here outline any positive *blueprint* for ethics. Indeed, he is suspicious of all idealistic 'ethics', as he terms it, which attempts to generate absolutist and universally binding ethical laws [*2Ro*, 462]. His, in contrast, is an actualistically conceived ethics of the situation, or "command of the moment", which he calls "Christian exhortation" [*1Ro*, 485]. Nevertheless, this Christian exhortation is not altogether a stumbling around in the dark in lacking any concrete "norms". One's journeying is partially lit by the directing light of the resurrection, albeit only in the immediacy of a concrete ethical situation [*CPS*, 296].[125] A certain affinity is admitted with Kant in that Barth aims for a theologically universalist ethic, with the 'good' being that of which God approves [*2Ro*, 468]. As shall be more fully discussed in Chapter 7, Barth's eschatological discourse, then, functions as determinative and constitutive for a proper grounding and regulating of human hope's activity.[126] His ethic of *2Ro* thereby becomes an "ethic of witness", as Ruschke describes it, being conceived from within the context of an appeal to analogy. In other words, he provides a model of human activity following the pattern of the divine as a *Gleichnis* (parable) or sign pointing to the coming world, an appeal that stands in rudimentary continuity with the *analogia fidei* of the *CD*.[127]

In *2Ro*, this activity is propelled particularly, and indeed primarily, through the provision of a "critical comparative" which functions to

---

[123] Citation from *2Ro*, 28.
[124] *CPS*, 296; *2Ro*, 316, 318, 320.
[125] See McCormack, 1995, 278. In this "between the times" Barth conceives 'the good' as not wholly natural to us, but actualistically in the sense of needing to be realised anew in each moment.
[126] See *CPS*, 290, 296, 308, 311f.; *RD*, 149.
[127] Citation from McCormack, 1995 275. See *2Ro*, 435.

sustain the sense of eschatological reservation.[128] This necessitates that we must be set in radical opposition to this life, since "There is peace only in prospect of the *overcoming* of the *enemy*" [*RD*, 178]. Ours becomes, then, a "*priestly agitation*" through our being "drawn into taking sides with the Attacker" of the world's fallenness [*CPS*, 316, 282].

It is in this thematic context that Barth, in contrast to Luther, justifies his exhortation to "no-revolution" *negatively*. God abrogates *all existing systems of order* and refuses to approve of the revolutionary option. The Christian is to witness to God's eschatological Revolution by her activity of "not-doing": non-anger, non-attacking and destroying, etc. In other words, she is to deprive the existing order of power, and thereby starve it out of existence [see *1Ro*, 508]. This is "The Great Negative Possibility" [*2Ro*, 475-492].

Herein, Barth limits all illusory claims and ambitions of human praxis to ultimacy without intending to put an end to all activity.

> Though we are alive to the limitation of our own work there will arise in us a will to do good, sound, finished work; for the spark *might* come from above, and the eternal be brought to light in the transitory [*CPS*, 308].

As Gorringe argues, Barth

> Makes any idea of 'progress' or normal movement impossible. Far from leading us into the fervid and privatized world of individualist decision, Barth refuses to identify eschatology with the lukewarm progressivism of Ebner's republic. He is arguing, as he did in the first edition, that Christianity is far more revolutionary than current 'revolutionary' programmes. The cross casts a shadow on all 'healthy' humanity, where our most secure standing place is shattered, set ablaze and finally dissolved.[129]

Passivity is as much sin as revolution and although politics remains "essentially a game", it nevertheless remains a game to be riskily played, while one simultaneously remembers the hubristic, provisional and

---

[128] This is Eberhard Jüngel's term [Jüngel (1989), *Theological Essays, Volume 1*, trans. J.B. Webster, T&T Clark, Edinburgh, 183].

[129] Gorringe, 'Eschatology', 97.

fragile character of all human activity.[130]   This doing or not-doing, Barth argues, will be forgiven by God only if the agent eschews an idolatrous identification of her activity with God's.   The task, then, is to learn the significance of true revolution, and to manifest that meaning in one's own agency.

In a somewhat parallel manner, Rahner declares that even "the nets of our plans" are frequently torn up by the Absolute Future, permitting them "no promise of abiding relevance" [*TI*, 10:237, 240].   Consequently, Rahner distinguishes between eschatology's Absolute Future (Moltmann's *Adventus/Zukunft*), which is "just another name for what is really meant by 'God'", and the intramundane future (Moltmann's *Futurum/Futur*), the foreseeable future which can be "described in categories and be planned", calculated and controlled.[131]

However, in the second place, albeit somewhat muted in *2Ro*, the Barth of this period maintains that it is only out of affirmation of the world that this "genuine, radical denial" in our movements of protest derive [*CPS*, 299].   Refusal of a world without God is only done in order to commit ourselves to a world with God [*CPS*, 300].   In a similar vein, the Barth of 1938 urges that

> Christians would, in point of fact, become enemies of the State if, when the State threatens their freedom, they did *not* resist, or if they concealed their resistance – although this resistance would be very calm and dignified. ... If the State has perverted its God-given authority, it cannot be honoured better than by this *criticism* which is due to it in all circumstances.[132]

For the Barth of the 1930s and beyond, despite *2Ro*'s rejection of the revolutionary option, the perspective is developed that possibly not all resistance will be calm and dignified.   On the contrary, Barth even sets out three relative criteria for the issue of the last resort overthrowing a government:

1. the government's "behaviour show[ing] such a measure of injustice and inhumanity";
2. all other remedying means have been exhausted;

---

[130] Citation from Zahrnt, 34.

[131] *TI*, 6:62, 59; cf. Moltmann, 1996, 25ff.

[132] Barth, 1939, 69.

3. the opportunity must be present for a real betterment of the situation.[133]

Moreover, with the earlier plot against Hitler in mind he admits that the Decalogue's prohibition of killing refers to specifically to the act of *murder*, and lamentably, and tragically, "One might have to kill" in spite of one's necessary efforts to achieve peace. In other words,

> There may be revolution in obedience to God's order: an obedience in compliance to civic duty and as such not against God. But then revolution would not be against but *for* the State. Here there is no question of overthrowing the *State* [as such], but only the present rulers in order to institute better government.[134]

What one discovers here in Barth's agapeistic ethics, "the truly revolutionary activity of love", is not only a critique of individualism, but also a stress on neighbour-love since life is to be lived before God and with other people.[135] It constitutes a divine emancipation from self-relatedness and the creation of a community of fellowship and freedom [e.g., *1Ro*, 247, 475]. This is "the Great Positive Possibility" that stands in contradiction with the present state of affairs:

> in it there is brought to light the revolutionary aspect of all ethical behaviour, and ... it is veritably concerned with the denial and breaking up of the existing order [*das Bestehende*]. It is love that places the reactionary also finally in the wrong, despite the wrongness of the revolutionary. Inasmuch as we love one another we cannot wish to uphold the present order as such, for by love we do the 'new' by which the 'old' is overthrown [*2Ro*, 493].

In order to achieve this action of love, which Gorringe suggests could be construed as being "impossibly utopian and careless of realization",[136] Barth's Tambach lecture permits more room for social reform and less for revolutionary hubris. Indeed, Barth even declares that

---

[133] Barth, 1963, 76f.

[134] Ibid., 79.

[135] Citation from Gorringe, *Karl Barth*, 66. See *2Ro*, 492ff.

[136] Gorringe, 'Eschatology', 99.

one acts *within* democracy, not as religious socialists, but "as hope-sharing and guilt-sharing comrades" [*WGWM*, 319]. However, as indicated above, the theme of revolutionary action becomes present again later under the pressure of the political events of the 1930s.

Chapter 4

Barth's Christological Hermeneutic of Eschatological Assertions (*GD-CD*, I)

Introduction: Barth's Learning to Speak Theologically as Eschatology's Change of Mood

In the previous chapter it was suggested that Barth was not attempting to subsume time into an eschatological given, as Roberts and Moltmann suppose. The eschatological Future plays an extensive role for Barth (and, to some degree, Christ's past of death and resurrection also does). For it is that 'place' from where God, whose presence is indicated by the sign of the empty shell-crater or dried up canal structure, comes to his creation. This 'futurist' eschatology provides a certain dynamic to an apparently 'stilted' conception of time, and is reinforced by the ethical implications of Barth's eschatology. As Barth admits in 1922, for example, "The present is worth living only in reference to the eternal future, to the hoped-for latter day" which lies at the present's door [*WGWM*, 208].

The problem at this stage is that while *2Ro* served to distinguish God and world, its predominant eternity-time model is limited in any expression of the form of *unity*-in-distinction, and thereby unwittingly creates the danger of expressing, or perhaps rather of *sounding as if* it expresses, simple opposition. Its account of the world and humanity's selfhood and agency thereby creates a difficulty for any positive ethical expression and regulation. When pressed, which is not necessarily an appropriate move given Barth's unsystematic intentions in composing *2Ro*, the revelational actualism could endanger the human subject's freedom and spontaneity, with the latter being overwhelmed in the Moment of crisis and thereby reduced to a mere object of that divine act.[1] So, for example, famously Bonhoeffer felt that Barth's revelational actualism "splinters the self and community into discrete moments of divine encounter", therein

---

[1] On human passivity in Barth, see Wingren, 112.

undermining the person's social and historical locatedness.[2] Moreover, Barth tends to undermine the sense in which Christians could be mirrors or agents of God's action in the world, apart from some scattered references to parable and analogy. Although Mehnert exaggerates when claiming that Barth's is a "theologically based anarchism", Barth's emphasis on the sovereignty of God, even though it is not intended to deny anything about human beings' agency, is dangerously close to failing to, as Webster describes, prevent "man as the subject and agent of his own history" from vanishing.[3] That this was not Barth's intention is recognised by Frei:

> One hears Barth constantly asserting during the dialectical
> period that man's question, the question that *is* man, i.e.,
> human spontaneity and subjectivity, cannot be overwhelmed
> by the answer.[4]

On the other hand, Barth's placing of a relatively positive assessment of social relations and alluding to a form of agapeistic ethics alongside and within an interrogative reading of divine sovereignty, indicates the direction that he would later move in the later ethics of volume IV.

Although Barth never comes to relax his insistence on the sovereignty of God, its original context, in his post-1914 sense of crisis and anger against relationalism does fade in the 1920s.

Thereafter is generated a mood-shift from *2Ro's* primarily condemnatory connotations to something much more creative. So, although Barth cannot later come to wholly reject *2Ro*, he does seriously qualify it by admitting its one-sidedness.[5] Several factors contributed to facilitating this change: Barth's 1921 transition from pastor to Göttingen academic; reading Reformed systematics, rather than the protesters, Overbeck, Kierkegaard, *et al*, seeking training for the preacher's voice, and being open to, and specifically considering, the criticisms that had been levelled against his work. However, Barr misses this last point when over-

---

[2] Marsh, 39.

[3] Gottfried Mehnert, cited in Kitchen, 188; John Webster (1987), '"On the Frontiers of What is Observable": Barth's *Römerbrief* and Negative Theology', *Downside Review* vol. 105, 169-180 (175).

[4] Frei, 1956, 567f.

[5] See *2Ro*, 25 (1928 preface); *CD*, I.1, vii; *HG*, 34-42. Frei acknowledges that this one-sidedness "was one of those risks theology had to take, since the primacy of God must be asserted in it" [1956, 560].

generalising that Barth "paid little attention to other people's opinions", and theologically vetoed all forms of public discourse.[6]

The resultant eschatology, while bearing significantly different marks from that of his Safenwil period, and thereby appearing almost as a substitution of the sweet tasting for the bitter, nevertheless grows on the ground that had been ploughed earlier. It develops certain underexposed, but certainly identifiably implicit, elements such as the place of christology in eschatological discourse and the nature of the hope that that furnishes.

While attempting to avoid the self-assured and eschatologically realised nuance of the word, Barth comes to seek some form of theological 'stability' in his reading of the bible's strange new world. Although he is not advocating unrevisable theological axioms, he declares that "What is needed is the discovery of basic principles" [*GD*, 29]. This move leads Wallace to explain that

> Barth's theological hermeneutic risks the belief that the Bible, as the church's Scripture, does have a relatively stable though never fully determinate and self-present extrahistorical and extralinguistic referent, the referent of the divine life itself as that life encounters the reader whenever and wherever it is graciously disposed to do so.[7]

It is in Göttingen that Barth, in his daring to rebegin his work from the very beginning [*GD*, 13], learns to speak in a certain theological voice and therein drown out *2Ro*'s tone of ironic self-dissolution. Barth here ascertains how the sovereignty of God theme could function positively for a dogmatics which operates "by way of reflection on the Word of God" without necessitating the intellect's being sacrificed [*GD*, 30]. Thus, by *GD*,

> Gone is not only the bewildering array of dialectical pyrotechnics, but also the heavily one-sided emphasis on polemic at the expense of constructive theological work. The shift, in other words, is impressive both substantively and rhetorically.[8]

---

[6] James Barr (1993), *Biblical Faith and Natural Theology*, Clarendon Press, Oxford, 131.

[7] Mark I. Wallace (1990), *The Second Naiveté: Barth, Ricoeur, and the New Yale Theology*, Mercer University Press, Macon, 24.

[8] George Hunsinger (1993), 'Article Review: Karl Barth's *The Göttingen Dogmatics*', *SJT* vol. 46, 371-382 (372).

"Nothing less was at stake," Hunsinger asserts, "than a radically new standpoint which promised to safeguard the integrity of theology."[9] This *Standpunkt*, which Barth establishes and intensifies in the years at and after Göttingen, becomes what Barth describes as a "Christological concentration", albeit it is only after *CD* I that his thinking becomes less Logos-focused than concretely Christ-centred.[10]   Or, more accurately, Barth's becomes an incarnationally grounded trinitarian methodology. Thus, temporally speaking, it would be inaccurate to claim with Jenson that

> Not one word of what is said in ... *Romans* is withdrawn. But
> where abstract eternity was, Jesus of Nazareth now stands.[11]

Eschatology, and the hope that it both generates and sustains, is thereby rooted in a christological context, a procedure that parallels Rahner's important 1954 essay, 'The Hermeneutics of Eschatological Assertions' [*TI*, 4:326-346]. As in Rahner, christology comes to function for Barth as the hermeneutical key to eschatological discourse.   For instance, in a deliberate allusion to Johannine soteriology, Barth declares that

> God has so loved the world that he gave his only begotten
> Son. Christian hope rests on the basis of this extravagant *so*
> [*GD*, 35.II].[12]

Eschatology becomes a positive articulation of the form of that christologically-centred theological method, and only secondarily the expression of the negative aspect of the divine judgment, rather than being *almost* exclusively a blasting of any ground upon which theological, social and political homes were being constructed.

Moreover, as Chapter 5 will describe, teasing out and developing the possibilities of an 'eschatology' defined by God's loving manoeuvring his creation into his Ultimate Future, occurs over the following years through this christological matrix.   In preparing the ground for this discussion, the present chapter depicts Barth's theological turn to the Particular: i.e., Jesus Christ. It subsequently moves into a discussion of how Barth maintains a location of the present's temporality within an

---

[9] Hunsinger, 1976, 217.

[10] Barth, 1969, 43. On Barth's move toward an incarnational perspective, see Hunsinger, 1993, 378f.

[11] Jenson, 71.

[12] Cited in Migliore, 1991, lviii.

eschatological scheme characterised by the tension between actuality and provisionality. This he primarily does through the christologically controlled dialectic of revelational veiling and unveiling. However, the concern remains that at this stage Barth's eschatological discourse may still somewhat 'float free' from the contingencies of the redemptive event.

Eschatology's Christological Configuration

Turning to the Contingent and Particular: Barth's Christological Reading of Dogmatics[13]

Prior to *GD*, Barth had been criticised by Erich Przywara for not explaining the grounds of the unity of God and humanity, instead relegating God into the untouchable and unknowable transcendence of the *totaliter aliter*. Leaving aside the erroneous identification of his thought with "pure negation", a theological way explicitly rejected by Barth in 1922 in favour of the carefully designed eclectic dialectical way, Przywara had detected an important problem area: "the lack of an adequate doctrine of the Incarnation."[14] Directed by this, and also by conflict with Paul Tillich over revelation, Barth felt forced to place the relation of revelation and contingency at the top of his agenda.

The resultant christological 'turn', first significantly expressed in the *GD*, sees Barth embark on a "radically Christocentric", to cite von Balthasar's description, or more especially a christologically focused trinitarian intellectual voyage.[15] What Barth rejects in *GD* when he declares that theology should not be "christocentric" is rather the cult of the heroic religious personality of Jesus of Nazareth than a "more objective and valiant" theocentric christology [*GD*, 91]. "Theology will really be theology," Barth argues in 1929, "...when from beginning to end it is christology" [*FI*, 60]. No longer does Barth reduce the 'site' of revelation to the single 'mathematical' points of cross and/or revelational contemporaneousness, although these events remain integral to giving a

---

[13] For a more detailed exposition of Barth's christology to the *CD*, see McCormack, 1995; Torrance, 1962, 139ff. On *CD*'s christology, see Thompson, 1978; Bruce D. Marshall (1987), *Christology in Conflict: The Identity of a Saviour in Rahner and Barth*, Basil Blackwell, Oxford.

[14] Citation from McCormack, 1995, 321.

[15] von Balthasar, 1972, 25.

full account of the story. Barth's turn to the contingent, historical, concrete, and particular [see *GD*, 91] is being marked by an increased fear of generality. As Barth later proclaims, "*Latet periculum in generalibus*" [*CD*, II.2, 48]. This is a dread that comes to be focused in both his particularist form of theological rationality, and a critique of 'natural theologies'.

In *GD* Barth expresses a version of theological rationality, or of dogmatic *Wissenschaft*, that has particularly become famous because of his Anselm study, and has further been carried into the *CD*'s 'prolegomena'. Thus, contrary to Veitch's account, for example, one notices that the methodological similarities between *GD* and *FQI* are striking, as McCormack argues.[16]

Without either defining this conception from a general conception of 'science', or *a priori* ruling out the possibility of overlap between theological and other types of science, Barth intends for theological rationality to take its rise from, and be wholly determined by, the nature of the object that is given to be known. Since *Deus non est in genere* in the sense that other objects are, Barth argues that God cannot be known in the same way as other objects, and therefore theological rationality remains relatively independent from other forms of rationality.[17]

Barth does not, therefore, begin with and expound 'faith', even the content of 'faith', as would 'fideism' and 'subjectivism', as some critics accuse him of doing.[18] Rather his starting-point lies in the correspondence of the human noetic *ratio* to the *Ratio* inherent in the object of theology. Theology becomes, henceforth, if it is to be scientific (*Sachlichkeit*) and rational, a faithful and obedient *Nachdenken* [*FQI*, 40]. In other words, it has to be a thankful, realistic, and *a posteriori* reflection upon and explication of the divine object of faith's speaking [*GD*, 3, 8, 11]. This move Barth famously articulates through the Anselmian slogans, *fides quaerens intellectum* and *credo ut intelligam*, later arguing, with respect to the former, that this is "What distinguishes faith from blind assent" [*ET*, 44]. Faith for Barth, of course, contains knowledge (*notitia*), assent

---

[16] McCormack, 1995, 422; see J.A. Veitch (1971), 'Revelation and Religion in Karl Barth', *SJT* vol. 24, 1-22 (7). Hence, "it is clear that what is 'new' in the Anselm book is at most a *relatively* more faithful unfolding of the dogmatic method which Barth had been employing since 1924", although that was itself quite significant for Barth, and not a paradigm shift and new *Denkform*, as Barth himself exaggeratedly supposed [McCormack, 1995, 441; cf. Barth, 1969, 42ff.; *FQI,* 11].

[17] E.g., *CD*, I.1, 3, 5, 10f.

[18] The first charge is levelled against Barth by Robert Brecher (1983), 'Karl Barth: Wittgensteinian Theologian Manqué', *Heythrop Journal* vol. 24, 290-300 (299); James Richmond (1970), *Theology and Metaphysics*, SCM Press, London, 13; the second by Pannenberg (1991), *Systematic Theology I*, T&T Clark, Edinburgh, 42ff.

(*assensus*), and commitment (*fiducia*), and is not merely voluntaristic 'risk' as Pannenberg supposes.[19] Consequently, rational demonstration is an *explication* of the meaning and content of faith's incarnate Object, and not the apologetic strategy that modernity had determined it to be. And such a process of faithful knowing, for Barth, could never be irrational since it is rather the proper form and location of rationality, an emphasis that moves some way to extricating Barth from the charge of making his faith decision "on 'non-rational' factors ... [i.e.,] simply a response to the gospel", as Markham improperly contends.[20] In postulating this, Markham has, therefore, missed the complexity of Barth's epistemic reflections and is quite wrong to suppose that

> The Barthian [i.e., Barth and all who follow his position] is only able to repeat that it is a matter of faith: a matter of trusting the Christian community that gives us Christ.[21]

In Barth's mind, it was rather the God of Descartes that was hopelessly enchained within the human mind, having its origin in the human subject's thinking and knowing.[22] Consequently, Schleiermacher's theology of religious feeling, something that is generally derived from this type of epistemic method, is understood by Barth to be

> dependent on human feelings and will, ... [a faith with] no ground, object, or content other than itself. ... Faith as the Christian's commerce with God could first and last be only the Christian's commerce with himself. ... Theology was still being penalised for accepting the Renaissance discovery that man was the measure of all things, including Christian things [*HG*, 25f.].

---

[19] See Molnar, 1995, 317; Stephen G. Smith (1984), 'Karl Barth and Fideism: A Reconsideration', *Anglican Theological Review* vol. 66, 64-78; James J. Buckley and William McF. Wilson (1985), 'A Dialogue with Barth and Farrer on Theological Method', *Heythrop Journal* vol. 26, 274-293 (276).

[20] Ian Markham (1998), *Truth and the Reality of God: An Essay in Natural Theology*, T&T Clark, Edinburgh, 1.

[21] Ibid., 2.

[22] See *CD*, II.1, 360; Barth (1959), *From Rousseau to Ritschl*, trans. Brian Cozens and John Bowden, SCM Press, London, 335. Cf. Cushman, 103-122; Fergus Kerr (1996), 'Cartesianism According to Karl Barth', *New Blackfriars* vol. 77, 358-368.

Barth is not here opposing all theo-anthropological procedures, as Pannenberg, for example, supposes in classifying Barth as the pre-eminent modern exponent of "the christological procedure 'from above to below'".[23]   Later talk of a properly pneumatologically grounded anthropology,[24] has been preceded by Barth's christologically determined anthropology. Instead, his objection is to a theology that attempts to stand anywhere but under the hearing of the *Deus dixit*. And this, Barth believes, is precisely what Schleiermacher's theology of "man's religious consciousness", and Cartesianism's *cogito* do [*CD*, III.1, 314]. For Barth, the test case is christology, and Christ fits badly into Schleiermacher's theology of the 'composite life'.[25]

Without challenging Feuerbach's materialist and atheistic humanism, Barth holds out Feuerbach's theological non-realism as a diagnosis of the fatal malaise affecting theology on the way of Schleiermacher.   For example, the nineteenth-century Ritschlians constructed a ramp "so that one may easily ('casually'!) climb to the top, that is, to revelation" [*GD*, 61]. Feuerbach, however, indicated that the anthropocentrically conceived god of post-Cartesianism is the idolatrous positing of "myself as the subject", "a voice ... from this unredeemed world", a creation of a "God for himself after his own image", and therefore a failure to hear the divine speech.[26] Barth's *2Ro* treatment of religion as the expression of the sinful human mind, as a factory of idols, therefore emphatically endures into *CD*, I.2.[27]

Gunton's claim that Barth's project is a conscious attempt "to replace the Enlightenment project with something altogether different" by reordering its "epistemological direction" is misleading, however.[28] Firstly, it implies that Barth was interested in the generalities of epistemology when, rather, his own theological iconoclasm is precisely an effort to advance a more appropriate model for understanding the nature of *theology*.   Secondly, it sets Barth in strict opposition with the Enlightenment and its successors. Tracy's concern not to over-react to the heritage of the Enlightenment, but to ascribe to it a combination of some admirable concerns (for example with freedom) with overly narrow and misleading, Gunton would say "alienating", understandings of rationality

---

[23] Wolfhart Pannenberg (1968), *Jesus - God and Man*, trans. Lewis L. Wilkins and Duane A. Priebe, SCM Press, London, 33.

[24] *HG*, 23f.

[25] Barth, 1959, 313, 342.

[26] *GD*, 48; 92; *CD*, I.2, 6.

[27] See, e.g., 293f.

[28] Colin E. Gunton (1988), 'No Other Foundation. One Englishman's Reading of *Church Dogmatics*', in Biggar (ed.), 61-79 (64).

and autonomy better fits Barth's consciously loose appropriation of conceptual frameworks.[29] One should not forget, moreover, that as an historical and socially located being Barth could not, and would not attempt to pretend otherwise, rise to the Archimedian heights from which to uncommitedly observe all else.

Barth even expresses a reluctance to follow modernity's path in opening his dogmatics with a prolegomena, conceding only in order to articulate (as opposed to 'discover') his starting-point [*GD*, 18]. His project is an attempt to conceive Christian faith beyond the end of humanly generated religion, and is concerned to maintain the theme of God's sovereignty over and against all human attempts to domesticate and possess him. In so doing, he raises a powerful question-mark against forms of post-Enlightenment rationality that seek to control the theological knowing-process from some neutral Archimedian point.[30]

Barth identifies a similar procedure of control operating in the *analogia entis'* premature objectivisation of God, with its postulation of a common being shared by God and creation alike, and the subsequently possible human epistemic movement to the divine 'It'.[31] Both moves fall under his general condemnation of 'natural theology', by which he intends all forms of theology which do not begin exclusively from the known *Ratio* of God [*CD*, I.1, 36, 219]. In a parallel manner, while he does utilise Kant's metaphysics-critique, Barth theologically rejects any *a priori* philosophical agnosticism as a negative natural theology.[32] Natural theology, in both its epistemically Pelagian (human discovery of God) and Semi-Pelagian (human discovery of God aided by grace) forms, operates as a "good and useful narthex or first stage on the way to the true Christian revelation", gained quite apart from that revelation [*GD*, 91]. And for Barth, Buckley and Wilson summarise, all natural theologies

---

[29] Tracy, 1987, 31; Colin Gunton (1985), *Enlightenment and Alienation: An Essay Towards a Trinitarian Theology*, Marshall Morgan & Scott, Basingstoke.

[30] See Buckley and Wilson, 276f. This makes Barth an attractive figure in the post-modern context.

[31] See, on the former, *FI*, 33, 38, 42f.; *CD*, II.1, 81ff.; *ET*, 16; on the latter, *CD*, II.1, 231; *ET*, 152f.

[32] See *FI*, 55; *CD*, I.2, 29f.; 244f.

begin their journey with their backs turned towards God and, with all brilliance and ingenuity, end at a deity who cannot be the God of Christian grace whom they seek.[33]

Barth attempts to argue for a faith beyond religion through 'reversing' the orientation of the subject-object schemes of post-Cartesian epistemology, albeit this is not a simple 'reversal' which denies the possibility of a christologically regulated anthropology. Cushman is right to argue that Barth "cannot fairly be charged with swallowing up man in the sovereignty of God", in contrast to Wingren who simplistically and misleadingly reads Barth's project as a simple inversion of the Liberal scheme so that God's transcendence banishes his immanence and overwhelms humanity.[34] This concern is particularly prominent after *CD*, I, and consequently Williams' claim that humanity is utterly passive before and in the event of revelation is unwarranted in respect of these writings, and is also so even in relation to the discussion in *CD*, I.1, 148.[35]

Combined with this qualified 'reversal' is a stress on God's freedom which functions both in a manner similar to the earlier stress on the divine transcendence over all human ethical, political and religious constructs (God's freedom *from*), and, crucially, to identify the movement of grace (God's freedom *for*).[36] Through this second element within the concept of divine freedom Barth avoids implicating God in arbitrariness and caprice in a manner missed by Moltmann, for example.[37] In other words, God is free *for*, and not merely *from*, creation out of his free love, and is continually faithful to what he has created. Barth especially comes later to explicate this theme through the concept of "The Humanity of God" [*HG*, 33]. "[T]he God of the Gospel is no lonely God, self-sufficient and self-contained", an absolute who is imprisoned in his own majesty [*ET*, 18].

Consequently, the Subject for Barth becomes the *divine Subject* who freely and graciously gives himself to be known to the human *object* of revelation, in a movement that necessarily becomes the indexical point of all theological thinking [*GD*, 87]. This human knowing is thereby asymmetrically characterised as one in which the human subject does not

---

[33] Buckley and Wilson, 286.

[34] Cushman, 120; Wingren, 25.

[35] Rowan D. Williams (1979), 'Barth on the Triune God', in *Karl Barth: Studies in His Theological Method*, ed. S.W. Sykes, Clarendon Press, Oxford, 147-193 (174).

[36] On God's freedom: *from* all forms of external necessity, see *CD*, I.1, 112, 158f., 178f., 195f.; I.2, 7, 135, 160, 231, 349f.; *for* humanity, see, e.g., *CD*, I.2, 135f., 395; *HG*, 66f., 69.

[37] Jürgen Moltmann (1985), *God in Creation: An Ecological Doctrine of Creation*, Trans. M. Kohl, SCM Press, London, 81ff.

master the object known, but is rather mastered by the divine Subject. An expression of this may be found in the statement that "As knowers they are got at by the known object" [*CD*, I.1, 214]. In this way, Barth rejects Idealist constructivism as a placing of the creatively human subject in the place of the creative divine Subject, although he does have positive words to say about Idealism's aspiring to take God's hiddenness seriously, and therein standing as an antidote to all correlations of human thought and speech with the divine [*FI*, 46f.]. Idealism has, Barth accuses, an inherent tendency towards ideology by its reference to "timeless truths of reason, directly accessible to everyone", which undermine realism's "accidental and particular truths of history" [*FI*, 47]. In contrast, human knowledge, for Barth, is not constitutive of, but derivative from the Reality. Moreover, in an eschatologically significant statement, it is argued that revelation is not a *datum* (given) but a *dandum* (to be given) [*HGCL*, 16]. It is this rejection of God as an Unmoved Mover whose depths are openly penetrable by human thinking, in whatever form that thinking may be done, that entails that Barth defends a stress on the unprovability of God in his self-attesting revelation.

If *FQI* is notable for its abstract-sounding theological methodology, the earlier *GD* and the later *CD* make it clear that revelation is a uniquely particular story, albeit not one which merely recedes into the memory, rather than a general or universal event.[38] Revelation, or "God['s] communicating himself", embraces an ontologically localised, contingent, and self-objectified form in Jesus Christ, in a unique and once-for-all "being ... in becoming" or incarnation.[39]

Barth has, for the sake of theological consistency, then to reconceive the order of possibility-actuality questions of the incarnation between the *GD* and the *CD*. In *GD* Barth discusses the incarnation's possibility before treating its historicity and reality. Moreover, 'Man and his Question' stands prior to Trinity (§5) and incarnation (§6), albeit it does follow '*Deus Dixit*' (§3). *CD* I.2's consistent application of this christological principle emends this architecture: revelation's objective reality is explicated prior to its objective possibility. This architecture expresses the ineffability of the *how*, therein highlighting the *miraculous*

---

[38] On the importance of narrative in Barth, see, e.g., D.F. Ford (1979), 'Barth's Interpretation of the Bible', in Sykes (ed.), 1979, 55-87; William Werpehowski (1986), 'Narrative and Ethics in Barth', *Theology Today* vol. 43, 334-353.

[39] *GD*, 58; Eberhard Jüngel (1976), *The Doctrine of the Trinity: God's Being in Becoming*, trans. Horton Harris, Edinburgh and London, 63.

nature of divine revelatory and reconciliatory activity. Barth even claims later, somewhat echoing his earlier lament that a prolegomena is "a symptom that we do not live in a classical age of theology", that issues of epistemology and methodology, as understood in modernity to be necessary preliminaries to the act of doing one's research, can be presented as *postlegomena* rather than *prolegomena*.[40]

> Methodology and epistemology could come at the end of dogmatics – or even in the middle.

Nonetheless, the conceptual content of *GD* and *CD*, I.2 is similar: God gives, reveals, and identifies *himself* in the person of Jesus Christ [*GD*, 153]. In making this claim one needs to note that what Barth did not intend by his architecture of *GD* is clear from the statement that

> I have not been talking hypothetically about a hypothetical entity but about the actual existent possibility of revelation, about Jesus Christ, about the way that God comes to us as it is known and confessed in the Christian church [*GD*, 141].

The reason for the problematic structure is that he had not wanted to prematurely anticipate that which is not obvious to some, a necessity that he lamented in the process. Furthermore, Barth later does not declare that his 1927 *Christliche Dogmatik* was existential in *content*. Rather what he discards in *CD* is

> everything that ... might give even the slightest *appearance* of giving to theology a basis, support, or even a mere justification in the way of existential philosophy [*CD*, I.1, ix, my italics].

Barth has begun, materially even if not formally, with the particular man, the God in Christ, and not, as John Godsey claims, "with God and not man".[41] In so doing, as Torrance describes, Barth

> threw out the old dialectic between eternity and time and all talk of a timeless crisis, and interpreted the Word of God in the most concrete and positive way, strictly in terms of the person of Jesus Christ, the Incarnate Son of God, who is true God and true Man in one Person, and even more strictly in

---

[40] GD, 18; 1963, 13.

[41] John Godsey (1956), 'The Architecture of Karl Barth's *Church Dogmatics*', *SJT* vol. 9, 236-250 (239).

terms of the Holy Trinity as the ground and basis of everything.[42]

Such a strongly incarnational account draws its semantic inspiration and conceptual guiding lines, albeit not uncritically, from the Chalcedonian *vere Deus et vere homo* formula, and has its scriptural antecedents especially in the Johannine accounts (especially cardinal is Jn. 1:14).[43] "By God alone can God be known", and in Christ this *Deus revelatus* is conceived to be the embodiment of the *Deus in se* [*CD*, II.1, 86].

> 'The content of revelation is *wholly* God.' The point here is simply that God is not just half revealed or partly revealed, so that another part of his being or attributes or acts will have to remain hidden or will have to be imparted in some other way than by revelation [*GD*, 5.91].

Walter Kreck claims that

> God is here inseparable from the name and person of Jesus Christ; apart from him God has no shape or form (*kein Gesicht*) for us.[44]

Given this, Barth proposes christology as the *sole* and regulative location of the objectivity of divine being and speaking. "God is free for us at this point, and not elsewhere" [*CD*, I.2, 29]. This is "the narrow isolation" of the revelation-event, for it is in Christ *alone* that God reveals himself.[45]

The Eschatological 'Tension' in Barth's Doctrine of Revelation

This *Ereignis* of God's self-revelation in Christ comes to be expressed in pre-eminently eschatological terms, or rather eschatology comes to receive a distinctly christological shape from this "epiphany of Jesus Christ" [*CD*, I.1, 334]. Suggestive of II.2's treatment of election, Barth understands

---

[42] Torrance, 1962, 139.

[43] *CD*, I.2, 125; *R*, 45f.

[44] Cited in Marshall, 1987, 166. See Jüngel on the *logos asarkos* [1976, 80].

[45] Barth (1986), *The Way of Theology in Karl Barth: Essays and Comments*, ed. H. Martin Rumscheidt, Pickwick Publications, Allison Park, Pennsylvania, 77.

revelation as "the fullness of time", and indeed fulfilled time itself or "real time" breaking "in as new time".[46] Therefore, greatly enthusiastic notes of actuality and completion are prolifically sounded, with "the consummation to which Jesus Christ pointed" becoming a work of restoration that has *already taken place* for us, and is therefore to be recollected [*CD*, I.2, 428]. In this second, heavenly, Adam, a new humanity has been created.[47]

> 'In Christ' means that in Him we are reconciled to God, in Him we are elect from eternity, in Him we are called, in Him we are justified and sanctified, in Him our sin is carried to the grave, in His resurrection our death is overcome, with Him our life is hid in God, in Him everything that has to be done for us, to us, and by us, has already been done, has previously been removed and put in its place, in Him we are children in the Father's house, just as He is by nature [*CD*, I.2, 240].

While this stress on the eschatological actuality of revelation functions to direct Christian God-talk, it is also pressed into the service of the ethically significant critical theme so prominent in Barth's *krisis*-period, with its stress on eschatological provisionality: that of eschatological critique of existing affairs. This divine Subject's giving himself to be known is portrayed as the insertion of an eschatological *novum* into the affairs of the world. In Jüngel's phrase, this is "the interruption of the continuity of the world".[48]

Eschatology, for Barth, thus prevents human self-divinisation since, given the novelty of the revelational event with the knowledge of God and reconciliation that it brings, humanity cannot justify herself [*HGCL*, 74]. As he argues against Brunner's use of *Offenbarungsmächtigkeit* (capacity for revelation) and *Anknüpfungspunkt* (point of contact) in the early 1930s, and continues to maintain as theologically crucial, there is no creaturely 'capacity' for revelation in any shape or form.[49] Neither is the incarnation an eternal relation, nor an

---

[46] *CD*, I.1, 4; I.2, 53.

[47] *GD*, 161; *CD*, I.2, 189.

[48] Eberhard Jüngel (1995), *Theological Essays Volume 2*, trans. J.B. Webster, T&T Clark, Edinburgh, 91. Cf. *CD*, I.2, 63ff; *R*, 45, 55; Ingolf U. Dalferth (1989), 'Karl Barth's Eschatological Realism', in S.W. Sykes (ed.), *Karl Barth: Centenary Essays*, Cambridge, 14-45 (21).

[49] E.g., *CD*, I.1, 29ff., 273ff.; I.2, 280. The political situation of the early 1930s may help to account for the ferocity of the debate in 1934, and also Barth's rather single-minded critique. But it cannot wholly explain it. Barth's concerns over natural theology had been expressed much earlier, as also had been his growing dissatisfaction with Brunner [*FI*, 39f.; see Stephen Andrews (1994), 'The Ambiguity of Capacity: A Rejoinder to Trevor Hart',

inherent possibility of the creaturely [*GD*, 156]. The event of the cross, so powerful an image in *2Ro*, stands as an iconoclastic exposure of human being as existing in a state of sinful rebellion from God. At Golgotha, Barth declares starkly, "Man unveils himself here as really and finally guilty ... by killing God" [*CD*, I.2, 92]. Hence, "it is monstrous to describe the uniqueness of God as an object of 'natural knowledge'".[50] Moreover, any talk of humanity's 'coming of age', devoid of an eschatological reference-point, is foolish self-assertion and an illegitimate self-justification that dispenses with its only proper Teacher, and which thereby refuses to acknowledge the proper creaturely limits of dependence on God.

On the contrary, human knowing of God is a miraculous gift of free divine grace, an association of themes that provides Barth with both a warrant for the irreversibility of the *ordo essendi* of the asymmetrical God-human relations, and a critique of 'natural theology' and synergism. Humanity's 'faculty', or possibility for hearing and appropriating this Word, is understood as being divinely imported or 'lent'. Therefore, Barth's thought is in agreement with Brunner's claim that the new creation is

> in no wise a perfection of the old, but comes into being exclusively through destruction of the old and is a replacement of the old man by the new.[51]

The question here, however, is whether Barth could further admit Brunner's concern, albeit the latter subsequently trod a treacherous methodological path, that

---

Tyndale Bulletin vol. 45, 169-179 (170)]. Trevor A. Hart misses the debate's underlying issue of election, when claiming that Barth's theology necessitates the application of Brunner's 'formal capacity' [Hart (1993), 'A Capacity for Ambiguity? The Barth-Brunner Debate Revisited', *Tyndale Bulletin* vol. 44, 289-305]. Even a 'formal capacity' would set the terms of God's action in the world and thereby threaten God's freedom. The 'point of contact' is a christological and eschatological concept [see Joan E. Donovan (1986), 'Man in the Image of God: The Disagreement between Barth and Brunner Reconsidered', *SJT* vol. 39, 433-459 (442, 445)].

[50] Inaccurately cited by Jung Young Lee as *CD*, IV.1, 453 [Lee (1969), 'Karl Barth's Use of Analogy in his Church Dogmatics', *SJT* vol. 22, 129-151 (134)].

[51] Emil Brunner (1946), 'Nature and Grace (1934)', in *Natural Theology*, trans. Peter Fraenkel, The Centenary Press, London, 15-64 (21).

the new creation is never mentioned without the picture of *reparatio*, of restoration, being used at the same time. It is not possible to repair what no longer exists.[52]

Does Barth's emphasis on revelation's 'interruption' entail a dualism of eschatological discontinuity with the present? Has Barth unconsciously retained his earlier *tendency* towards revelation's eschatological immediacy, so that it floats with no contact with contingent being? Roberts' charge of a Barthian theological isolationism precisely accords to Barth a revelational immediacy and discontinuity with 'commonplace reality'. Frequently the problem is apparently detected in Barth's christocentrism, which John Baillie describes as a denial "that except in His incarnation in Jesus of Nazareth God has ever spoken to man at all", since this alone is revelation.[53] Critics particularly lament the implication that Barth expensively denies creation's place as revelation; and a similar concern underlies some Evangelical complaints over Barth's denial of scripture as revelation.[54]

Without attempting to expose their own problematic presuppositions, these critics pre-eminently misrepresent Barth as rejecting revelation's mediatedness, mediatedness particularly through scripture and proclamation (and creation?). It is precisely revelation's *essential* mediatedness, and therefore indirectness, that prevents Barth from slipping into a fully realised eschatology that is narratable *exclusively* in the past tense. Thus provisionality is secured by the connection between God's mystery, in the sense of unfathomable depths rather than logical puzzle, and the worldliness of the Word.[55]

As mentioned earlier, Barth equates revelation with God's *self*-giving as the 'Word'. Herein, revelation is presented as an event of *personal* I-Thou encounter of God in Christ with human beings, rather than as divinely authoritative propositions, for example [see *CD*, I.1, 310ff.]. An uncompromisable distinction between God's *being* as revelation and all creaturely elements, including Christ's humanity and the scriptures, is consequently devised [e.g., *R*, 46, 73]. Baillie in particular confuses

---

[52] Ibid., 34.

[53] John Baillie (1939), *Our Knowledge of God*, Oxford, 17f.

[54] On the former, see e.g., Barr, 124; Ned Wisnefske (1990), *Our Natural Knowledge of God: A Prospect for Natural Theology After Kant and Barth*, Peter Lang, New York, Bern, Frankfurt am Main, Paris, 69. On the latter, see Klaas Runia (n.d.), *Karl Barth and the Word of God*, Leicester, Inter Varsity Press, 25; Geoffrey W. Bromiley (1986), 'The Authority of Scripture in Karl Barth', in *Hermeneutics, Authority and Canon*, eds. D. A. Carson and John D. Woodbridge, Leicester, 275-294 (290f.).

[55] *CD*, I.1, 188. Moreover, immediacy is somewhat qualified by Barth's discussions of Christ's manifestation as the expected One in Israel [*CD*, I.2, §14.2].

Barth's primary emphasis here on 'revelation' as the *content* of the encounter (God's *Self* in Christ) with the *means* (scripture, etc.) by which that revelation becomes present.[56] To suggest that content and means are identical, therefore, would be tantamount to declaring the latter's divinisation, which can either be a docetic embarrassment of revelation's use of the fragile and contingent, or an attempt to undermine eschatological provisionality in the quest for certainty, as Barth detected in Roman Catholic ecclesiology and in the "paper pope" theories of biblical inerrancy.[57]

Williams, however, suggests, echoing much in Donald Baillie's earlier critique of Barth's christology,

> the awkwardness of a scheme which so divorces the substance of revelation from its historical form, in making the latter's relation to the former basically external.[58]

This, he believes, is a consequence of Barth's too Nestorian (or radically Calvinist) theology, and especially of his lack of a doctrine of creation. The feel of these early volumes is then contrasted with Williams' belief in the divine self-abnegation in the face of created evil.[59]

A possible response to this charge, and to that of Spence who claims that God's revelation through God detracts from the incarnational and pneumatological mediation of revelation, is already suggested in Barth's writings at this time, implying that Williams has somewhat caricatured his thinking.[60] Barth may not be exactly hitting the right key for Williams' ear to recognise, but it is arguable that he is at least frailly trying to hum the same tune.

Given Barth's stress on the divine selection of, and self-chosen identification with, the instrument by which he will be revealed - particularly and wholly in that of the incarnation - it is just not true that the

---

[56] Similarly, John Macken (1990), *The Autonomy Theme in the* Church Dogmatics: *Karl Barth and his Critics*, Cambridge, 171. On this distinction, see Ronald F. Thiemann (1986), 'Response to George Lindbeck', *Theology Today* vol. 43, 377-382 (378).

[57] *GD*, 217; *CD*, I.2, 525.

[58] Williams, 1979, 153; cf. D.M. Baillie (1948), *God Was in Christ: An Essay on Incarnation and Atonement*, Faber, London.

[59] Ibid., 189.

[60] Alan Spence (1992), 'Christ's Humanity and Ours', in *Persons, Divine and Human: King's College Essays in Theological Anthropology*, eds. Christoph Schwöbel and Colin E. Gunton, T&T Clark, Edinburgh, 74-97.

event of revelation is external to the means. That is so only to the extent that Barth places the elements in the divine *choice*, so that they have no *intrinsic* value of their own by which to determine the nature of God's eternal choosing (this is the issue that divided Barth from Brunner) [e.g., *R*, 64].

Nevertheless, although distinct from it, the identified sacramental *means* of revelation (scripture and proclamation) function *indispensably* as what Torrance calls the "earthen vessels" and "corporeality" of revelation in order to mediate revelation's contemporaneity [see *GD*, 201].[61] They function *appropriately* as divinely chosen sacramental means through which God freely makes himself present. Thereby, Barth refers to the divine presence as a "contingent contemporaneousness" [*CD*, I.1, 164]. Indeed, he even claims that

> The power of Jesus Christ is *not operative*, however, *save through* these instruments, these secondary and therefore conditioned means of revelation [*R*, 64, my emphasis].

Accordingly, they are invaluable witnesses to, tokens of, and, to adopt Kelsey's description of scripture, "identity-descriptions" of God in the event of revelation, even though they are not that revelation themselves.[62] Moreover, even specifically non-ecclesially structured elements can become witnesses, and are perceivable as such in the light of a christological hermeneutic.[63] On this Marshall correctly argues that Barth's christocentrism does not stipulate about the details of the process of revelation's subjective appropriation, since, as Thiemann indicates, Barth means by the term 'revelation' primarily the *content* of our knowing of God.[64] In a statement not unrelated, Barth himself affirmed,

---

61 T.F. Torrance (1990), *Karl Barth: Biblical and Evangelical Theologian*, T&T Clark, Edinburgh, 105.

62 David H. Kelsey (1975), *The Uses of Scripture in Recent Theology*, SCM Press, London, 45. On the biblical writers as 'witnesses', see, e.g., *CD*, I.1, 125ff. The Spirit makes the scriptures authoritative for us [e.g., *CD*, I.1, 113], but *only* because he *had inspired* their authors to witness to Christ [*GD*, 219; *CD*, I.2, 505, 514ff.]. Scripture is an "authentic copy of revelation" [*CD*, I.2, 544] through which God will speak in each present [*GD*, 201, 206; *CD*, I.2, 457].

63 See *GD*, 92; *CD*, I.1, 176.

64 Marshall, 1987, 148f.; Ronald F. Thiemann (1991), *Constructing a Public Theology: The Church in a Pluralistic Culture*, John Knox Press, Louisville, Westminster, 84.

> No one can say how this is done, not even the most devout
> and learned theologians of all times have been able to hear
> the Christmas message.[65]

Consequently Barth eclectically comes to make positive, albeit critical, use of extra-ecclesial anthropologies [*CD*, III.2], Mozart's music [*CD*, III.3, 297ff.], and various philosophical elements.[66] For example, the last's perceivable role in the processes of Barth's theological ruminations and articulations is too complex to be reduced to any single systematic scheme of an opposition of relations. Barth uses philosophy eclectically in the service of theology, while intending to take care not to allow it to undermine or overwhelm the particularity of theology's witness to God in Christ. Thiemann describes this as "the temporary borrowing of a tool to help us better understand the complex meaning of the Christian Gospel."[67] A statement of Barth's renders the flavour of what he intends here. He admits that

> The central affirmations of the Bible are not self-evident ...
> Every possible means must be used ... not the least, the
> enlistment of every device of the conjectural imagination.

in order to interpret it [*ET*, 37f.]. In this thematic context he famously declares

> God may speak to us through Russian communism, through a
> flute concerto, through a blossoming shrub or through a dead
> dog. We shall do well to listen to him if he really does so. ...
> God may speak to us through a pagan or an atheist, and in
> that way give us to understand that the boundary between the
> Church and the profane world still and repeatedly takes a
> course quite different from that which we hitherto thought we
> saw [*CD*, I.1, 60f.].

Anderson is mistaken, therefore, when arguing that the later Barth has *changed direction* on the issue of 'natural theology' (although the use of that term is questionable in relation to Barth in any case), albeit it does

---

[65] Barth, 1959, *Christmas*, 25.

[66] Barth, 1933, 63-78.

[67] Thiemann, 1991, 82.

appear that Barth has *extended* the 'witness' concept to include creation in IV.3.1.[68]

However, Barth insists that God does not identify himself through these with the specificity that he does in the incarnation and scripture, but remains free in his choice of which non-ecclesial elements to utilise. Von Balthasar claims that Barth

> is as open to the world as any theologian could be. But he can never abstract from the relationship between God and man in Jesus Christ, as he goes about building his 'intensive universalism'.[69]

Nevertheless, in speaking of this actualistically presented divine choice without reference to election and creation, Barth does leave himself open to the suspicion that his presentation of creation is that of a formal provision of the stage upon which humanity is encountered by the Word. So Hendrikus Berkhof, for example, alleges that creation in Barth never materially becomes part of the drama of redemption itself.[70]

The revelation-contingency *identification*-in-difference is later developed to a greater extent in *CD*, II.1 whenever Barth begins to associate the revelational veiling with a kenotic-sounding divine self-negation and "self-emptying" [*CD*, II.1, 516]. Herein Barth declares that God "makes Himself foreign and improper to Himself" by lowering himself to us in revelation [*CD*, II.1, 55]. This he does by coming in a form which is different from himself in the corporeality and worldliness (*Welthaftigkeit*) of Christ's life, or in the entextualised narration of its story. This is particularly the case in "God's self-humiliation and self-alienation" of the cross. A twofold risk is taken in this movement, therein suggesting that Barth's understanding of revelation is not the epistemic parallel to Calvin's "irresistible grace" as Williams claims that it is: that of risking revelation-sacrament identification, and also of the possibility of non-recognition of the Word.[71]

It is certainly true that because of his theological christocentricity Barth cannot undertake an ontology of unbelief, and can thereby

---

68 Ray S. Anderson, 'Barth and a New Direction for Natural Theology', in *Theology Beyond Christendom: Essays on the Centenary of the Birth of Karl Barth*, ed. John Thompson, Pickwick Publications, Allison Park, Pennsylvania, 241-266 (244f.); cf. *CD*, IV.3.1, 117f., 139; *CL*, 375.

69 von Balthasar, 1972, 157.

70 Cited in Ronald Spjuth (1995), *Creation, Contingency and Divine Presence in the Theologies of Thomas F. Torrance and Eberhard Jüngel*, Lund University Press, 15. Cf. Barth, 1963, 52 on nature as "the theatre of God's work with man".

71 Williams, 1979, 158.

unwittingly create the impression that unbelief is not an actual state of affairs. But he does, nevertheless, come in I.2 to speak of unbelief in the negative terms so characteristic of *CD*, III.3. For example, it is "the impossible, the excluded and the absurd" [*CD*, I.2, 398f.]. That is why it can be explained that revelation "does not enforce faith. It does not even exclude unbelief" [*CD*, I.2, 5].

So Barth announces that although the sacramental reality serves revelation,

> it can also not serve it; it can even hinder and prevent it. The very thing can fail to happen which, because this form is given, ought to happen. The direct opposite can even happen. The blindness of man can continue in face of the work and sign of God. ... God Himself can be rejected in the grace of His condescension to the creature [*CD*, II.1, 55f.].

Hence, identification-in-differentiation between God's revelation and the sacramental elements does not entail, for Barth, the transparency of the revelation-event. Barth is consequently led in I.1 to speak of the veiledness, mediacy, and indirectness of revelation.[72] Accordingly, because "This veil is very thick", we must there "halt before an enigma".[73] As Ward argues with reference to II.1,

> The Word is always compromised by its necessary incorporation within a semiotic system - a system of object-signs that is 'different from' the Word.[74]

This compromise entails that revelation cannot be read directly off the sacramental text, so that those who came into direct confrontation with Jesus, or scripture, did not necessarily encounter revelation.

In a number of places Barth argues that blindness to revelation is a result of sin, so that faith, being illuminated by the Spirit, perceives an unveiling [*CD*, I.2, 241]. Sinfulness creates a material incapacity for apprehending the Word that is recreated only in the revelation-event [*CD*, I.1, 220, 271]. This notion, however, if left unqualified, could seriously

---

[72] *CD*, I.1, 188f. Cf. *GD*, 209, 248f.; *R*, 64.

[73] *CD*, I.1, 188, 236; cf. 191.

[74] Graham Ward (1993), 'The Revelation of the Holy Other as the Wholly Other: Between Barth's Theology of the Word and Levinas' Philosophy of Saying', *Modern Theology* vol. 9, 159-180 (163).

undermine thoughts of eschatological provisionality, hence Williams declares that this dialectic of veiling-unveiling, which is similar for all saving events alike, entails a 'homogenisation' of salvific event.[75] Revelation's veil is lifted and the faithful are enabled to see.[76] Is this, rather than fear of theological anthropocentrism, why Barth does not dwell on questions of human spirituality and development: the believer is overwhelmed by God's eschatological self-giving in the event of revelation?

Nevertheless, this potentially generalised discourse of 'unveiling' inhabits a specific context that significantly qualifies it.

- It is important to recognise, for instance, that this concept does not feature as frequently as its antonym of 'veiling'.
- Barth maintains the emphasis on "God's *mystery* in His revelation" [*CD*, II.1, 38, my emphasis].
- The unveiling comes, paradoxically, only through the veiling, and therefore a veiled-unveiling remains [*CD*, I.1, 192].
- Unveiling, without its reverse movement, is an eschatological concept relevant only to the consummation [*CD*, I.1, 203].
- Moreover, although generally implicit in *CD*, I, humanity remains a sinner even in the event of revelational-encounter, and therefore cannot wholly appropriate that which is being revealed [*CD*, I.1, 189f.].
- Finally, albeit stated too infrequently in Barth, Hunsinger shows that even the eschatological move from faith into sight will be protected from God's naked objectivity.[77]

Williams' complaint that Barth's early *CD* exhibits an irresistible and infallible divine self-knowing into which the human is (passively?) incorporated does not take note of the dialectical complexity of the revelation-event.[78] Cushman, therefore, identifies Barth's thinking as a "critical realism".[79] Certainly although Barth does not adequately examine epistemological and hermeneutical questions of human shaping in the reception of revelation, his emphases on the place of the hearing of the Word in the *ecclesia*, the ecclesial location of theology, and the remaining frailty and sinful nature of all human knowing, do suggestively point in

---

[75] Williams, 1979, 156.

[76] E.g., *GD*, 58; *CD*, I.1, 192, 198f.; I.2, 506.

[77] Hunsinger, 1991, 88f., commenting on *CD*, II.1, 209.

[78] Williams, 1979, 158.

[79] Cushman, 112.

this direction somewhat. Hinted at, albeit requiring fuller development in order not to lose or misconstrue the concreteness of Barth's theology, is the idea that as a human being the knower/reader perspectivally inhabits (in Polanyian language, "indwells") certain patterns of tradition, a theme similar to Calvin's use of an ocular image of the function of ecclesial tradition, and develops specific and appropriate habits of reading and responding to that encountered in and through this particular society. Of course no group or society is self-contained. One lives with one's feet in many overlapping places. And yet some sense of hermeneutical continuity, although what that is and entails would need to be more fully specified and qualified, is provided by the traditions within which one lives, or can come to live in. Loss of these particular memories, therefore, would be mortifying for the traditions (in the sense of the French word *mort*), and alienating for the identities of those inhabiting the present. On these thematic roads Barth is suggestively travelling.

However, due to the fact that these suggestions remain undeveloped, one remains somewhat sympathetic to the tone of Richmond's identification of a problem-area in Barth's "disregard for man in his concreteness and historicity", as Ford has complained with reference to Barth's unconcern with the natural sciences.[80] Where Richmond misdirectedly exaggerates the significance of this, however, is in perceiving in it a dehumanisation of humanity given Barth's inclusion of anthropology within a christological hermeneutic.

Frei specifies the cause of this lack of attention to anthropological detail as deriving from Barth's practice of placing primary, if not even sole, emphasis on the divine act.[81] Barth's non-articulation of the content of human freedom and spontaneity entail that they remain assertions at this stage. Frei's subsequent proposal is that theological anthropology does not rule out, but in fact greatly helps "toward the achievement of objectivity" and the specificities of a "content-filled doctrine of human freedom". In theory at least, one cannot see how Barth would disagree, given his use of 'non-ecclesial' elements. And yet, how far Barth actually puts this into practice is a question to which a satisfactory answer would be difficult to give to Frei and Ford, never mind Roberts.

Frei further suggests that, in the earlier volumes of the *CD*, the content given to the name 'Jesus Christ' operates at a purely formal level.

---

[80] James Richmond (1966), *Faith and Philosophy*, Hodder and Stoughton, London, 148; 1981, 172.
[81] Frei, 1956, 569.

In other words, apart from talk of virgin birth, cross and resurrection, Barth understands Jesus to be God's revelation of God's-self in hiddenness (one would have to add that even Barth's use of the Chalcedonian categories serve to formally and ontologically identify the being of this One). In a similar vein, von Balthasar implies the problem of a lack of revelational-contingency through his critique of the early *CD*'s *extra-Calvinisticum* style of christology, a style of christology in which the Word/Son is never fully incarnate.[82] Frei describes the weakness as "a sort of epistemological monophysitism".[83]

> As a human, historical figure [Jesus] is simply 'there', but neither his life nor his teaching seems to have much connection with his personhood or with the historical revelatory person's connection with us.[84]

Talk of the mediatedness of revelation, the true incarnate humanity of the Word in Jesus, etc., as Hart does, therefore, is not sufficient to alleviate the suspicions over how these things actually operate in, particularly, the first volume of the *CD*.[85]

Barth solves the problem, Frei continues, through the theological application of the hermeneutical category of narrative, particularly in *CD*, IV. In other words, Barth's attention shifts to the shape of Jesus' person as enacted intention and passion undergone over time.

> Jesus was what he did and underwent, and not simply his understanding or self-understanding. He was an agent in a narrative plot, in his particular narratable plot, that is, the restoration of the broken covenant which is also the realization of the aim of divine creation.[86]

This criticism has significance for Barth's eschatology since any eschatology founded upon generalities stands in danger of either wandering into unwarranted speculations, or becoming too general to be of any use in the concrete realities of temporality. As will be argued later,

---

[82] von Balthasar, 1972, 95.

[83] Frei, 1956, 576.

[84] Ibid., 106.

[85] Trevor Hart (1999), *Regarding Karl Barth: Essays Toward a Reading of His Theology*, Paternoster Press, Carlisle, ch. 1.

[86] Hans Frei (1993), 'Barth and Schleiermacher: Divergence and Convergence', in *Theology and Narrative: Selected Essays*, ed. George Hunsinger and William C. Placher, Oxford, 177-199 (184).

particularly in the Conclusion, while Barth manages not to succumb to either temptation, his eschatological discourse, at a significant point *even in volume IV*, does unwittingly sound like a free-floating hope unconnected with the contingencies of the redemptive event. Nevertheless, that Barth's eschatologically understood anthropology was generally moving in the right direction is something that will also be maintained.

It is not easy to assimilate Barth's theology into a form of conceptual closure as is so characteristic of the proposals that he is consciously seeking to avoid. At the very least, eschatological provisionality is written into Barth's discourse of veiling and unveiling. Moreover, a strong sense of eschatological reservation comes to be focused in what may be termed a 'hermeneutic of suspicion' for the dogmatic enterprise, i.e., a recognition of the provisionality and amendability of all human language about God.[87] In human reflection, therefore, in its endless critical service of 'pure doctrine' for ecclesiastical proclamation, there can be no inerrant product or theological stabilisation. That is why Barth speaks of the scriptural writers' fallibility, their *capacity* for and consequent *possibility* of error, although this is not to admit the *actuality of errors*, as Bromiley wrongly believes Barth is guilty of doing.[88]

Escaping finitude through the closure of securing externally verifiable certitudes is not a proper theological option for Barth. Rather, such a move is understood as an expression of sin, since in the event of revelation humanity remains human [e.g., *GD*, 126, 138]. Accordingly, *all* human (and therefore even ecclesial) thought is located "between the times" [*CD*, I.1, 334].[89] It is *necessarily* fallible, fragile, broken, penultimate, and dis-coloured by sin. Theological language and meaning, as human constructs, occupy a space that is to be continually set in motion through fresh openness to the self-giving of the Word [e.g., *CD*, I.1, 12, 53, 258ff.]. Certainty and assurance cannot pertain to any human endeavours, but can only be obtained momentarily in fresh renewals of the revelatory

---

[87] See Hunsinger, 1991, 70; A. Torrance, 38.
[88] Bromiley, 1986, 291; see, e.g., *CD*, I.2, 509. Barth speaks of the humanity of scripture [e.g., *CD*, I.2, 513] and dogma [e.g., *CD*, I.2, 513; 474, 636].
[89] Temporality is eschatologically conceived as a time of: "not yet", "between times", "interim period" [*CD*, I.1, 51; I.2, 408, 421, 423, 430f., 643; *C*, 114; *R*, 81]; interval between the ascension and second coming [*CD*, I.2, 676ff., 692f.]; human standing in the midst of conflict and tension [*GD*, 208, 216; *CD*, I.2, 269, 363, 431]. Nevertheless, it is a time "which is determined by the Word of God in the prophetic and apostolic witness" [*CD*, I.2, 693], a time of authentic joy [*R*, 81].

event. This is why Barth eschews all conceptual foreclosures or, what he calls 'systematisation'.

Of course, Barth's opposition to 'systems' is not a rejection of ordered thinking. On the contrary, his reflections on the order of knowing and of the necessary overlaps and interrelation of the things known positively necessitates that "Christian thinking is both free and ordered; it is never loose but always disciplined thinking".[90]

A useful summary of this perspective can be found in Torrance's claim that

> Theological knowledge can never come to an end, but is by its very nature, at least for mortals on earth and pilgrims in history, a perpetual inquiry and a perpetual prayer that take place in the interval between the inception of faith and final vision. There will be no possibility, therefore, of abstracting from the substance of theology some final theological method which can then be wielded magisterially to subdue all doctrines to some rigid pattern, and there will be no possibility of reaching final solutions to theological problems.[91]

Embracing this recognition of one's proper eschatological locatedness will render to theology's broken words the proper service of a humble witness. It will remind any *theologia gloriae* of its prematurity. The revelation event, Barth later argues suggestively for the interrelation of the triadic nature of theological time,

> is not, therefore, an event which has merely happened and is now a past fact of history. God's revelation is this as well. But it is also an event happening in the present, here and now. Again, it is not this in such a way that it exhausts itself in the momentary movement from the past to the present, that is, in our to-day. But it is also an event that took place once and for all, and an accomplished fact. And it is also future - the event which lies completely and wholly in front of us, which has not yet happened, but which simply comes upon us. Again, this happens without detriment to the historical completeness and its full contemporaneity. On the contrary,

---

[90] Barth, 1959, *Christmas*, 9.
[91] Torrance, 1990, 72.

it is in its historical completeness and its full contemporaneity
that it is truly future [*CD*, II.1, 262].[92]

Explaining this paradoxical statement is something that occurs
over the coming years. It comes to be particularly through II.2's doctrine
of election that these themes, and also the apparent difficulties in Barth's
eschatology, are distinctly displayed. For now, it is sufficient to note that
eschatological fulfilment is futural, something in the *Endzeit* [*C*, 115].
Therefore contemporary theology is characterised both as a *theologia
viatorum* and a *theologia crucis*. Indeed, Barth submits the Pannenberg-
like comments that God "in the strictest sense is future", and is present as
the coming God.[93] In a way that parallels Pannenberg's 'ontology of the
future', Barth even claims that the future exists "first and then the present",
and also speaks of the asymmetrical priority of the coming world over that
of the present, themes that are given flesh in the doctrine of election [*CD*,
I.1, 531; I.2, 410]. God, as the content of humanity's future, comes to
fulfil and complete his reconciliatory work in the redemption, which is
"God's still outstanding future" [*CD*, I.1, 468].

Of this Ultimate Future we are not yet possessors but rather those
to whom possession is promised on the basis of revelation already made
[*HGCL*, 79]. And so we await Christ, who will hand the kingdom over to
the Father and bring us to fulfilment.[94] As yet, we live in the midst of the
valley of death, in the time of the conflict between old and new (Christ and
sin) in which we still are afflicted. Then, in the expected and promised
consummation, we shall see God, who *is himself* the *eschaton* and our
hope, "face to face", whereas now we live in hope by faith.[95] However,
also suggestive is Barth's comment that

---

[92] Barth distinguishes between "the revelation that happened" and "the revelation
promised" [*CD*, I.1, 15].
[93] *CD*, I.1, 221; I.2, 113. Cf. *TKG*, 56. Barth speaks in unequivocal terms of God as Lord
both over and in the world, whereas Pannenberg speaks of God as the coming Lord. And
yet, Barth qualifies this by claiming that Jesus Christ's lordship over the world is not yet
visible [see *GD*, 165, 414; *CD*, I.2, 409].
[94] Barth describes this future as the end of time [*C*, 114]; kingdom of God [*CD*, I.2, 686,
882f.]; God's doing away with the veil of death [*HGCL*, 76]; bodily resurrection [*CD*, I.2,
449] and *futurum resurrectionis* [*GD*, 414]; eternal life [*CD*, I.2, 438, 499, 883]; an eternal
inheritance [*CD*, I.2, 241]; a new heaven and a new earth [*CD*, I.2, 882].
[95] *GD*, 155, 339; *CD*, I.1, 279. Barth contrasts faith and sight: *GD*, 339; *CD*, I.1, 529; I.2,
705f.; *C*, 115.

> even in the eternal redemption, we shall not be at the goal,
> and the blessedness of our perfect knowing of God will
> consist in a being on the way, so that it too will have to be
> described as *theologia viatorum* [*CD*, II.1, 209].

It is toward this "genuine, qualitatively, and indeed infinitely better future" that we advance in the present which exists only as a shadow of the future [*CD*, I.2, 883]. Barth, however, is careful to prevent any suggestion here that the kingdom of God is either a human construct, or is identifiable with the church [e.g., *C*, 112]. God relates our world to the coming world that he is creating, and accordingly sets the world in hope in the life lived through the Holy Spirit [e.g., *HGCL*, 80].

> On a second and final comprehensive Easter Day the
> exaltation of the Lord will be repeated. The interim period is
> running towards that Easter as the Day of the Lord. The
> Church with all creatures in their sighing is, in this interim
> period, waiting and watching joyfully for that day [*C*, 122].

Moreover, anticipating II.2 on election, Barth declares this to be the reason for creation and grace, and also the room given for repentance by the divine patience [*HGCL*, 73; *C*, 114, 120].

Chapter 5

Contriving Creation Eschatologically under Christological Control: The Doctrine of Election (*CD*, II-III)

Tentatively Dispelling the Time-Eternity Problem

It is with II.2's move into an eternal perspective that Barth's critics feel that the legitimacy of their criticisms is pre-eminently displayed. Chapter 2 has illustrated an account of Barth's revelation that perceives temporality's having been pressed into a systematically realised and eternal trajectory. History's contingency is thereby overwhelmed and negated, and its 'openness' to the future, and with it the framework for hope, is emptied of its content.

However, it is not clear that Barth uses a time-eternity model that is simply, and parasitically, related to general philosophical conceptions. Roberts and Gunton, for instance, recognise Barth's Boethian language but fail to notice that he does not *identically repeat* the Boethian conceptuality.[1] Rather, Barth 'baptises' 'pre-theological' concepts for theological use, and in so doing questions their previous conceptualisation. Moreover, Barth's time-eternity model derives from his involvement in a much more modest intellectual project than that of advocating a philosophical resolution to an academic puzzle. As Ford comments, albeit in a different context, there can be no such intellectual settlement for Barth.[2] Without commenting on his model's success, Barth at least intends to maintain two *theological* maxims.

Firstly, he plans to prevent an *a priori* exclusion of God and contingency by arguing that God's freedom is not a freedom-nullifying straitjacket or "prison" that prevents his incarnational relating to creation [*CD*, IV.2, 84]. On the contrary, the gracious trinitarian God can *freely* identify with, transfigure, and lead creation to its redemptive rest through

---

[1] *KBDT*, 116; *IR*, 173; Gunton, 1978, 180.

[2] Ford, 1979, 75.

the Passioned existence of his incarnate Son [*CD*, II.1, 304]. Creation is presented as the consequence of the free "overflowing of His [inner-trinitarian] glory" *ad extra*, with 'glory' here being understood as "God Himself in the truth and capacity and act in which He makes Himself known as God", at the core of which lies God's "freedom to love".[3] Consequently, this is the freedom of the trinitarian God who

> does not will to live only for Himself but also for another distinct from Himself..., working and creating beneficently in this desire and love. He lives as the God who so loved man that He condescended to become man Himself in His only begotten Son [*CD*, III.1, 363].[4]

As such, divine freedom, and its relation to creation, is both carefully distinguished from models of "absolute freedom of choice" and potentially arbitrary (non-christologically controlled) accounts of freedom [*CD*, II.2, 25]. Barth is able to do this more consistently since, from *CD*, II.1 onwards, the *Extra Calvinisticum* begins to disappear as a consequence of the emphasis on the Word's never being *Logos asarkos* but eternally *Logos ensarkos*. Barth would radically emphasise, then, that "it is precisely God's *deity* which, rightly understood, includes his *humanity*", presenting creation as the result of the inner-trinitarian love God freely flowing 'outwards'. This, moreover, is a conception which suggests a more powerful concept of the *lovedness* of creation than does that of the *creative necessity* of God's inner-trinitarian being in Moltmann's theology, for example.

Eternity conceived as pure 'timelessness' renders this account problematic, and reduces God to a remote and impassible deity, although Barth does deny an *external* necessary passibility to God [*CD*, II.1, 370]. However, any concept of God (and also that of humanity) that does not begin from revelation, but imagines a deity without humanity (*Menschenlos*), is an idol of human creation [*HG*, 47]. Hence, Barth's is a theological suggestion that *God has time for us*, that "True eternity includes this possibility ... [and] potentiality of time", and that

> without ceasing to be eternity, in its very power as eternity, eternity became time ... [i]n Jesus Christ ... submitting Himself to it, and permitting created time to become and be the form of His eternity [*CD*, II.1, 616].

---

[3] *CD*, II.2, 121; II.1, 643.
[4] See, e.g., Moltmann, 1981, 53ff.; 1985, 75ff.

Consequently, eternity is neither opposed to, nor is the negation of, temporality.[5] It does not abolish distinctions between past, present, and future, although it is not itself subject to these. Rather, in a move that Owen argues to be "sheer self-contradiction", Barth paradoxically declares eternity to be "pure duration" (*reine Dauer*), albeit a duration of divine simultaneity (*Gleichzeitigkeit*) in which beginning, succession and end are one and not three, without separation, distance, or contradiction [*CD*, III.2, 526f.].[6]

This is the hermeneutical context of Barth's talk of eternity as "real time" (*wirkliche Zeit*), and therefore as prototypical of created time [*CD*, II.1, 611]. It is crucial, however, to notice that Barth does not lend prototypicality to eternity's full range of conceptual content, but rather, and more particularly, to the triadic distinction of past-present-future. Roberts' assertion that eternity's prototypical basis had rendered created time as temporally problematic, thus mis-attributes temporality's being patterned on eternity as *simultaneity*.

Moreover, Barth's talk of the forty days of the resurrected Christ's presence as the "new time" and "real time", depicts the God-human reconciliation in Christ rather than the formal structure of temporality in itself [*CD*, I.2, 52; III.1, 76]. This renewed 'time', lived as fully reconciled human being, contrasts with our experience of time as "fallen" and "improper" by virtue of sin, since allotted and created time has been "lost" to creation [*CD*, I.2, 46ff., 66ff.]. In this "time of grace" created time has its meaning, purpose, and fulfilment [*CD*, III.1, 76].

Secondly, as in *2Ro*, God's *aseity*, or freedom *from* external constraint, is served by distinguishing eternity from time, and therein Creator from creature [e.g., *CD*, II.1, 311, 614]. Divine perfections such as constancy (contrasted with *immutability*), unchangeableness, and therefore reliability in this *freedom from* time are located in this concept of *freedom from* time [*CD*, II.1, 609]. What derives from this theological topography is that Barth denies that this relational trinitarian God is lonely and in *need* of creating [*ET*, 16]. Temporality itself is a creature, Barth declares, and where its difference from eternity is particularly evidenced is in the latter's simultaneity, or coinherence, of pre-, supra-, and post-temporality [*CD*, II.1, 619]. Thus "Time can have nothing to do with God" in the sense that God is not a prisoner, but rather Lord, of time [*CD*, II.2, 608]. Hence,

---

[5] *CD*, II.1, 610, 611, 615; III.2, 526, 558.

[6] H.P. Owen (1971), *Concepts of Deity*, London, 107; cf. Gunton, 1978, 179.

although God does assume specific spatio-temporal co-ordinates in Christ, revelation remains veiled apart from the contemporaneous unveiling by the Spirit.

Barth's time-eternity model, therefore, functions to safeguard the dual nature of divine freedom, which is why the discussion of eternity is located within that of the perfections of divine freedom [*CD*, II.2, 608]. Indeed, not only does the discussion of 'eternity' parallel Barth's concept of 'God', it even occasionally appears as a synonym for it. "Eternity is God Himself", Barth insists, "His own dimension" [*CD*, III.2, 526].

As well as misconceiving Barth's *dipolar* categorisation of eternity, Roberts problematically presses Barth's model by identifying it as *CD*'s hermeneutical key, and thereby he surmounts the confines of its intended boundaries.[7] All overarching hermeneutical keys are suspect, and care must be taken not to overlook Barth's diverse and revisionistic forms of expression. His theology:

> 1. is an indication of the never fully textualised, but eternally rich, divine Subject [*ET*, 37];
> 2. is a self-consciously *provisional*, fallible and stumbling thinking of the theological *Gegenstand* (although Barth's tendency for confident verbosity could detract from this) [e.g., *CD*, I.2, 483, 861f.];
> 3. exhibits recapitulatory self-critique. Barth himself describes his theology as exhibiting a polyphonic, rather than monotonous, testimony to the divine act [*ET*, 36];
> 4. involves tension creating and never resolving dialectic and paradox (e.g., eternal 'dipolarity', and revelational veiling-unveiling).

Returning to material matters, it is noteworthy that while Roberts certainly notes he does not pursue Barth's connecting eternity and divine freedom [*IR*, 173]. Indeed, what he specifically fails to recognise, as Marshall indicates, is that this dual understanding of the nature of God's freedom determines, and hence logically precedes, Barth's theological engagement with temporality.[8]

Barth's talk of eternity's threefold *distinctions* and potentiality for temporal becoming, raises questions as to the ease of *past-oriented* readings of Barth's eschatology. If Barth had presented a de-

---

[7] *KBDT*, 89,102; *IR*, 166.

[8] Bruce D. Marshall (1993), '*A Theology on its Way? Essays on Karl Barth*. By Richard H. Roberts [a Review]', *JTS* vol. 44, 453-458 (457).

eschatologised revelation in *2Ro*, as Chapters 3 and 4 have already doubted anyway, then he certainly is moving beyond suggesting this with *CD*'s christologically determined eschatology. *2Ro* is de-eschatologised only in the sense that Barth found it difficult to portray the divine coming to creation, something that later led to him admitting that the problem was the result of over-emphasising *post*-temporality [*CD*, II.1, 635]. The mistake, in other words, is to understand this earlier work as overplaying *supra*-temporality, something implied by critics' readings emphasising revelation's eschatological Moment.

Apart from the misleading comment about Barth's pre-1940 eschatology, Willis correctly argues that in most clearly by II.1 in particular, "Barth begins to find a way to take eschatology and the temporal future more seriously".[9] Thus, at least in principle, Barth's account of eternity's openness for temporality comes to retain a highly important eschatological dimension. Hence, God "precedes its [creation's] beginning, He accompanies its duration, and He exists after its end" [*CD*, II.1, 619].

This chapter contends that in 1942 (*CD*, II.2) in particular, Barth discovers the tools to forge an eschatological understanding of creation and history through a dramatic christological perspective.[10] This, which further raises issues of evil and human autonomy, will be explicated below; and an explanation will be made of how Barth's discussions rule out certain models of eschatology: notably immortality of the soul, evolutionary eschatology, and 'predictive' eschatology. What emerges is an eschatology that views Christ as both creation's *Prótos* and *Eschatos* who has realised reconciliation and redemption in our place. Chapter 6 will tackle the question of how this realisation relates to eschatological provisionality, with respect to *CD*, IV.3 and IV.4.

---

[9] W. Waite Willis (1987), *Theism, Atheism and the Doctrine of the Trinity: The Trinitarian Theologies of Karl Barth and Jürgen Moltmann in response to protest Atheism*, Scholars Press, Atlanta, Georgia, 155.

[10] In his brief discussions of election and eschatology, Thompson never makes the connection between them [1978, chs. 8 and 10]. On II.2's importance, see *CD*, II.2, 3, 76f., 91; von Balthasar, 1972, 145.

Election as Creation in Eschatological Perspective

In 1936, Barth came under the impress of Pierre Maury's lecture on election's proper christological grounding.[11] This helped Barth achieve two things.

The first thing that this lecture helps Barth to achieve is that he is able to concretise and develop his focus on the Word into a burgeoning christocentrism. Christ has steadily become Barth's theology's methodological 'rule' and regulative 'principle'.[12] Comprehensively being unfolded is the 'systematic' (i.e., coherentist) significance of God's self-revelation in Christ Dogmatic Christ-centeredness, something that enables Barth to distinguish between an "unauthorised systematisation" and "authorised systematisation", although Sykes understands this to be unconvincing rhetoric ('in practice', one should add) [*CD*, I.2, 868f.].[13] In making this distinction Barth is concerned to avoid an unrevisable and monotonous dogmatic 'systematisation' attained through an impersonal Christ-*Prinzip*, or *a priori* first principles (*Grundanschauung*) [*CD*, I.2, 861]. Hence he comes to favour talk of "Christian truth" as "a globe, where every point points to the centre", over it as having an "architecture". The latter "connotes 'building' or 'system'".[14]

In the second place, the 'systematic' implications of his christological theology for election, and thereafter also creation and eschatology, are what this lecture enables him to pursue. In so doing, it takes him beyond the actualistic (*aktuellen*) presentation of election of *GD*, with the latter's focus on the recipient of revelation's situation in the *hic et nunc*.

As in *GD*, highly significantly election is located in the doctrine of God. Gunton, for example, comments that "It is failure to understand that election is about God that has led to fruitless arguments about Barth's alleged universalism".[15] However, this comment is misleading. God's self-election precisely functions to ground God's *election of creatures*, and therefore the question of *apokatastasis* cannot be so simply dismissed. God could *freely*, i.e. without any external necessity, elect and save *all* humankind.

---

[11] Barth (1960), 'Foreword', in Pierre Maury, *Predestination and Other Papers*, trans. Edwin Hudson, SCM Press, London, 15-18 (16).

[12] *GD*, 131, 322; *CD*, II.2, 59.

[13] Sykes, 1979, 46.

[14] Barth, 1963, 13.

[15] Gunton (1974), 'Karl Barth's Doctrine of Election as Part of his Doctrine of God', *JTS* vol. 25, 381-392 (384 n.7).

The significance of Barth's *theo*-logical move with his discourse about election is rather to be sought in the fact that primarily, albeit not exclusively, election speaks of God, and of his primary act 'before' all others (logically, rather than temporally) which grounds and determines his consequent activity.[16] As is demonstrated in Christ, the electing God behind whom there can be no inscrutable divine figure untrinitarianly conceived, God, Barth's story unfolds, "did not remain satisfied with His own being in Himself" but elected another; although it is clear that this *free* activity is motivated solely by God himself and not by any necessity external to himself, hence the concept of God's free *self-election* [*CD*, II.2, 168].

Moreover, it is primarily through the image of Christ as *electing God* that Barth speaks of the revelation of God's eternal will, negating any unchristological and untrinitarian idea of an inscrutable decree of a hidden God [e.g., *CD*, II.2, 111]. God, and also the content of election, cannot be anyone other than the God incarnate in Christ [e.g., *CD*, II.2, 94].

However, Barth's discussion now comes to incorporate creation and anthropology within a christological perspective [*CD*, III.2, 390]. What it means to be human and creaturely has a christological basis since, originally and properly, God's election of *another* takes a particular christological form [*CD*, II.2, 107]. It is this *Other* who is the "Real man", the type and "prototype", and ground of others' election, since from, in, and for him everything else receives existence [*CD*, III.2, 132; 50]. Others "are what they are only in their confrontation and connexion with the fact of this one man" [*CD*, III.2, 161]. That is why Matheney can legitimately claim that "Christology does not dissolve anthropology, but complements and completes it".[17] As its origin it also shapes it.

By coming to reject the *Logos asarkos* in favour of the *Logos ensarkos*, Barth does not entertain the existence of a human being *temporally before* creation. Even his use of the Pauline image of Christ as creation's firstborn also has a logical, rather than temporal, *prius*.[18] Moreover, this eternal election does not undermine incarnational historicity by promoting an *accomplishment of reconciliation* in a remote

---

[16] See *CD*, II.2, 54, 84, 101f. Moltmann misrepresents this 'before' and 'after' talk as temporal [1981, 54; see *GD*, 466; Colwell, 1989, 228].

[17] Paul D. Matheney (1990), *Dogmatics and Ethics: The Theological Realism and Ethics of Karl Barth's Church Dogmatics*, Verlag Peter Lang, 170.

[18] *CD*, II.2, 99; IV.1, 48; cf. Col. 1:15.

eternal past, as Brunner and others suggest.[19] On the contrary, Barth's account of eternity's temporal simultaneity implies that God's eternal decision is an *anticipatory* determination for Christ's consequent temporal history.[20] Furthermore, Barth insists that this election necessitates the creation of a stage on which election is fulfilled [e.g., *CD*, II.2, 94]. "[T]he primal history [*Urgeschichte*]," Gunton proclaims, "is not the negation of the temporal story but its ground."[21]

Creation (and history, as creation's temporality) has its origin, centre, meaning and goal in Christ. History is, consequently, a salvation history which is hidden in general world-occurrence, and "reaches its goal in the appearance, death and resurrection of the Messiah Jesus" [*CD*, III.1, 24]. For he is the eschatological Man, *des zweiten, erlöften Adam*, even though in election he also is the first Man.[22] In such a eschatological view Wisnefske's attempt to revive natural theology through Barth's theology, when presented as "knowledge of nature *without* God", should be viewed as being careless.[23] There simply cannot be any form of nature *without* God.

In opposition to his earlier writings [e.g., *GD*, 155], Barth does not here understand eschatology as the *reditus* to an original creation-order. Although it does include this, eschatology is now conceived as history's moving towards God in Christ, or rather his (Second) coming as the universal revelation of God's kingdom [e.g., *C*, 121; *DO*, 131]. Webster recognises that

> Creation is wholly ordered towards its redemptive fulfilment:
> its meaning lies not in its original ordering *per se*, but in that
> ordering as the external condition for covenantal grace.[24]

One important function of this discourse in Barth is to rule out any suggestion that "we must laboriously build the road to" the goal [*DO*, 133]. The question of what this does to other (contingent) human hopes and goals (what Rahner terms "intramundane futures") is not discussed, although Barth does, in principle, clearly retain their legitimate place [*TI*, 6:59; cf. *DO*, 131]. His is not a 'hope against all hope', understood in any straightforward sense. What they are denied, as is perceivable in Barth's

---

[19] Brunner, 1949, 347; Zahrnt, 107, 112f.; *TG*, 254; *SL*, 168.

[20] *CD*, II.2, 53, 94, 160f., 173, 184.

[21] Gunton, 1974, 388.

[22] *C*, German, 144; trans. 167.

[23] Wisnefske, 2 my emphasis.

[24] Webster, 1995, 64.

earlier presentation of political activity and the kingdom-signs distinction, is ultimacy [*GD*, 413]. Ultimacy, and therefore the content of eschatological discourse, refers to God alone as

> the absolute, unsurpassable future of all time and of all that is in time.... There is no history in time that can end except with Him, i.e., under the judgment which He holds over it, and the results which He gives it [*CD*, II.1, 630].

This theme negates any *purely* immanentistic and contingently constructed hope. Barth would, therefore, be able to agree with Pannenberg that the "hope against all hope" cliché makes sense in the context of contrasting Christian hope with hopes for salvation through intramundane planning and acting.[25] His rejection, for instance, of Liberal accounts of the Kingdom as a present reality in human love, on the basis of an Overbeckian-inspired eschatology, is well-known. Moreover, *CD*, I.2, volume II, and the early parts of volume III were composed at the time of National Socialism in Germany, and strongly suggest that Barth's opposition to its religious-like claims to ultimacy and its shaping of the hopes of the German peoples was no less theologically generated and sustained than his earlier critiques of the *Kriegstheologie* and *völkisch* ideology. Writing in 1938 he argues that

> When the State begins to claim 'love' it is in process of becoming a Church, the Church of false God, and thus an unjust State. The just State requires, not love, but simple, resolute, and responsible attitude on the part of its members.[26]

It was a sense that these boundaries between church and state, and the divine and human constructions were being blurred that made Barth suspicious also of North American politics and the preaching of the 'American way of life'.[27]

Excluded also is Leibnizian optimism's 'evolutionary' style eschatology on the basis not only that it too comfortably undermines tragic

---

[25] See Wolfhart Pannenberg (1998), *Systematic Theology, Volume 3*, trans. Geoffrey W. Bromiley, T&T Clark, Edinburgh, 177.

[26] Barth, 1939, 77.

[27] See Barth, 1963, 24f.

conditions [*CD*, III.1, 406], although the fact that this is mentioned is important and suggestive in itself, but also, and more importantly, because it "does not really need ... God" since its "mode of entry is purely and simply an act of human self-confidence" [*CD*, III.1, 410]. So, for example, more recently Hick's evolutionary-eschatology has only had a 'need' for God in the sense that, as Creator, he sets the "soul-making or person-making process" in movement and 'guides' it through its multiple worlds to completion.[28]   By contrast, Barth emphatically relates that a properly christologically configured eschatology, with Christ as the coming One, bars all such human attempts at self-divinisation [see *HGCL*, 74].

It also excludes the form of eschatology to which post-Enlightenment thinking had reduced eschatological-discourse to, at most: the soul's immortality. In *GD* Barth appears to understand this concept as referring to a continuing existence based on something *innate within human being*, or, in theological accounts, on the divine creation.[29]

Barth's critiques of 'natural theology' and Brunner's *Offenbarungsmächtigkeit*, however, deny that there is anything *inherent* within human beings that leads to knowledge of God. His rejection of 'natural' immortality parallels this.   No guarantee for hope can be discovered in ourselves, since only God possesses immortal life, as if his granting us eternal life is an externally imposed necessity on him   [*CD*, IV.3.1, 310f.]. Rather, that *God* is the One who elects asserts his freedom from external constraint, and generates the asymmetrical God-human relationality.

> God does not owe us anything; either our existence, or that He should establish and maintain fellowship with us, or that He should lead us to a goal in this fellowship, to a hereafter which has a place in His own hereafter. ... For He could have done without it, because He is before it and without it [*CD*, II.1, 621f.].

Therefore,

> it will depend on God's decision alone if, contrary to all appearances, there is for man an ascent above the dust. No immortality of the body or soul, no eternal destiny or expectation necessarily linked with man's existence as such, can guarantee it. God alone can give this guarantee [*CD*, III.1, 247].

---

[28] John Hick (1976), *Death and Eternal Life*, Collins, London, 408.

[29] See Migliore, lxiii.

Secondly, for Barth, body and soul are a unity, whereas immortality separates the latter from the former at death.[30] Furthermore, Barth claims that since the concept of the immortality of the soul implies that individual souls are indestructible, it denies death's rupturing of life.[31] Here, there can be no comfortless absurdity of death since

> death ... is merely a passing privation, an unfortunate compression of life, the disintegration of a distinct and notable function of the living creature. Yet the creature survives this transformation both in soul and body, and thus attains to a new life. Hence even in death there is no real disruption or disintegration of the continuity of creaturely existence [*CD*, III.3, 317].

This conception of immortality, psychologically as well as conceptually, escapes finitude's limitations (knowing its future). Hence, Barth acclaims it to be

> a typical thought inspired by fear. For it would be so consoling if things were different, if the frontier of dying towards which we are hurrying, the contradiction which awaits us, were not quite so dangerous but could somehow be overcome [*CD*, III.4, 590].[32]

Instead, Barth intends to be "loyal to the earth" by being true to humanity's permanent belonging-to-the-world and opposing both human conflicting with temporality's flux and any attempt to escape one's life-span's definite temporal allottedness, which is ended by death [*CD*, III.2, 6]. Barth even attributes temporality to humanity's eternal life [*CD*, III.2, 521]. So Kerr regards Barth as "celebrating our finitude", thereby taking seriously Wittgenstein's concern to acknowledge human limitation as non-affliction.[33] Createdness, that declared 'good' by the Creator, is life's *proper* framework: "we are not in an empty or alien place" [*CD*, III.3, 48].

---

[30] See Migliore, lxix; *FC*, 136f. On body-soul unity, see *CD*, III.1, 243; III.2, 366-393.

[31] Cf. *TI*, 13:177f.; Simon Tugwell (1990), *Human Immortality and the Redemption of Death*, Darton, Longman and Todd, London, 157.

[32] Similarly, Nicholas Lash (1979), *Theology on Dover Beach*, Darton, Longman and Todd, London, 164f.

[33] Fergus Kerr (1997), *Immortal Longings: Versions of Transcending Humanity*, SPCK, London, 24; cf. viif., 23.

And those words are significantly written by Barth at a time when Europe is facing rebuilding after the horrors of Auschwitz and the war's ravaging of the continent. Barth continues, both creatureliness and

> the body formed by God's fingers cannot be a disgrace or a prison or a threat to the soul. Man is what he is as this divinely willed and posited totality. ... Creatureliness can be regarded as humiliating only where the creature is thought to be in partial or total opposition to God [*CD*, III.1, 243].[34]

Barth is careful not to suggest any form of escape from these proper limitations of creaturehood since human being eschatologically becomes a person not *in flight from*, but only *in orientation to*, the world and history.

> The Christian hope does not lead us away from this life; it is rather the uncovering of the truth in which God sees our life [*DO*, 154].

This is primarily why Barth utilises the image of bodily resurrection, although he does also imply a sense in which language of immortality could properly inhabit a context of describing the divinely given eternal life of the resurrected [*CD*, III.2, 624]. Redemption, Barth here argues, is *more than* the soul's immortality, i.e. bodily resurrection, thus implying that he sees no need to dispense *completely* with the conceptually limited and potentially misleading immortality symbol.[35] As a possessing of a much fuller conceptuality, the theme of bodily resurrection maintains eternal life's miraculous character as divine gift. Moreover, it suggests both a holistic sense of eternal life, and the continuity of person in the event of being resurrected.

> Resurrection of the flesh [*Auferstehung des fleisches*] does not mean that the man ceases to be a man [*aufhört, ein Mensch zu sein*] in order to become a god or an angel, but that he may, according to 1 Cor. xv. 42f., be a man in *incorruption, power* and *honour, redeemed* from that contradiction and so *redeemed* from the separation of body and soul [*Scheidung von Leib und Seele*] by which this

---

[34] *CD*, III.2, 520ff., 524f., 526f.
[35] See Migliore, lix.

contradiction is sealed, and so in the totality [*Totalität*] of his human existence *awakened* from the dead.[36]

Schmitt misunderstands this passage as suggesting a body-soul separation, whereas Barth claims the opposite. The redemption includes the healing from any temptation to separate body and soul. Another biblical metaphor, that of a new heaven and earth, functions in a similar fashion by indicating that creation is not eschatologically annihilated, but, rather, fulfilled and consummated.[37]

In other words, what Barth advocates is a theological anthropology of personal integrity, one that is to be read with an eye on a christologically shaped eschatology, and one that seeks to thematise the idea that people "become really human", and not less human, as he expressed it in 1931.[38] Here, however, Barth uses the term "ideal" to describe this eschatological humanity in Christ, whereas he will later more consistently define it as the 'real'.

Finally, eternal life is not a neutral endlessness or continuing life. As IV.3 later indicates, Barth understands eternal life in the positive sense of a divinely given life *lived for God* [*CD*, IV.3.1, 310f.]. Indeed, Barth focuses his eschatological discourse not primarily on *ta eschata*, a general *eschaton*, or any other neutral conception (e.g., Kingdom of God, eternal life, End), since such impersonal nouns are potentially abstractly fillable. Rather he emphasises that Christ is *Eschatos*, he who also is *Prótos*, something that Berkouwer, for example, fails to appreciate the significance of in his limiting of his discussion of Barth's eschatology to themes of death and the form of post-mortem life [*TG*, ch. VI].[39]

> Christian Eschatology ... is not primarily expectation [*Erwartung*] of something, even if this something were called resurrection of the flesh and eternal life, but expectation of the *Lord*.[40]

---

[36] *C*, 169; German, 145f. Keith Randall Schmitt (1985), *Death and After-Life in the Theologies of Karl Barth and John Hick: A Comparative Study*, Amsterdam, 46.

[37] E.g., *C*, 170; *DO*, 153f.

[38] Barth, 1959, 48.

[39] See *GD*, §7.Intro; *CD*, III.2, 490. On the *Eschaton-Eschatos* distinction, see Ingolf U. Dalferth (1995), 'The Eschatological Roots of the Doctrine of the Trinity', in *Trinitarian Theology Today: Essays on Divine Being and Act*, ed. Christoph Schwöbel, T&T Clark, Edinburgh, 147-170 (158).

[40] *C*, 166; German, 143.

As Rahner claims, in similar fashion, and yet is something strangely missed by some of his critics, Christ is the hermeneutic principle "of all eschatological assertions". Hence,

> Anything that cannot be read and understood as a christological assertion is not a genuine eschatological assertion [*TI*, 4:342f.].[41]

Consequently, Barth's thinking here negates those predictive-style eschatologies, mentioned in Chapter 1, that confidently blue-print world-history's future.   In these, eschatology becomes a sub-set of God's historical providence, with Christ functioning, at most, as the divine Revealer of that plan.   Such a family of models (e.g., Dispensationalism, Chiliasm, etc.) would infringe Barth's christologically constructed ban against eschatological speculation.   Eschatological discourse cannot be motivated by idle curiosity, or speculative knowledge [*GD*, §38.I].   Presumably Barth had just such eschatological models in mind when claiming that the older eschatologies were constantly in danger of this idle speculation: they tended to make the impersonal events at the end of history, rather than the *Person* of Christ, the theme of eschatological discourse.   In contrast, Barth's is a discourse which is conscious of Feuerbach's theological reductionism, and therefore seeks firm and realistic grounding in Christ as the *Real*.[42]

Subsequently, Barth's future-talk rings with a distinctly nescient sound. No one, he declares, has an idea of this life beyond, or the form of the passage to it.

> We have only what came to pass in Jesus Christ, in his reign, which is present with us through faith, and which is declared to us. What we dare to believe, is that we participate in this change, in the effects of human sanctification that occurred in the resurrection of Jesus Christ [*FC*, 40].

Although Barth continues to use these neutral nouns, testifying to their biblical basis, they are christologically controlled.   Hence, he identifies the kingdom with revelation and incarnation, and claims that

---

[41] Adrio König (1989), *The Eclipse of Christ in Eschatology: Toward a Christ-Centered Approach*, Marshall Morgan and Scott, London, 37; Peter C. Phan (1988), *Eternity in Time: A Study of Karl Rahner's Eschatology*, Associated University Press, London and Toronto, 206.

[42] See Ludwig Feuerbach (1989), *The Essence of Christianity*, trans. George Eliot, Prometheus Books, New York, 135f., 170ff.

Christ "is the kingdom of God in person", i.e., God's perfect lordship over human being [*CD*, III.2, 144].

> [*E*]*ternal* life [*ewige Leben*] is the name given to this new
> form of our unity with Jesus Christ [*C*, 169; German, 146].

Outlining election's meaning and purpose leads into the theme of covenant fellowship, a significant departure, Gunton thinks, from the 'other-worldly' descriptions of election in the Augustinian tradition.[43] Hence, when speaking of the elect community's being 'called' to witness, he is not supplying a different conception of election's *telos*, but rather intends the service of calling others into that fellowship [*CD*, II.2, 196f.]. In other words, creation is presented by Barth as the external basis of, and formal presupposition for, the covenant. The covenant (the asymmetrically ordered God-human relationship/fellowship/communion in reciprocal love) is the reason for, and therefore the inner ground of, God's creative will. Pressing the "strikingly intimate and personal" [*CD*, III.1, 247] nature of the relational language further, Barth argues that, in imparting *himself* to his human creatures, God

> promotes him to the indestructible position of His child and
> brother , His intimate and friend. What God is, He wills to be
> for man also. What He can do is meant for the benefit of
> man also. ... [A]nd in fellowship every need of man is to be
> met; he is to be refreshed, exalted and glorified far beyond all
> need [*CD*, II.2, 238].

Through this concept, one that gives weight to Webster's rejection of any suggestion that Barth's God stands at humanity's expense, Barth rehearses the formula of divine promise ('I will be your God') and imperatival divine command for appropriate human ethical response ('You shall be my people') [*CD*, IV.1, 47].[44] Human freedom is herein presented positively, as freedom *for* obedience to God, rather than freedom as self-

---

[43] Gunton (1989), 'The Triune God and the Freedom of the Creature', in Sykes, 1989, 46-68 (51).

[44] Webster, 1995, 88f. On Barth's themes of 'Personalism' and 'Truth as Encounter', see Hunsinger, 1991, ch. 6. Hunsinger notes Barth's distinction between "external and casual" and "internal and essential" fellowship [*CD*, IV.1, 757], with Barth's favouring the latter as the act of the heart [1991, 174]. On the 'I-Thou' encounter between God and humanity, see *CD*, III.2, 245-8.

defining, self-initiated, and neutral *choice*. There is no neutral position from which to choose from equally appropriate and valid states of affairs. Hence, Barth opposes Brunner's account of human freedom since he feels that it promotes the notion of freedom as neutrality, freedom to choose God or withdraw from covenant-partnership [*CD*, III.2, 131]. Moreover, Barth emphasises, the attempt to live as one's own master lies at the heart of sin, the infantile delusion of exclusive self-motivation [*CD*, III.3, 305]. Instead, *proper*, *authentic* and *true* human life, that for which humanity is only free, is that lived in the *responsiveness* of free human obedience and thankfulness to God, with the concomitant expression of joy at the humanly unmerited grace. Following Augustine, Barth claims that even Christ's life was an offering of absolute gratitude, obedience, and submission before God [*CD*, II.2, 120f.]. In so freely living for God in this way, humanity exists as the covenant partner for which it was "destined and disposed" [*CD*, III.1, 97]. Humanity

> can and actually does accept the self-giving of God. ... There is, then, a simple but comprehensive autonomy of the creature which is constituted originally by the act of eternal divine election and which has in this act its ultimate reality [*CD*, II.2, 177].

Language of 'autonomy', here, serves to insist that this response is a spontaneously free "self-determination", albeit Barth clearly demarcates it from much post-enlightenment use [*CD*, II.2, 510]. It is an 'autonomy' with the force of a 'theonomy', i.e., a 'situated freedom', or a freedom clearly placed within a divinely chosen and created space. It is this that Webster terms Barth's "moral ontology, an extensive account of the situation in which human agents act", and the space that they occupy.[45]

Barth, however, emphatically rejects suspicions of divine coercion [*CD*, II.2, 510]. God created humanity distinct from himself, and continues to respect that human integrity and individuality [*CD*, II.2, 178]. In this context Barth attests, suggestively for the issue of *apokatastasis*, that God risked that humanity would not live by his Word but would rather reject the freedom that is proper to its nature, and therein conjure up the divinely rejected shadow of *das Nichtige* [*CD*, III.1, 109; cf. Genesis 1:2]. Human and divine freedoms are here presented in a *co-operative*, rather than *competitive*, manner.[46]   In election, therefore, Barth presents

---

[45] Webster, 1995, 1.

[46] For a discussion of the reconcilability of divine sovereignty and human freedom in Barth in "the Chalcedonian pattern", see Hunsinger, 1991, 177-180. Gunton shows that Barth predicates human freedom analogically from the inner-trinitarian relationality [1989, 50ff.].

humanity as receiving a specific determination, and therein he strenuously opposes passive and spectatorial models of human subjectivity, based on the neutrality of the thinking and ethical subject before God [*CD*, III.1, 35]. This determination is portrayed as entailing that true (i.e., eschatological) human being is a spontaneously responsive agent before God, one "confirming and glorifying" God's sovereignty [*CD*, II.2, 178]. Language of *constraint to obey* therein functions not to signal the impersonal "compulsion of force"; but rather "the compelling power of divine love exerted in our favour" [*CD*, III.1, 387]. This sovereign love

> did not will to exercise mechanical force, to move the immovable from without, to rule over puppets or slaves, but willed rather to triumph in faithful servants and friends, not in their overthrow, but in their obedience, in their own free decision for Him [*CD*, II.2, 178].

Human freedom is restricted by all other commands, "powers and dominions and authorities", and obedience to them is servile [*CD*, II.2, 585]. But, obedience to the only true God is freedom because it is gospel, as the doctrine of election impresses. Only the Lordship of "The true God" is non-coercive and person-affirming, thus allowing humanity to fulfil its created purpose [*CD*, III.3, 87]. That is why, as early as 1927, Barth could argue that

> To join in the Creed should not be an obligation (which it cannot really be) but privilege, a freedom to profess what is both true and expedient, the wonder of Christmas.[47]

Consequently, in a statement that distinctly raises questions of theodicy, Barth rhetorically argues that humanity is free to obey and "never to sin" [*CD*, III.2, 196]. God compels humanity

> with the compulsion which excludes all choice and gives him freedom for the only true choice, viz. the acceptance of his election [*CD*, III.1, 364].

Hence, Barth draws the analogy between the relations of God's inner life, God's relations with humanity, and inter-humanity relations [*CD*, III.2. 16, 50f., 219].

[47] Barth, 1959, 23.

Hence, there can be no *valid* or *divinely legitimated* and *approved*, choosing of disobedience and godlessness.

It is in this theological context that Barth uses axiological and theologically rich, albeit frequently misunderstood, paradoxical and negative terms to depict the nature and status of sin. So later he shows that, because of its absurdity, the godless forces could be spoken of "only in consciously mythological terms" [*CL*, 216]. Barth, given his christologically eschatological description of the *Real*, comes to consciously reverse *2Ro*'s talk of faith as the (humanly) "impossible" by reapplying that negative term to sin and evil (in I.2 and II.2).[48] This then, in III.2, expands into the paradoxical "impossible possibility" (*unmögliche Möglichkeit*). Similarly it is also referred to as "the absurd (irrational) possibility of the absurd (irrational)", and an "ontological impossibility" [*CD*, III.3, 178; III.2, 146]. The addition of this noun in this first citation from III.2 clarifies that Barth is not denying, or at least intending to deny (which may have a different result altogether), evil's actuality. In fact, although Barth views it as an extremely foolish and irrational act,

> the covenant-partner of God can break the covenant ... [and is] able to sin, and actually does so [*CD*, III.2, 205].

In II.2, Barth places his discussion of sin as "the impossible" within a specific framework of the divine 'permission', thereby avoiding any suggestion of Manichaean dualism and implicitly rejecting Marcionite dualism. Divine 'permission' may be the formal requirement for recognising sin's actuality, but Barth comes to speak more theologically and axiologically in volume III of the divine "non-willing" [*CD*, III.3, 73f.].

Several critics, most notably Hick, here claim that Barth is saying too much about sin, thereby infringing "his [own] ban against speculative theorizing".[49] In response to this idea of Barthian speculation through use of the theme of election, one should note on a general level that it is the recognition of grace in Christ that necessitates Barth's talk of the election of grace (*die Gnadenwahl*) and the sum of the Gospel [*CD*, II.2, 3]. Barth is pursuing the theological implications of the scriptural narratives, rather than any narrative overstraining or peering into the Trinity's script, as

---

48 See *CD*, I.2, 370; II.2, 170; cf. *2R*, 300.

49 John Hick (1977), *Evil and the God of Love*, 2nd ed., Macmillan, London, 135. Cf. Colin Brown (1961-2), 'Karl Barth's Doctrine of the Creation', *The Churchman* vols. 75-6 99-105 (102); Paul Ricoeur (1985), 'Evil, A Challenge to Philosophy and Theology', *Journal of the American Academy of Religion* vol. 53, 635-648 (644); George S. Hendry (1982-3), 'Nothing', *Theology Today* vol. 39, 274-289 (284).

Zahrnt implies.[50] Whether Barth's reading of grace was overly-speculative cannot be discussed at this juncture.

Secondly, and more importantly for the issue of the nature of evil in Barth's discourse, this, however, fails to appreciate Barth's theologico-poetics of evil as a quasi-reality, and his rhetoric of its being extant only in negative relation to the divine willing. Such discourse functions to deny any possibility that evil/sin is either divinely created or necessary to creation [e.g., *CD*, III.3, 77]. After all, Barth rejects 'modern' theodicies in which evil and sin is worked into the whole system, and therein entail that they become necessary and even good [*CD*, IV.1, 374-387].

It is true, certainly, that on one occasion, however, Barth does unwittingly appear to imply sin's inevitability in creation when he declares that

> God wills evil only because He wills not to keep to Himself
> the light of His glory but to let it shine outside Himself [*CD*,
> II.2, 170].

Hick tentatively claims that Barth maintains the *O felix culpa* in the sense that evil 'exists' in order "to make possible the supreme good of redemption".[51] But, for Barth it is *creation*, and not *evil*, that exists *in order to* make redemption possible. Moreover, Barth's theology does not appear to be a 'problem-oriented approach' (i.e., postulating the incarnate history as a response to sin), although this statement must be qualified by noting that Barth *never* abstractly discusses the question of an incarnation in a sinless world since creation *is* sinful, and therefore the incarnation is always placed within that context in a manner reminiscent of Rev. 13:8 [*CD*, II.2, 122; IV.1, 36].[52] So Barth speaks of the world's reconciliation, resolved in eternity and fulfilled on Calvary [*CD*, IV.2, 314].

Instead of suggesting that evil is an intrinsic necessity to creation, perhaps as the means to some 'greater good', Barth specifically rejects Schopenhauerian pessimism [*CD*, III.1, 335ff.] and emphasises that evil is an "alien" factor that is abhorrent to God, since God's creating is wholly beneficent to creatures, and the result of that creating is wholly good [*CD*, III.3, 302]. As Barth explicates in II.2, there is no divine fore-ordination of

---

[50] Zahrnt, 112.

[51] Hick, 1977, 139.

[52] See J.L. Scott (1964), 'The Covenant in the Theology of Karl Barth', *SJT* vol. 17, 182-198 (184, 196); Thompson, 1978, 23f.; cf. *CD*, IV.1, 48.

humanity to sin, but rather to blessedness and eternal life [*CD*, II.2, 170, 171]. Humanity, as created good, has been

> ordained and equipped ... only for what is good, ... [and therefore been] cut off from evil, i.e., from what He [God] Himself as Creator negated and rejected [*CD*, III.1, 263f.].

This is a possibility passed over and rejected as a *legitimate reality* by God. As *das Nichtige* it has no autonomous *being* like that of creaturehood, but rather receives its quasi-reality in a relation of negation or privation, following Augustine, of the 'good' [*CD*, II.2, 170f.].[53] Thus Barth argues that "when a man sins", therein implying this to be an actual state of affairs,

> he has renounced his freedom. Something takes place which does not flow from his creation by God, his creatureliness of his humanity as such, and cannot be explained on these grounds [*CD*, III.2, 197].

That is why one needs to note with Oden that disobedience in Barth's thinking is not

> freedom being *misused*, since true freedom for God, self and for neighbour *cannot* be misused. It can only be put to use or nonuse. Disobedience consists simply in the neglect, ignorance and disregard of true human freedom.[54]

Barth is not here seeking to provide a theoretical *solution* to the theodicy question, by accounting for evil's origins, what an exasperated Hick calls a "leaving the problem hanging in the air, without presuming to settle it".[55] It is arguable that he is doing something similar to MacKinnon, when the latter calls for a "phenomenology of moral evil",

> a descriptive study aimed at achieving a *Wesenschau* into the substance of the thing. Such an enterprise is not a contribution to the discussion of the so-called 'problem of evil'.[56]

---

[53] For a discussion of the logic and meaning of the theological and philosophical uses of the word 'nothing', see Hendry, 1982-3.

[54] Thomas C. Oden (1969), *The Promise of Barth: The Ethics of Freedom*, J.B. Lippincott Co., Philadelphia and New York, 66.

[55] Hick, 1977, 143.

[56] MacKinnon, 1966, 176-7.

As *CD*, IV.4 indicates, this description operates by way of focusing one's prayerful attentions on the immediate sources of evil in human affairs.   Barth, as with MacKinnon's agnostic preference for paradox over synthesis, in view of the mystery of the paradox of the existence of evil alongside the sovereignty of God in the world, refuses to attempt to justify God.   Rather God justifies himself in the event of encounter.   Barth contents himself instead with seeing evil both as under the 'unwilling' of God and as having been overcome in Jesus Christ.   The question of the reason for God's 'permission' of the existence of that which opposes is left an unresolved mystery, expressing its absurd existence in paradoxical terms.

Nor does he intend in any way to minimise sin's demonic power, as Wingren, Berkouwer, and others appear to imply [see *CD*, IV.3, 177].[57] Thus Hartwell speaks of *das Nichtige*'s existence

> in a most terrifying and menacing manner, as is clearly
> revealed in the reality of the Nihil which God faces in Jesus
> Christ, above all in the agony of the Cross.[58]

Barth recognises the "absurdity" of evil, and therefore refuses to capitulate to philosophical drives for conceptual systematisation in theodicy-projects.   As Highfield recognises,

> Barth's point in using the term 'nothingness' to denote sin is
> to communicate its irrational, merely factual nature. In order
> to give sin a rationale one would have to show how it has a
> place in the will and plan of God.[59]

Rather, Barth intends to maintain creation's blessedness and God's gracious beneficence, that which Barth found so striking in his detection of Mozart's pervading theme of creation's praising of its Creator [*CD*, III.3, 298f.]; the sheer irrational and inexplicable actuality of this "surd element

---

[57]   Wingren, 110; *TG*, 232, 272.

[58]   Herbert Hartwell (1964), *The Theology of Karl Barth: An Introduction*, London, 120.

[59]   Ron Highfield (1989), *Barth and Rahner in Dialogue: Toward an Ecumenical Understanding of Sin and Evil*, Peter Lang, 158.

in the universe", as MacKinnon describes, which menaces creation; and the ultimate divine control over it.[60]

If Barth's discussion appears to involve over-generalised abstractions and ideals, one must recall that underlying his account is that of the covenant fulfilled by Christ in the actual appropriate human response to God's electing grace. This is what *real* humanity is [*CD*, III.2, 32, 144, 147].[61] It is *he* who is the divine good pleasure and purpose for God's creation, and he who has actually trodden the road of human covenant obedience to its very end.

Particularly, it is *he* who, through his obedience, has realised and accomplished glorification, the salvation from death, exaltation to fellowship with God and eternal life, and it is *he* who possesses, therefore, "the foretaste of blessedness" [*CD*, II.2, 173]. In so doing, he has destroyed humanity's 'old' life and creation's fallen time, and triumphantly inaugurated the gracious coming of the New in his resurrection. It is *he* who "is the beginning of a new, different time from that which we know, ... real time" [*DO*, 130].

What is striking about Barth's soteriology is the pronounced emphasis on themes of Christ's vicarious life, suffering and death [*CD*, II.2, 441]. The precise nature and implications of this, in reading Barthian eschatology, will be discussed in the following chapter. For the moment, it is recognised that this is consequent on Barth's talk of election in Christ [*CD*, II.2, 51, 94]. Consequently,

> In the One in whom they are elected, that is to say, in the death which the Son of God has died for them, they themselves have died as sinners. And that means their radical sanctification and purification for participation in a true creaturely independence, and more than that, for the divine sonship of the creature which is the grace for which from all eternity they are elected in the election of the man Jesus [*CD*, II.2, 125].

Present in II.2, but developed at length in IV.1, is the theme of the 'Judge judged in our place', with humanity being acquitted in this event [*CD*, II.2, 125]. Using an image that echoes several of the Greek Fathers, Barth declares that eternal life is "man's portion in the amazing exchange between God and man as it was realised in time in Jesus Christ" [*CD*, II.2,

---

[60] Donald M. MacKinnon (1995), 'Teleology and Redemption', in *Justice the True and Only Mercy: Essays on the Life and Theology of Peter Taylor Forsyth*, ed. T.A. Hart, T&T Clark, Edinburgh, 105-109 (109).

[61] See W.A. Whitehouse (1949), 'The Christian View of Man: An Examination of Karl Barth's Doctrine', *SJT* vol. 2, 57-74 (62).

173]. Hence, as our Representative, he is the cause and instrument of our exaltation into participation and sonship. These he realised for us while standing in our place so that we could have eternal life in fellowship with God [*CD*, II.2, 116f., 195].

> This seeking and creating finds its crown and final confirmation in the future destiny of mankind as redeemed in Jesus Christ, in his destiny for eternal salvation and life [*CD*, II.1, 274].

Therefore, it is in Christ, and the eschatological existence that he has vicariously opened up for human beings, that Barth speaks of the ontological impossibility of godlessness [*CD*, III.2, 136]. There can be no justification for sin, whether that be the excuse of one's defencelessness or evil's inevitability. It is ontologically impossible because of both God's creation of good alone, and his subsequent rejection of chaos in the "triumph inaugurated" by Christ [*CD*, III.2, 146].

> The freedom of his being in its responsibility before God includes the fact that man is kept from evil; *potest non peccare* and *non potest peccare* [*CD*, III.2, 196f.].

Consequently, humanity cannot evade, or be lost to, God. Even in sin, humanity still belongs to God, because of his original determination in Christ. Sin cannot destroy either that fact or subsequent human responsibility.

Conclusion

Chapter 1 has imagined the predictive type of eschatology to be an optimistic disdain of the tragic and a foreclosure of the future through its esoteric revelation. Both the immortality of the soul and evolutionary or Utopian progressivisms similarly *know* their futures: through human powers of rationality, the power of history's evolutionary progress, or the Utopian potential of Marxist revolutions.

Barth rejects all of these options, since for him Christ alone is our hope [*C*, 120]. Does this imply that his hope can take the tragic seriously? Barth at least intends for eschatology to remain loyal to the world, and to endure nescience over the details of the Future, by speaking of Christ as

Eschatos. Chapter 2, however, claimed that it is apparently precisely Barth's christological reading of eschatological assertions that creates the difficulties for hope's fragility. Zahrnt, for example, presents Barth "knowing too much".[62]

Roberts, the first section has argued, misunderstands Barth's account of eternity's openness for temporality, and thereafter misconceives Barth's eschatology of creation and history. Creation does have a temporal eschatological Future: that of the coming of its *telos*, Jesus Christ. Hence, Barth expands the claim that God (logically and, in a sense, temporally) precedes, accompanies, and succeeds created time, into the eschatologically significant statement, of being the One who was, and is, and is to come [*CD*, II.1, 619ff.].

Nevertheless, Barth declares that this *future* time of redemption is an unveiling (*Enthüllung*), "enforcing, emphasising and unfolding of truth already perceived and known" (*schon erkannter und bekannter*).[63] Creation and history may have a temporal Future, but how is this Future an eschatological one when it has already been realised in Christ's election and eschatologically vicarious humanity? Does this recognition not necessitate the conclusion (in a tacit nod to Roberts' thesis) that Barth has de-temporalised eschatology?[64]

Barth's discussion of the absurdity of sin's actuality suggests a theology that has not forgotten what day it is, and promotes an eschatological sighing, and indeed crying, for coming of the divine consummation. Moreover, the discussion of election's *telos* through concepts of fellowship, covenant partnership, communion, obedience, etc., further implies that a reading of the eschatological Future as the mere cognitive comprehension of the christologically determined truth of our lives is seriously inadequate. Chapter 6 is the place for the exposition of these suggestions.

---

[62] Zahrnt, cited in Colwell, 1989, 202.

[63] *C*, 162; German, 140.

[64] So Migliore, lxii.

Being Placed in Hope: Christ's Prophetic Work (*CD*, IV.3, IV.4)

Introduction

Hoping for an Attentive Appraisal of Barth

Reading texts can be a hazardous enterprise. Personal sanctuaries can be breached, dark corners uncomfortably radiated, and readers' pretensions exploded. Good reading, or interaction between interpreter and text, should entail a recogntion of 'otherness' of the text confronting one as "an unexpected claim to truth", and which then places one's pre-understanding at risk of contradiction and transfiguring.[1] However, because of the nature of textual inscription, the communicative act can become submerged in the depths of an excessive formalism in which the text is cognitively dissected and its content unaffectedly received. As Tracy argues with respect to what he names a "narrow scholasticism",

> the original insight is buried under a centograph of dazzling technical virtuosity and unacknowledged sterility.[2]

Furthermore, one's own interpretative framework can be exclusively cherished, and subsequently secured, above the risky potentialities of conversation and transformation resulting from the interaction with the 'other' through the text.

To Bromiley, in 1961, Barth complains that certain questioners have superficially ignored his writings' details, because "They are closed to anything else" than their orthodoxy, and "they will cling to it at all

---

[1] David Tracy (1987), *Plurality and Ambiguity: Hermeneutics, Religion, Hope*, SCM Press, London, 15.

[2] Ibid., 30.

costs".[3] A failure to listen attentively characterises a number of critiques
of Barth. No doubt fuel is provided by the fact that Barth's texts are so
slippery, often taking away with one hand what he had appeared to present
with the other. Hence the misreadings may be occasions of tone-deafness
to the Barthian rhythms. "Mistakes", Barth declares, "arise when only a
part of a sentence is heard".[4] And, given that six million words are not
easily digested, the manifold perspectives are not readily graspable. Hence
the attractiveness, but nevertheless ultimately "misguided enterprise", of
seeking a hermeneutical *Konstruktionsprinzip*.

The reading of Barth's theology as a potentially unrestrained
christologically eschatological optimism, which receives its
eschatologically predictive bearings from a wholly completed
christological past, is just such a tone-deafness to the Barthian symphony.
Something much more subtle is taking place which makes Barth's
treatment of hope, and thereby also his discussion of eschatological
completion (*Vollendung*), much more interesting.

Christ's Prophetic Work

IV.1 and IV.2 discuss the nature and accomplishment of reconciliation in
the Person of the Royal Man in his Kingly and Priestly offices. IV.1
proceeds in the direction of the divine *exitus*, the way of the Son of God
into the far country (Barth's analogy with the Prodigal Son). IV.2 speaks
of the Son's homecoming in the corresponding movement of atonement's
reditus. In Christ's vicarious existence, as has already been noted,

> there takes place all the life-acts of those who as free subjects
> (within their determined limits) are the creatures of God. ...
> To live as man is to live in the proximity and sphere of this
> One and therefore of this Lord and Servant ..., so that,
> whether we realise it or not, the decision is made that ... there
> is this union between God and each of us men, and that it is
> indestructible [*CD*, IV.3.1, 41].

Barth, however, is clear that Christ's work is not yet complete,
hence IV.3's discussion of his Prophetic office. Herein Christ, as the Light
of Life or atonement's truth, continues to be active in triumphantly
demonstrating himself in the world's darkness and overcoming it in his
resurrection power. God in Christ makes effective provision to interrupt

---

[3] Karl Barth (1981), *Karl Barth: Letters, 1961-1968*, ed. and trans. Geoffrey W. Bromiley,
T&T Clark, Edinburgh, 7f.
[4] Barth, 1963, 63.

people's evil dreams by indicating both that these dreams are *evil* and that they are really *dreams*, and he subsequently awakens them to their true ontology in the Reality of God's being for humanity (and vice versa) in Christ. Consequently, Christ as "the true Witness", by the Spirit creates a reconciled community that undertakes a missionary witness for the world's sake [*CD*, IV.3.1, 303].

Although IV.3's concern appears, at first, to lie in a recapitulation of Barth's methodological reflections, its more interesting component pertains to the explication and intensification of Barth's eschatological perspective. As the preceding three chapters have demonstrated, the location of the most eschatologically significant part-volume last in the series on reconciliation is not to be attributed to theological 'chronology' (i.e., eschatology and hope's relegation to a theological appendix). In Barth's coherentist dogmatics, eschatology is not a self-enclosed unit safely fileable at dogmatics' end without any conceptual relation to the previous explicated doctrines.

Once Barth opens the *CD* with reflections on the Word of God (a concession to modernity), he follows the Creed's trinitarian structure: God (II) has created heaven and earth (III), into which the Son has come as our Saviour (IV), and the Holy Spirit is redeeming us through him (the proposed V). IV.3 then functions as a link between Christ's reconciliatory work in IV and his redemptive work in the Spirit in V.

This part-volume explicitly discusses the relation of the threefold coming of Christ (Easter, Pentecost, and the Consummation), and questions the 'theologies of hope' that were becoming popular at the time, pre-eminently through Moltmann's *TH*. This eschatological perspective generates and shapes the dimension of Christian hope, and exhibits the practical nature of that hope. What is thereby displayed, Chapter 7 will argue, is an eschatology that encourages a hope of practical, and indeed provisional and fragile, engagement.

In preparation for this, this chapter discusses Barth's eschatology of actuality and provisionality in relation to the theme of Christ's threefold *parousia*. Although in Christ's history redemption has in some sense ended, IV.3 reminds that in another sense his history, and therein ours also, has not yet ended. Consequently, the critics' version of Barth's Future misreads the significance of his noetic discourse, and therein also his treatment of the temporality of eschatological completion-provisionality (i.e., the structure of fulfilment-promise in Barth's theology of the interim).

Christ's Ongoing Prophetic Work and the Creation of a Hope-Filled Dimension

In IV.3's final section, 'The Holy Spirit and Christian Hope', Barth investigates 'hope' as the product of Christ's prophetic work's impact on the individual Christian [*CD*, IV.3.2, §73]. Suggestively, he contends that hope arises because Christ has begun, but has not yet completed, his prophetic work. In a pregnant statement, the themes of which will be unpacked as the chapter proceeds, Barth claims:

> [hope's] final and decisive basis lies in the fact that the prophetic action of Jesus Christ, and therefore the revelation of the name of God already hallowed, the kingdom of God come and the will of God done in Him, and therefore the revelation of the man already justified and sanctified in Him, while it is complete in itself, is only moving towards its fulfilment, i.e., not to an amplification or transcending of its content or declaration, which is neither necessary or possible, but to a supremely radical alteration and extension of the mode and manner and form of its occurrence [*CD*, IV.3.2, 903].

Triumphant Eschatological Actuality

In one sense, however, this suggestion that hope has its *basis* (*begründung*) in the *incomplete* nature of Christ's prophetic work is misleading. Certainly hope exists only in a time of incompletion and provisionality, as, so to speak, the *external basis* of hope's existence. Nevertheless, Barth's version of hope takes its rise from, or has its *internal basis* in, Christ's *completed* work (albeit, paradoxically, an incomplete-completed work) and parallels his discussion of faith as a sure and confident knowledge of God's being for us in Christ. Consequently, Barth speaks of the "most striking determination of the time" of the present as being only *apparently* "this Not Yet", since

> Primarily and decisively it is positively determined by that which Jesus Christ already is and means in it, by its beginning in His resurrection and its continuation in the mighty operation of His Holy Spirit [*CD*, IV.3.2, 903f.].

IV.3 continues the narrative encountered in the previous volumes that in Christ the kingdom of God has *already* (*schon*) come, humanity is already justified and sanctified in him, and the reconciliatory work is already complete in itself:

that *our* new and eternal has begun, that *our* deliverance, conversion and even glorification are accomplished, that *we* are already dead and risen again, that *we* are already citizens of the future world, i.e., of the new and true world to be revealed as the dominion of God and His Christ. *We* are those who are eternally loved and elected by God in Jesus Christ, and called to the grateful realisation of their election in time, each in his own time. This is what is said by the reconciliation accomplished in Jesus Christ [*CD*, IV.3.1, 107].

In Christ's vicarious existence, the incursion of the presence of a new humanity has become an actuality (*Wirklichkeit*), and therein the world's great transformation, or "turn", has already taken place [*DO*, 122]. As well as speaking of the kingdom of God come, however, Barth also mentions Jesus' image of the kingdom drawn near [*CD*, IV.3.1, 84, 309]. Nevertheless, this must be read within Barth's emphatic announcing that this Future, determined for the world in and with its reconciliation, has become its true and concrete present [*CD*, IV.3.1, 315]. Christ's Prophetic work is revelation's disclosure of this reconciliatory completion (*Vollendung*), the unveiling (*Enthüllung*) of that which is a once-for-all fact in Jesus Christ, and which needs no supplementation or amplification. It is the manifestation of an "ontological connexion" (*ein ontologischer Zusammenhang*) of humanity to Christ that is independent of the former's noetic awareness and acknowledgment (*anerkennen*) of it.[5]

Barth accentuates this sense of eschatological actuality by depicting Christ's post-Easter forty days in eschatological terms: as the *parousia*, or "effective presence" [*CD*, IV.3.1, 293f.]. Reist, however, complains that this unwarrantedly excludes Christ's whole incarnate existence, and particularly the crucifixion.[6] In this move, Reist discovers in Barth the tendency for a *theologia gloriae* and triumphalism, an 'already' of resurrection in Christian life that excludes the simultaneous crucifixion and self-denial of the penultimate.

These criticisms, nonetheless, fail to entertain several themes in Barth which indicate that it is appropriate to reserve eschatological terminology for the resurrection, rather than the Incarnate's life. Firstly, the resurrection is the manifestation of Christ's glory, the unveiling only

---

[5] *CD*, IV.2, 275; *KD*, IV.2, 305.

[6] Reist, 1987, 210f.

anticipated in, and *veiled* by, his ministry (particularly through the miraculous signs, and the transfiguration-event) [*C*, 96, 164]. That is why it is occasionally portrayed as Christ's "self-revelation", in other words the retrospective manifestation of that incarnate life's significance [*CD*, IV.1, 301; IV.3.2, 613].

Secondly, in some sense, the resurrection is the culmination of Christ's ministry, since it is the obedient One's being raised to *eschatological life*, and in this sense, it is the salvific dawning of the eschatological *Novum* [*CD*, IV.1, 95; IV.3.1, 300].

However, when Barth stresses the resurrection as the revelation of Jesus' life-acts, the resurrection's salvifically eschatological nature may be missed. On the other hand, however, in qualification of this point one needs to recognise that for Barth 'revelation' is itself an eschatological concept, particularly signifying Future eschatological divine unveiling. Moreover, later it will be argued that Barth understands by his noetic concepts more than mere cognitive impartation. Furthermore, later discussion of Barth's sense of eschatological provisionality will also undermine Reist's diagnosis of a *theologia gloriae*, although he does correctly observe the importance of the triumphal perspective in Barth.

While chastising Berkouwer for the *concept* or *principle* of 'grace', rather than identifying grace with the *Person* of Jesus Christ, Barth accepts that his theology bears witness to the triumph of *Christ*, a highly significant statement the depths of which will be excavated later in this chapter [*CD*, IV.3.1, 173ff.]. Particularly through this image of "*Jesus ist Sieger*" Barth powerfully expresses the theme of eschatological 'actuality'.[7] His cue here is taken from the outcome of the conflict between Christ and sin, as revealed in the resurrection, of which there can be no room for doubt, according to Barth [*CD*, IV.3.1, 176]. As he claims, the "is", in the slogan "Jesus is Victor", expresses a concealed drama and history, an eschatological event, a *becoming*. "It is a drama which can only be followed, or rather experienced and recounted" [*CD*, IV.3.1, 166].

However, as cited earlier, Barth qualifies this eschatological 'actuality' with reference to the eschatological Future. Although this victory "is complete in itself", he is insistent that it is, through continuing conflict in the present sphere, "only moving towards its fulfilment" [*CD*, IV.3.2, 903].

---

[7] *KD*, IV.3.1, 188; *CD*, 165.

From Victory Unto Victory: Proleptically Identifying the Eschatological Future

What Barth intends when he claims that Christ's "prophetic action ... is only moving towards its fulfilment" will be discussed in the following subsections [*CD*, IV.3.2, 903]. For the moment one needs to recognise that in Barth's doctrine of reconciliation there remains an 'and yet' or 'not yet'. The eschatological nature of the Easter-event includes within itself, by way of anticipation, a necessary speaking in the future tense. As he had expressed earlier,

> The Christian perfect is not an imperfect; but the rightly understood perfect has the force of the future [*DO*, 132].

By this Barth specifically denotes two things. Firstly, the Christian recognises that Christ's contemporaneous presence, known in faith, will give way to his manifestation as presented to sight. Secondly, the present remains a time of sinful conflict and opposition to the work of Christ, and therefore there remains the need for the future annihilation of this sin in the universal manifestation of the kingdom of God.

In one sense, the former is included within the latter, since Christian experience recognises that there is a fulfilment to come, and that therefore the present period is one of provisionality and expectation since there still remains sin's assaults. And yet, in another sense, the first cannot dominate reflections on eschatological discourse, given that Barth's recognition of the provisionality of contemporary existence does not arise as the

> Minus-sign of an anxious 'Not-Yet' which has to be removed, but [rather as] the Plus-sign of an 'Already', in virtue of which the living Christ becomes greater to them altogether great [*CD*, IV.1, 327].

The eschatological perspective develops, not out of a humanly felt lack or need or anxiety over a *delay* in Christ's promised return, but rather "from the joy at the fulness with which it [his eschatological presence] has taken place in the resurrection" [*CD*, IV.3.1, 324]. The resurrection's "immeasurable power" is too great to be limited to the one event which took place then and there. To see His return in the event of this one day [Easter Day, the day of all days] is to be given willy-nilly an expectation of the last day which recapitulates and judges but also fulfils all history [*CD*, IV.3.1, 324].

Barth's perspective here appears to stand contrary to Pannenberg's assertion that

To hope as such there simply belongs to it a sense of the incompleteness of life as it now is, related to the confidence that is oriented to its possible fulfillment.[8]

However, although Barth does emphasise the sense of completeness, his point about 'fulfilment' is that the existence of a Future can only be known in the promises focused on the coming Christ that had been made by that Christ who is also contemporaneous with us in our present. It is from the implications of much of Moltmann's *TH* that Barth's thoughts are distinguishable at this point. Similarly, Pannenberg complains that Moltmann

asserted too sharply and one-sidedly the element of contradiction between the promise (and the hope based on it) and the reality that we now grasp.[9]

Hence, for Barth it is from Jesus Christ that Christians come to expect a removal of the present's temporal barrier between themselves and Christ, something, however, which does not lead to any lessening of their contemporary being 'in him'. "[R]ather it is augmented ... [and] immeasurably deepened and enriched in its extent" [*CD*, IV.1, 328].

Not only for Christians, however, is this the Future, but it is learnt that it is the "Absolute future", which is also a "temporal future" in the sense that it completes temporality, with a universal scope [*CD*, IV.4, 89f.]. This is the "still awaited redemption of the world reconciled in Him", "the presence of the future of salvation of their [i.e., Christians'] own and all existence" [*CD*, IV.3.1, 343]. Then, God will be all in all, and we will know and see him "face to face" [*CD*, IV.4, 40]. As will be detailed later, the eschatological fullness has come in Christ, while the universal fulfilment is yet to come.

---

[8] Pannenberg, 1998, 173.

[9] Ibid., 176.

> The determination then given to the world and us [at Easter] is on a small scale, but with no less totality, the same as will then be given conclusively on a big scale [*CD*, IV.3.l, 306].

Barth is profoundly aware of the presence of sin, and thereby rejects a monistic conception of the God-sin relation.

> The power of light is not so overwhelming in relation to that of darkness that darkness has lost its power altogether, as though its antithesis were already removed, its opposition brushed aside, its challenging and restricting of light of no account [*CD*, IV.3.1, 168].

The opposition has not yet been driven from the battlefield, despite the fact that its defeat has already been accomplished. "It [*still*] has to happen that he is driven from the field" [*CD*, IV.3.1, 191]. Hence, Christ's Prophetic ministry still faces sin's

> assaults and temptations and acts of violence. The defeated enemy is still capable of attack in his dangerous death-throes, and we for our part are still vulnerable to his efforts [*CD*, IV.3.1, 336].

Barth is concerned to negate Berkouwer's charge that he does not take sin and evil seriously, and that he thereby cheapens grace by weakening sin's power. Certainly the opponent has to be taken seriously; but, drawing heavily upon Christ's resurrection event and its subsequent revealing of the status of sin, one is forbidden to take light and darkness with equal seriousness. Defended, therefore, is his use of negative and paradoxical terms for evil's mysterious, perverse and absurd actuality. By its very nature, sin defies explanation or understanding. Even as a simple brute fact, it is an impossible possibility which is both intractable to rational presentation and simply alien to the "true subject-matter of dogmatics" [*CD*, IV.3.1, 469]. Taking the situation seriously entails only a brief pointing

> to these depths without trying to plumb them, to recall in a few sentences the well-known painfulness of the situation in which man finds himself when he exists as though Jesus Christ did not exist [*CD*, IV.3.1, 469].

And it is precisely this pointing that Barth does with respect to the themes of the ignorance of God in the world, the dishonouring of his name, and the idolatrous domestication of the divine in religion and even in the church [*CL*, 127, 130].

However, Barth can only accord these sinful affairs a *relative* and *provisional* seriousness, because of Christ's victorious action. They are powers,

> victoriously assailed and profoundly shaken and radically
> swept aside to impotence by the power of the resurrection
> [*CD*, IV.3.1, 307].

In explaining what Barth is doing here, Zahrnt indicates the proleptic direction of Barth's eschatological discourse by highlighting how the historic eschatological event of resurrection 'victory' provides one with the confidence that Christ will also conquer in the future.[10] This the Light (i.e., Christ) does step by step in his ongoing history. The nature of this conflict is spoken of, in opposition to monism and dualism, as a "dynamic teleology" (*dynamisch-teleologisch*) in which the Prophetic Word is "active in great superiority" but "yet has not so far attained its goal but is still wrestling toward it" [*CD*, IV.3.1, 168].

> A history is here taking place; a drama is being enacted; a
> war is waged to a successful conclusion [*CD*, IV.3.1, 168].

Thus the adversary cannot win or even achieve equality with God. She can only be felled and destroyed.

> Darkness still threatens light. But with a far more serious
> threat, the light now threatens his darkness. ... What we have
> in the antithesis is a 'still' and 'already', not the equivocal
> balance of a 'partly-partly' or a 'both-and'. The movement is
> quite definitely from ignorance to knowledge. The conflict is
> still in full course, but already in the course of it there can be
> no doubt as to the outcome [*CD*, IV.3.1, 197].

Victory becomes an event in the place where the Prophet's Light is confirmed by its being recognised in its truth and clarity as the reconciliation of the world. In this event, or rather sets of particular events, Christ's resurrection victory becomes a self-multiplying history which evokes its own reflection in the world in the form of Christian

---

[10] Zahrnt, 56. Cf. *CD*, IV.3.1, 263ff., 274.

knowledge. The final Word, however, will be definitively spoken in Christ's "final, universal and definitive manifestation ... and of what has already taken place in Him", at temporality's concluding consummation [*CD*, IV.3.2, 715].

Barth's conception of the future operates, therefore, protologically from the past. Consequently, Biggar's statement that Barth's "emphasis falls heavily upon the openness of the present to the future", as opposed to "the formative impact of the past upon the present", is an odd one.[11] As Barth declares, with a christological reference in mind, eschatology is a repetition "from the standpoint of the future all that has been said from the standpoint of the present" [*C*, 163]. It anticipates the future coming of the eschatological human being who has already come, "the Eschatos [who] is no other than the Protos",

> and that the meaning, novum and proprium of his coming is - fortunately - very definitely determined and already characterized by the fact that he has come and is.[12]

So Barth depicts temporality as having "a goal and horizon in a future analogous to the Easter revelation of Jesus Christ" [*CD*, IV.3.2, 642]. As such, the Easter event provides the "primal and basic pattern" of the other forms of Christ's coming [*CD*, IV.3.1, 293]. They all therefore "have the character, colours and accents of the Easter event" [*CD*, IV.3.1, 294].

In III.2 Barth had spoken of the "single event" of Christ's coming, which was "for us" "two [temporally] separable events": "the resurrection and the *parousia*" [*CD*, III.2, 290]. By IV.3, the term *parousia* has become expanded to include Pentecost also. This description indicates the eschatological nature of these events and the singular identity of the One who came and comes with the One who will come. In a similar manner, Barth consciously broadens the general conception of eschatology, referring not "merely to the final stage of the *parousia*", but also to "the last time": "the time which is still left to the world and human history and all men ... [as] running towards its appointed end" [*CD*, IV.3.1, 295f.]. That end is "the manifestation and effective presence of Jesus Christ in their definitive form" [*CD*, IV.3.1, 295].

---

[11] Nigel Bigger (1993), *The Hastening that waits: Karl Barth's Ethics*, Clarendon Press, Oxford, 136.

[12] Barth, Letter to Dr. Tarjko Stadtland, 18 Jan. 1967, in Barth, 1981, 236.

Despite maintaining these (temporal) distinctions between the three forms of Christ's presence, Barth refuses to separate them into distinct events for Jesus. In analogy to the unity-in-distinction motif of the trinitarian concept of perichoresis, they are presented as three forms of the *one* event. Each "maintains its individuality and is inseparably bound to the others in this individuality" [*CD*, IV.3.2, 911]. Therefore,

> Even if in a different manner, it is the same person who was
> yesterday, is to-day, and will come to-morrow and for ever ...
> (Heb. 13:8) [*CD*, IV.3.2, 910].

This christological locus and directing of eschatological discourse, Barth feels, is seriously undermined in Moltmann's *TH*. To Moltmann, in 1964, Barth complains of "the unilateral way in which you subsume all theology in eschatology".[13] Such, Barth admits, constitutes "the baptized *principle* of hope of Mr. Bloch".

Any complaint about Moltmann's "new systematizing", as Barth makes in a letter to Richard Karwehl, here uncomfortably reminds one of Barth's own christological centring of dogmatics, with all dogmatic themes receiving their shape from that *Mitte*.[14] And yet, Barth's point is important: eschatology cannot be an abstract principle or concept that is potentially arbitrarily fillable. For this reason Barth complains to Stadtland that the procedure of a 'theology of hope' "can hardly be recognized or taken seriously as *Christian* eschatology", but rather is a pasting of the name of Christ "on its own futurism".[15] Is Rosato, for example, also not in danger of falling foul of this stricture when he fails to recognise the *Eschaton*'s dynamic and personal nature in Barth in lamenting that Barth's "*eschaton* is uniformly [and statically] present at each moment" [*SL*, 167]? Such a criticism of Rosato appears further warranted when one notes that for him the "as yet incomplete [future is] ... essentially open and available", whereas for Barth, the 'Absolute Future' is closed and determined in the sense that it is the fulfilling presence of Christ *pro* and *in nobis* [*SL*, 165].

Consequently, Barth proclaims that this "mere futurity" of the theologies of hope "announces *nothing new*".[16] It is a human creation, or at most a human co-operation with the divine, whereas the *Real/Absolute*

---

13 Barth, 1981, 175.
14 Ibid., 174.
15 Ibid., 235.
16 *C*, 118; 1981, 235.

Future, christologically identified, is purely that eschatological creation by God in Christ.

In contrast, Barth's eschatology, with its pronounced focus on Christ as himself the *Eschaton*, and therein the constructor of creation's Absolute Future, is precisely that arena in which human self-divinisation is deposed. The "real *future*" is the coming again of this new person, a singular absolute, in contrast to the multiple and relative humanly constructable contingent futures [*C*, 119]. It will be the universal manifestation of God's rule (*Herrschen*) and lordship (*Herrschaft*) over all things which has been established in Christ, "Whether known now or unknown" [*CD*, IV.3.1, 346]. God in Christ "is the future of all", and therefore "wittingly or unwittingly all move towards His appearing and judgment" [*CD*, IV.3.1, 346]. Consequently, the present time is definitively determined by Christ's eschatological existence. That is why Barth's designations for 'present' time (for example, as the "between the times") are eschatologically determined by the latter's place in relation to the three forms of the *parousia* [*CD*, IV.4, 89].

In similar mood, Barth contrasts eternal life with any form of creaturely continuity not conceived in terms of grace's novelty, for example, the "immortal life" inherently proper to creatureliness [*CD*, IV.3.1, 311]. Continuity, in spite of the emphasis on novelty, is itself conceived also in terms of grace, as the divine eschatological taking-up of the present form into the new form. In saying this, however, one must bear in mind the problem that an overuse of themes of newness, interruption, and divine advent can create by implying an undermining of the created order's value through an over-emphasis on occasionalistic eschatological actualism.[17] Barth's language here, on the other hand, is firmly placed in the thematic context of election, creation and covenant. Moreover, Christ's eschatological existence is instantiated within the whole framework of Israel's divine calling, as the latter's "goal and end" [*CD*, IV.3.2, 583]. In fact, in opposition to what he perceived to be an over-emphasis on the future in Moltmann, Barth believes his own eschatology to indicate better that "honour can still be shown to the kingdoms of nature and grace".[18] While a stress on novelty can create the impression of

---

[17] See Langdon Gilkey (1976), *Reaping the Whirlwind: A Christian Interpretation of History*, Seabury Press, New York, 233-6, 324f.

[18] Barth, 1981, 175f. Moltmann, however, also appears aware of the need to avoid this problem in his own eschatology [Moltmann (1979), *The Future of Creation*, trans. Margaret Kohl, SCM, London, 16].

discontinuity, Barth tends to use the concept in order to stress that the eschatological humanity is related to divine election, and therefore is not something within creaturely potentialities to possess or control, either by creation's structure and order or by creaturely effort [*CD*, IV.3.1, 246].

The Nature of Eschatological Provisionality in the Determined Future

There is, consequently, an 'and yet' or 'not yet' in Barth's theology of reconciliation. Christ's "prophetic action ... is only moving towards its fulfilment", since he

> has not yet spoken universally [immediately and definitively]
> of Himself and the act of reconciliation accomplished in Him
> [*CD*, IV.3.2, 903].

When he does, then we will know the truth of our being in him. Rosato correctly perceives that the Spirit, in Barth, noetically realises Christ's eschatological achievement in us [*SL*, 124, 164]. However, Rosato's subsequent mistake lies in his misunderstanding of the nature of Barth's eschatological noetic, and therefore misreads the nature of eschatological provisionality. In so doing Rosato stands in a tradition of misreading the nature of Barth's noetic thematics, appearing in Gunton's comment that Barth's stress on revelation is a prevention of

> adequate systematic weight from being given to divine action
> in salvation (or creation), so that the overall balance of ...
> [his] theology is disturbed. Revelation is given too
> prominent a role in the wrong place, so that other aspects of
> relationships between God and the world are crowded out
> and so are systematically distorted.[19]

It is true that for Barth faith contains propositional cognition since it takes its rise, realistically, from something that is believed. Nevertheless, reading Barth's 'noeticically' presented themes of revelation and knowledge in *exclusively* (or even primarily) epistemic and propositional terms is to mistake his project. On the contrary, Barth's conception of the noetic denotes more than mere cognitive impartation. Christian 'knowledge' of God is neither the 'intellectualist' acquisition of neutral or academic information expressible in statements, systems, and principles; nor passive contemplation of a being that exists beyond the

---

[19] Gunton, 1995, 18.

phenomenal world.[20]   In contrast, a more holistic understanding of revelation (and, by implication, also knowledge) is presented in which "God acts on the whole man" [*CD*, IV.3.2, 510].

Barth's Johannine-sounding language of the deafs' ears being opened, the shining of the Light on those in darkness, and the calling of those in bondage into freedom, must be placed in a context of God's revelational *self*-giving to those who do not know him and the active response of those who hear [*CD*, IV.3.1, 339].

Secondly, concepts of 'revelation' and 'knowledge' are explicated primarily through the themes of confrontation, encounter, and approach. Hunsinger, therefore, speaks of Barth's "personalist conception of truth", in which knowledge is a self-involving event, comprising God and human being in a personal encounter and which Gunton likens to Michael Polanyi's   personal-knowledge-by-acquaintance.[21]   In   this   event "reconciliation overcomes and destroys man's distance from" God [*CD*, IV.3.1, 183].

Barth even claims that 'salvation' refers not merely to something once-for-all achieved, but also to something contemporaneously realised, and which therefore "actually" occurs in the event of Christian knowledge [*CD*, IV.3.1, 218]. Similarly, earlier in *GD* Barth argues that the doctrine of revelation is not complete if faith and obedience are absent [*GD*, 191]. This soteriological movement Barth depicts pneumatologically, through Christ's continuing prophetic activity in a trinitarian soteriological and eschatological scheme. Colwell describes this as "determined by the Father, actualised by the Son, and realised in the power of the Holy Spirit".[22] So, the pneumatological freeing of humanity *actualiter*, in correspondence to the christological liberating *realiter*,

> is not a different work, a second work alongside, behind and after the work of the reconciling covenant action of the one God accomplished in the history of Jesus Christ and manifested in His resurrection. It is the one divine work in its movement, its concrete reference, to specific men, wherein for the first time it realises its goal [*CD*, IV.4, 29].

---

[20] *CD*, IV.3.1, 183, 216ff., 220, 256; IV.3.2, 510.

[21] George Hunsinger (1993), 'Truth as Self-Involving: Barth and Lindbeck on the Cognitive and Performative Aspects of Truth in Theological Discourse', *Journal of the American Academy of Religion* vol. 61, 41-56 (44); Gunton, 1988, 64-70.

[22] Colwell, 1989, 180.

Barth speaks of the reality of the promise of the Spirit as the drawing "into the history of salvation and ... [giving] a part in it"; and this pneumatologically promised presence stands ahead of those who have not yet received him [*CD*, IV.3.1, 350]. It is the Spirit who "communicates to us communion with God ... in communicating the glory of God to us" [*FC*, 144f.]. Therefore,

> the prophetic work of Jesus Christ is no mere appendage or echo of His high-priestly and kingly work. It is an integral element in the whole occurrence. Hence if the promise of the Spirit is one of the forms of the prophetic work of Jesus Christ, then quite apart from the dignity to be ascribed to the Holy Spirit on a sound doctrine of the Trinity, we cannot possibly think less of His work than we do of that of Jesus Christ Himself [*CD*, IV.3.1, 358].

Because of the Spirit's soteriological, and therein also an eschatologically promissory, function, Colwell rightly argues that in Barth, Christ's Future revelation will be a "causative as well as a cognitive event".[23] It will be an Absolute Future which will bring a

> setting aside [of] all suffering, wiping away all tears, hushing all crying, making a new heaven and a new earth, and bringing in the new man [*CD*, IV.4, 198].

In other words, in Barth's trinitarianly shaped eschatologically significant soteriology, the pneumatological work is

> no more of an addendum to the completed work of the Son than the work of the Son is ... to the eternal decision of the Father.[24]

Two further features arise, with reference to this event: the call to ethical response, and the "conversion" of the human person.

With regards the first, Barth intends by his holistic conception of revelation and knowledge to describe a history in which the human is encountered by the "alien history" from without in a way which compels her so that she cannot be neutral towards it [*CD*, IV.3.1, 183].

As the previous chapter explicated with reference to Barth's treatment of the covenant, the Word contains a necessary imperative with

---

[23] Ibid., 129.

[24] Ibid., 283.

the corresponding dangerous force of an offence. Certainly the Word's uttering of an indicative and an imperative must be maintained in their proper asymmetrical relationship: the *nosse*, for example, always follows the *esse*. But that does not mean that either side may be dispensed with, for ethics is integral to Barth's presentation of revelation. Hence, Macken is wrong to suppose that IV.4 exemplifies the emerging affirmation "of human and creaturely reality gradually won ground without contradicting the absolute claim of the divine subject".[25] As Webster's study timely indicates, Barth "has kept a firm eye on human persons as agents right from the beginning of his dogmatic argument".[26]

The human decision, in all its located freedom "is the goal of the divine change" [*CD*, IV.4, 41]. Revelation (by which Barth intends the *matter* and *content*, Christ, rather than the *form* of God's self-manifestation) summons one to give oneself in return,

> to demonstrate the acquaintance which he has been given with this other history in a corresponding alteration of his own being, action and conduct [*CD*, IV.3.1, 184].

To the term, "alteration", Barth further adds "transformation" and "conversion" [*CD*, IV.3.1, 299, 444]. By these, in a manner which Rosato has missed, Barth indicates that

> the divine noetic, God's self-declaration as the One He is in the being and action of Jesus Christ, the prophecy of divine-human Mediator, has the full force of the divine ontic. ... This means, however, that after the declaration of its reconciliation to God effected in this event the world is not the same as it was before [*CD*, IV.3.1, 298].

Similarly, Barth suggests that

> For me the noetic and the ontological are *one* here. ... That Christ died for all provides a common ontological basis for *all* men. However, we must remember that ontology is not something static and fixed. Within this ontological structure that is valid for all, there are ontological differences. When a man has faith and is baptised, then he *knows* (noetic)

---

[25] Macken, 85.
[26] Webster, 1995, 13.

something that changes his life (ontic). This *knowledge* is *reality*, so that the baptised man does undergo an ontological (noetic) change within the once-for-all ontological condition created for all men by Jesus Christ.[27]

In the event of conversion (*Umkehr*), there occurs a "renewal of life" (*Lebenserneuerung*) in which the person is "made different" from what she was: in thought and act [*CD*, IV.2, 560]. Therefore, despite "all the common features (and ontological unity), everything is totally different" between Christian and non-Christian,

> not merely subjectively in the thought and outlook and conduct of the men, but objectively in the form of the orders and relationships which determine them [*CD*, IV.3.1, 340].

Hence, Barth speaks of non-Christians, those who do not know Christ's significance for them, as being unable to express the freedom that God in Christ has provided them with [*CD*, IV.3.1, 337f.].

The more-than-cognitive nature of the Christian's liberation is accentuated through seven points [*CD*, IV.3.2, 664-672]. It is portrayed as a:

1. pulling out of solitariness into fellowship, with God and fellow-humanity;
2. "deliverance from the ocean of apparently unlimited possibilities by transference to the rock of the one necessity which as such is his only possibility" [*CD*, IV.3.2, 665f.];
3. movement out of the realm of things into that of the human;
4. shift from desiring and demanding to receiving;
5. deliverance from indecision and a setting in action;
6. replacing of the moral rule by forgiveness and gratitude;
7. release from anxiety to prayer.

It is also worth briefly indicating that Rosato's assertion that Barth's Future is a mere impartation of information inadequately accounts for Barth's portrayal of sin as pride (IV.1), sloth (IV.2), and falsehood (IV.3). Falsehood, for example, is painted by Barth in colours of a *conscious and wilful* falsifying of that which is True, "an attempt to claim God by and for" oneself, and not primarily as *ignorance* [*CD*, IV.3.1, 368]. And since sin is dehumanising, conflicting with Real human being, it involves an ongoing disintegration of True human existence and its

---

[27] Barth, 1963, 90ff.

existential situation [*CD*, IV.3.1, 470-3]. Hence, cognition of one's situation is not enough. A complete transformation of the person is required, an active becoming of what we are in Christ.

Certainly Hunsinger, for example, is correct to draw attention to the oddity of the fact that Barth explicates his existentially and ethically relevant theme of conversion primarily through noetic terms.[28] Nevertheless, one should not be misled into misreading how these terms operate. As Hunsinger continues, existential and ethical implications are not excluded but are rather included within the noetic dimension. They are consequently situated within the context of our inclusion in Christ.[29]

However, in articulating Barth's view of the future as 'ontically' and existentially creative, a further move must be made by way of support: that of depicting the relation between the particular christological actuality and its universal provisionality.

Hope's 'Temporality' in the Time of the Eschatologically Provisional

'Pro Nobis, In Nobis'

As has already been argued, Barth's theology is characterised by a strong account of Christ's vicarious existence *pro nobis*, on behalf and in the place of human beings. As our Representative, he objectively enacts our salvation as a gift which is universally valid and efficacious. This is why, in *CD*, Barth can lend serious voice to Kohlbrügge's claim that "he was converted on Golgotha" [*CD*, IV.3.2, 500]. This type of account is what James Torrance calls a proper "doctrine of realized eschatology".[30]

The disturbing connotations of this account of the soteriological 'in Christ' for eschatology have often been located in an ontically realised present with a noetically outstanding future. The Future for all has already come in Christ (ontic), whether one is aware of it or not (noetic), by virtue of Christ's incarnate and high-priestly inclusion of us in himself. This eschatological 'christomonistic' problem has been expressed by Rosato:

---

[28] Hunsinger, 1991, 163.

[29] Ibid., 181.

[30] J.B. Torrance (1956), 'The Priesthood of Jesus: A Study in the Doctrine of the Atonement', in *Essays in Christology for Karl Barth*, ed. T.H.L. Parker, Lutterworth Press, London, 155-173 (165).

> Barth's christological colouring of pneumatology leaves
> doubt as to whether there is any real gap between the man
> Jesus and other men [*SL*, 161].

It is instructive to note that even one as sympathetic to Barth's
project as Thomas F. Torrance can still criticise Barth for failing to provide

> a careful account of the priestly ministry of the ascended
> Jesus ... which would have been fully consistent with ... his
> persistent emphasis on the vicarious humanity of Christ.[31]

This lack Torrance attributes to a "docetic tendency" in Barth's
ascended Christ of *CD*, IV.3, with Christ's humanity being swallowed up
in God's transcendence and displaced by "the humanity of God".

While Rosato's complaint derives from his tendency to understand
human autonomy *over against* God, the puzzle remains how there exists
any 'space' in Barth for free human activity given that Christ has achieved
all eschatological human agency, and thereby realised the Future. In
eschatological terms, the question becomes how there can be any room (or
time) for a creative future, and therefore a provisional present, given the
eschatological actuality in Christ's vicarious humanity. How can there be
an "interim" period in which there is the sin of conflict against God and
fellow-human?

Barth appears to be aware of this problem. He asks why the
eschatological event, in its definitive universality, should not be
consummatedly manifest and wholly present without a creative future for
creation [*CD*, IV.3.1, 317]. Implicit, here, is the fact that Barth does intend
to maintain a stronger sense of eschatological provisionality than he is
often accredited for. In fact, to Stadtland, Barth expresses a weariness at
having to deal again with the highly unoriginal objection that "the future
brings 'nothing new', 'only' something noetic".[32]

Barth explicitly responds to his question with three points,
although he admits that none of them can provide a full answer to this
acute question [*CD*, IV.3.1, 318ff.].

In the first place, the eschatological event in Christ *does* engulf and
renew the world, although this is not yet universally apparent. Barth's
concern here is to indicate that the problem does not lie in the Christ-
event's incompletion or inefficacy in itself. Nevertheless, Christ is in the
process of definitively revealing himself and continually completing his
self-manifestation. All human words, therefore, are provisionally final,

---

[31] Torrance, 1990, 134.
[32] Barth, 1981, 235.

pointing to that final eschatological Word. Moreover, in an echo of *2Ro*, Barth implies that even all forms of human hearing of God's Word can be selective, or a misinterpretation, tainted, therefore, by sin's constructing falsehoods. The completed Word of reconciliation is known only incompletely in faith, and is not, therefore, directly experienceable.

In the second place, the Christ-event does engulf the world, but only in its first stage of *commencement* and therefore not in its final stage of *consummation*. The future of salvation is already present in Christ's resurrection in all its fullness, but it does not cease to be future to our sphere outside this event.

Barth's third point challenges the basis of the question by suggesting that it essentially fails to notice Christ's resurrection's "effects upon world-occurrence and the lives of countless individuals" [*CD*, IV.3.1, 320]. However, this ecclesial eschatological focus provides only ambiguous results, at best, being "exposed to some measure of haziness and doubt" [*CD*, IV.3.1, 322]. For as Barth likes to remind, the church still exists in "direct opposition ... [to] its Lord" [*CL*, 191].

What Barth has here developed is an eschatological programme in which the Future has been realised in Christ but remains temporally Future for creation. His three answers, therefore, must be situated within a context which focuses on christological *particularity* in the *Eschaton's* actualisation. It is this that permits Barth to give 'room' and 'time' for, as well as shape and content to, hope.

Barth's response to Berkouwer's charge of advocacy of a christologically conceived *apokatastasis*, at first glance appears to be an enigmatic avoidance of the accusation. And yet, the form of Barth's response suggests the opposite. While admitting that "grace" is undoubtedly an apt and profound and, in the right place, necessary paraphrase of the name "Jesus", Barth declares that it might misleadingly imply the victory of one principle (grace, or even Christianity) over another (evil, sin, devil or death) [*CD*, IV.3.1, 173]. Such a principle would be deductively derived from "a God ... and evil", and/or "a grace *in abstracto*" [*CD*, IV.3.1, 175f.]. Noticeably, would it be a conceptual synthesis. For Barth, on the contrary, the triumph is rather that of the particular Person, Jesus Christ, a fact that although Berkouwer does appear aware of it on one occasion it nevertheless plays little further part in his description so that in the latter's reading the triumph of grace almost becomes an a prioristic movement, achieved in a prior moment of the remote eternal past [*CD*, IV.3.1, 173].[33]

> He Himself is present as the Victor. ... It is in this self-declaration that He is superior to the contradiction and opposition brought against Him. In this context, therefore, 'Jesus is Victor' is better than 'The Triumph of Grace' [*CD*, IV.3.1, 173].

It is of this person, and not of any principle, that Barth speaks with an unconditional and final certainty. That, however, is very different, Barth admits, from any conceptual apprehension and control, although the answers that one gives/attempts to questions of Christ's identity do have implications for the developing of a coherent theology [*CD*, IV.3.2, 706].

Here, Barth highlights an important distinction: the victory of a principle would leave no place for responsible persons before God, offering their obedience in response to the prior grace of God. All would thereby be unilaterally subsumed within the impersonal, and monistic, process of grace's march. Perhaps, the antithetical principle of sin would be caught up in, and overcome by, the movement of the thesis. Some of Barth's dialectical talk in *2Ro* sounded like this. However, his christological focus provides a necessary particularisation, and therefore also a corrective, of this thought. That is why Barth argues that when he speaks of Jesus Christ as "the only real man for God" what he intends is not a denial of the *existence* of other people,

> but that there is a kind of existing that lacks reality. Man in sin exists, but is not 'real reality'. He does not accomplish what it means to be a man.[34]

In continuing his reflections on this theme, Barth asks certain questions that are suggestive of what he is intending here by the very manner of their being asked.

> How ... [should] this goal of the will and purpose and plan of God for His creature ... be reached there in the appearance of the one man Jesus in a way which in Him is valid for all ..., but in effect should be reached only in Him, whereas for the rest of the world ... it can only be a goal which is manifest, indicated and certain, yet unattainably distant in virtue of the

---

[33] One can be slightly less critical of Berkouwer when one recognises that Barth does speak of the "victory of grace" on two occasions in 1929 [*HGCL*, 29, 76].

[34] Barth, 1963, 15.

frontier of death which still divides Him and them? [*CD*, IV.3.1, 317].

What may be perceived is a distinction being drawn between what has happened in Christ, albeit *for us* (i.e., on our behalf), and what has happened *to* and *in us*. More fully and clearly does Barth do this in his 1962 essay, demarcating the *extra nos, pro nobis*, and *in nobis* aspects of Christ's vicarious work. Here, the event of the Christian life, the *in nobis*, is perceptibly presented as a 'temporally' distinct event.[35] The eschatological event has become a reality for Christ, already by, to and in him [*CD*, IV.3.1, 327]. However, it has not yet been decisively realised in others, so that, as O'Grady argues, "in this time between it has an earthly-historical, imperfect and incomplete form in the community".[36] Using certain descriptions that would later be somewhat paralleled by Pannenberg's talk of the kingdom of God as the universal rule of God anticipated for all in Jesus, Barth claims that the eschatological event/Future is present to us only "By way of anticipation", so that

> In this commencement, however, the goal is not yet reached except in Him. It is not yet reached in the situation of the world and man. It does not yet have the form of a world enlightened and irradiated by His revelation, of a redeemed and perfected man. ... In this conclusion of this return He Himself is still future [*CD*, IV.3.1, 327].[37]

To reduce this point to its most basic components (and therein risk possible distortion), one could say that it is *only Christ* who participates in eschatological fullness; and it is *in him*, through his pneumatologically mediated prophetic work, that our reconciliation is taking place in the here and now.[38] Salvific participation in God's self-knowing is trinitarianly imaged, as Alan Torrance acknowledges:

---

[35] Barth (1986), 'Extra Nos - Pro Nobis - In Nobis', trans. George Hunsinger, *The Thomist* vol. 50, 497-511 (504).

[36] Colm O'Grady (1970), *The Church in the Theology of Karl Barth, Volume 1*, Geoffrey Chapman, London, Dublin, Melbourne, 346.

[37] Cf., *TKG*, 55f.; Pannenberg (1994), *Systematic Theology Volume 2*, T&T Clark, Edinburgh, 54ff.; 136ff.

[38] Incomprehensibly, given his criticisms of Barth on the issue, Rosato recognises this eschatological dimension of the Spirit's work [*SL*, 101].

It is fully 'realised' in the Son alone and only open to us,
therefore, to the extent that the agency of the Spirit recreates
us for participation *en Christo*.[39]

This consummation of becoming what we are in Christ remains
futural, and thus full participation in the eschatological event, of the
creation of the new creature, is our Future in him. Barth has this in mind
when he claims that it is "not yet revealed in the situation of the world and
man" [*CD*, IV.3.1, 327]. Certainly, a more pronounced emphasis on the
continuing eternal high-priestly and intercessory ministry of the ascended
Christ could clarify this concern to present Christ's ministry *in nobis* on its
way to completion. Barth, it is true, underplays the fact that Christ is a
substitute here and now as the one who intercedes for all, with and in us
and was not only judged in our place once for all, but continues to present
himself to the Father as the eternal High Priest.[40]

Nevertheless, it is clear that for Barth Christ's "intrinsically perfect
work" is only as yet "on the way, moving and marching from the
commencement to the completion", bringing us into participation in it,
through repentance and conversion [*CD*, IV.3.1, 327]. The *extra nos*,
which is also a *pro nobis*, becomes an *in nobis* in which, because of
Christ's history, one's own history can become the story of

a new Christian life here and now, a life corresponding to the
transformation of their hearts and their persons which took
place there and then.[41]

But that movement, that in which Christ's work *extra nos* and *pro*
nobis creates in our present "the beginning of a new history, their history
as human beings become faithful to God", itself is denied a
'christomonistic' transition. In other words, Barth denies that Christ's
agency subsumes and negates every form of particular people's free and
spontaneous activity, that the *in nobis* is merely

a secondary extension, a mere reflection, of the act of
liberation accomplished in the history of Jesus Christ, and
thus *extra nos*.[42]

---

[39] A. Torrance, 223.

[40] See T.F. Torrance, 1990, 134; A. Torrance, 118.

[41] Barth, 1981, 509.

[42] Ibid., 505f.

Such a conception would entail that "humanity's reconciliation with God would have been effected omnipotently in Jesus Christ".[43] "All anthropology and soteriology would be swallowed up in Christology." Consequently, Christ would be "the only truly acting and effective subject", while other human beings' activity

> would simply be a passive human participation in that which God alone did in Jesus Christ. It would strictly a divine action, not a human action evoked by and responsive to God.

Critics point to the weakness of Barth's pneumatology when complaining of a 'christomonism'.[44] And yet, Barth suggestively turns to 'christocentricity', and argues that "Authentic 'christocentricity' will strictly forbid one" from making irrelevant the ethical problem of how the Christian life originates. Jesus' death creates a new humanity which *freely* corresponds in obedience to the divine initiative, and participates actively in the divinely created *newness* of being.

> It must rather be an inner change whereby one becomes a different person so that one freely, from within, and by one's own resolve, thinks, acts and conducts oneself differently from before.[45]

This discussion has implications for Barth's conception of the relationship between divine and human agencies, and the status of human beings in the event of encounter with God. According to Barth,

> As in general so here in particular, God's omnicausality must not be construed as God's sole causality. The divine change by virtue of which one becomes a Christian is an event of genuine intercourse between God and human beings. As certainly as it originates in God's initiative, so just as certainly human beings are not bypassed in it. Rather, they are taken seriously as independent creatures of God.[46]

---

[43] Ibid., 506.

[44] See the discussion of Rosato and Jenson in chapter 2.

[45] Barth, 1981, 504.

[46] Ibid., 511.

As Chapter 5 earlier suggested, Barth is concerned to prevent any suggestion of mystical depersonalising or merging of the Christian into Christ [*CD*, IV.3.2, 539]. Dickinson's exasperation that Barth reduces Christians to immature infants before an authoritarian God, therefore, is erroneous.[47] While Dickinson makes a valuable general point about the unqualified use of metaphors, he has precisely missed Barth's talk of humanity's mature development in response to God, and the fact that the 'childishness' that Barth promotes is that which avoids modernity's illusory coming of age without reference to any themes of fellowship as a two-partner personal encounter and mutual address (even if that be a symmetrically conceived). Or perhaps, with his modern-sounding discourse of "free, unfettered and autonomous use of their reason", Dickinson feels that this is nevertheless precisely the bondage of immaturity. In this way, Barth retains, and preserves from dissolution, the freedom, independence and uniqueness, of both God and the human partners [*CD*, IV.3.2, 540].

> They are not overrun and overpowered, but placed on their feet. They are not infantilized, but addressed and treated as adults. The history of Jesus Christ does not blot out the history of our own lives as human beings. By virtue of his history, the history of our lives is made new while still remaining ours. ... Just as there can be no anthropomonism, so also there can really be no christomonism.[48]

Provisional Time

Particularly before 1940, the theme of eschatological provisionality stood prominent in Barth's writings. In 1929, for example, Barth distinguished between Augustine's Spirit of fulfilment and his own Spirit of promise. Emphasised herein is time's being experienced as a dialectical paradox and an existence within the shadows of death. During this time, Barth argues, we are not yet the children of God [*HGCL*, 73-81]. Hope, therefore, here received a futurist-directing, the danger of which Barth later comes to explicate against the 'Theologies of hope'.

In 1936's *C*, Barth clearly used the eschatological language of promise (*Verheiszung*) and hope (*Hoffnung*) to suggest that something significant will happen to human beings at the manifestation of Christ's

---

47 Charles Dickinson (1981), 'Church Dogmatics IV/4', in *Karl Barth in Re-View: Posthumous Works Reviewed and Assessed*, ed. H. Martin Rumscheidt, The Pickwick Press, Pittsburgh, Pa., 43-53 (50f.); cf. *CD*, IV.4, 126.
48 Barth, 1981, 511.

universal presence. We have "the fulfilment only in the form of the promise that consoles us" [*C*, 166]:

> over against human history and society, time and world, there is a totally different existence of man [*eine künftige andere Existenz des Menschen*]. Man as he is to his own self-knowledge has a reflection of himself held up in front of him in which he appears as a completely new man [*ein vollständig neuer Mensch*]. And he now hears this reflection saying to him: You who here and now are *this*, will then and there be *that* [*du, der du jetzt und hier dies bist, wirst einst und dort das sein*].[49]

Because "*die Auferstehung ist noch nicht geschehen* [the resurrection has not yet taken place]", the new person in Christ "still belongs in himself to the old sin-ruined creation which sighs for redemption ... from death".[50] "*Noch müssen wir sterben* [We must still die]." Consequently,

> The present [*Die Gegenwart*] is the *regnum gratiae*, between the Ascension and the Second Coming [*zwischen der Himmelfahrt und der Wiederkunft*]. The future [*Die Zukunft*] is the *regnum gloriae* set open [*eröffnete*] by the Second Coming.[51]

Certainly, the tone of this changed after *C*, from the 'being in the midst' to the joyful moving from the light of Easter into the light of the Consummation, as Migliore observes.[52] In 1947, for instance, Barth accentuated thoughts of the world's eschatological turn's having been already achieved, Christ's resurrection as having inaugurated a new Aeon, and therefore the already of the future's presence [e.g., *DO*, 122f.].

And yet, Barth retained the characterisation of the present's eschatologically provisional time through various temporal and spatial metaphors. These express that this period has its beginning in Easter, continuing through Pentecost, to be fulfilled at the Consummation [cf. *CD*, IV.3.1, 348]. The present is thus an "interim space", "the time of the Church" and "the time of mission" [*DO*, 123, 127, 128]. The Christian

---

[49] *C*, 161f.; German, 139.

[50] *C*, German, 145; trans. 168.

[51] *C*, 164; German, 142.

[52] Migliore, lxi.

community is subsequently painted in eschatological colours as a "pilgrim church" involved in a teleological movement. With approval, Barth later paraphrases Luther to the effect that Christians have never become (fully eschatologically new), but are always becoming [*CL*, 78]. As such, there is a continuing transformation towards one's *telos*.

> The alteration which takes place in and characterises him is clear and definite and provisional enough in itself. But it is not yet accomplished. It is in process of accomplishment. Its outworking will always have limits which cannot be passed [*CD*, IV.3.2, 674].

The Christian, whose "life in transition ... between two worlds, will always be provisional" and incomplete [*CD*, IV.3.2, 674]. Citing the *Revelation to St. John*, Barth claims that, the Christian

> is still in the night, but he moves towards the day when 'God shall wipe away all tears from their eyes; and there shall be no more death, neither sorrow, nor crying, neither shall their be any more pain; for the former things are passed away' (Rev. 21:4) [*CD*, IV.3.2, 643].

Moreover, this time is a period of conflict in which Christ as Prophet moves on to victory without, as yet, his having come to an end of his continuing conflict with falsehood.[53] In *C*, Barth articulates this with reference to the continued existence of the old man in the interim period [*C*, 121]. Similarly, IV.3 declares that although the world has been reconciled to God in Christ, it

> is far from being a redeemed and perfected world, that wickedness, evil and death are still rampant in it and in each individual, that there is still within a whole sea of 'deserved' and 'undeserved' suffering, that we must still fight, and can only fight, under so many errors and in so much weakness [*CD*, IV.3.1, 328].

Even though this is portrayed as having been defeated, deprived of its right and ultimate power, Barth is emphatic in IV.3 that it seriously, and enigmatically, remains destructive [*CD*, IV.3.1, 186]. The sinful conflict

---

[53] Like Rosato, Rodin misconceives the nature of Christ's Prophetic work, and therefore also the nature of eschatological provisionality [52]. Accordingly, he puzzles over the continuation of "evil in the time between the resurrection and the final *parousia*", and asserts that Barth's "theology leaves no room for a viable alternative" to universalism [53].

of the world with God, the dark and difficult sphere in which the Prophet works, persists since the world is not yet redeemed. In unbelief, it still clings to its old reality as though Christ's prophetic revelation were an illusion, or, at most, a promised future and not a present fact [*CD*, IV.3.1, 249ff.].

Barth admits that this world would be in a worse condition than it actually is, were it not for provisional manifestations of the grace of truth and freedom [*CD*, IV.3.1, 476]. Nevertheless, despite the potential joys that may be found, Barth reminds one of the actuality of the painfulness of, and suffering during, this 'not yet' [*CD*, IV.3.1, 472f.]. Indeed, he earlier declares in *C* that the interim period (*Zwischenzeit*) to be "a repetition (*eine Wiederholung*) of the humiliation of the Lord Himself".[54]

Christians cannot be exempted from this situation, both in the sense of their own sin and in terms of their suffering at the hands of the sin of others. The church remains "the Church under the cross" [*C*, 121]. That is why Barth devotes a subsection to 'The Christian in Affliction' [*CD*, IV.3.2, 614-647], although he does rather generally and even facilely speak of the second form of affliction as being a good for us since it "testifies to the reality and aggressive power of the Gospel" [*CD*, IV.3.2, 641].

Reist's unqualified assertion of a Barthian *theologia gloriae* is incomprehensible, therefore. For example, speaking of the world's continuing wickedness, Barth claims that creation is "still bound and tortured", existing in "its aberration and confusion, its infirmity and misery ... which darkens everything" [*CD*, IV.3.1, 328]. On this world, Christ takes pity, "a pity which is not idle but active, angry, militant, aggressive and therefore genuine". And then, undermining Reist's claim that the cross does not figure heavily in Barth's eschatology, Barth propounds that

> It is not for nothing that Jn. 20:20f. speaks of the wounds borne by the Resurrected and proving to the disciples His identity with the Crucified. ... He first, who alone is a match for and superior to this enemy, even in the last round of the conflict, sighs and weeps and entreats and prays, as He previously did, in the open battle which has not yet been carried through to final triumph [*CD*, IV.3.1, 328f.].

---

[54] *C*, 121; German, 107.

Christ is victorious, paradoxically, only in complete defeat and remains the king crowned with thorns here and now in his prophetic work, the suffering servant of God [*CD*, IV.3.1, 389f.].[55] To miss this word of the cross is not to hear him, Barth emphasises.

Hence, the consummation brings both our awaited and hoped for "manifestation with Him", and the "new thing" of the lifting of "the cover of tears, death, suffering, crying, and pain that now lies over our present life".[56] In this,

> the decree of God fulfilled in Jesus Christ will stand before our eyes, and ... it will be the subject not only of our deepest shame but also of our joyful thanks and praise.

Conclusion

The primary reason for Christ's remaining on his way as Prophet, has been suggested as the calling of human beings to participate in their eschatological being in Christ. In other words, to become what they are in him. The *actual* victory is accomplished by Christ in the Spirit, which is why Barth speaks of the "grateful realisation of their election in time" [*CD*, IV.3.1, 107]. Thompson explains,

> Christ has included them in his reconciliation but they continue to exclude him; its *reality* for them has not become an *actuality* in them.[57]

This permission of the existence of the time of eschatological provisionality will be explained in the next chapter as a consequence of the God in Christ's pitying patience. Creation is given time to hear the Word of reconciliation, and to be responsibly incorporated into the service of an active obedient response to this grace of Christ. Consequently, in a very real sense, although the Future has been realised in Christ's participation in it and is also certainly anticipated in the present through Christ's Prophetic work, it nevertheless remains temporally Future for creation. Moreover, it is clear that for Barth this future consummation retains its creative dimension.

---

[55] However, Barth problematically rhetorically claims that all the sufferings of the world are incomparable with that of the Son [*CD*, IV.3.1, 414].

[56] Barth, 1981, 9.

[57] Thompson, 1991, 181.

None of this suggests, however, that Barth advocates an indeterminate Future. The Future is not 'open' in the sense of being *neutral*, a nothingness waiting to be filled by humanly creative acts. As he argues in *C*, "what it [the church] looks forward to cannot be any sort of neutral future [*nicht etwa irgendein neutrales 'futurum'*]", among other things.[58] However, that is not the same as saying that the *details* of the shape of that Future are being prematurely portrayed. Nor is it the same as saying that all possible human futures are determined, causally speaking, in advance. Rather, it is asserting that no matter how human futures develop they all will be brought to an End, in which the universal lordship of Christ will be manifested. How this Future then determines our present and futures, is the subject of the next chapter.

Any implication, as can be found in Rosato's writing, that 'eschatology' and 'christology' are competitive concepts neglects the fact that for Barth they are certainly not, which is why the latter is able to maintain a strong sense of eschatological provisionality and hope's anticipation of the future.

One may accordingly present Barth's eschatology as one fundamentally *open* to the future glory of creation, given by God in Christ, through the Spirit. Within the sphere of Christ's prophetic work, all contingent futures, and therefore also the detailed form of the Absolute Future, have not been actualised and pre-programmed mechanistically by eternity: if that understands temporality to possess no spontaneous agency of its own.

Clarification of this eschatological scheme could be found in dialogue with Pannenberg, especially with respect to his reflections on the Future's 'appearance' (*Schein*) in Jesus. Prominent in Pannenberg's presentation is the dimension of the futurity of creation's eschatological completion in God, and therefore also of God's lordship over creation. It is in this context that he utters the otherwise apparently enigmatic comment that

> In a restricted but important sense God does not yet exist. ...
> God's being is still in the process of coming to be [*TKG*, 56].

Nevertheless, what this Future will indicate, as one of its functions, is that this God has always been contemporary with our temporality [*TKG*, 63]. Pannenberg explicates the essential presence of God's future in the

---

[58] *C*, 118; German, 105.

Christ-event through a theology of 'appearance' and 'anticipation', particularly inculcated from Heinrich Barth's philosophical reflections. Indeed, this enables Pannenberg to speak of this God as creation's Future, albeit recognising the strong provisionality of all thinking and speaking. When something appears it is actually present.

However, the concept also implies that something manifests itself which is *more* 'in itself' than that which actually appears. This 'something' is not totally exhausted in the act of appearing.

> On the one hand, appearing and existence mean the same thing. But on the other hand, appearance, taken literally, points to a being transcending it [*TKG*, 128].

In a move indicative of retaining the theme of provisionality within eschatological discourse, Pannenberg suggests that what this entails is that

> The individual appearance always presents itself only as a partial realization of the possibilities of the *eidos* [or essence] appearing in it [*TKG*, 42].

Perhaps the image of 'unity-in-difference' encapsulates Pannenberg's intentions here. Like Karl Barth, he does not envisage the *eidos* as being something *different* from the appearance, but rather the difference is one of perceiving only a little of the richness of that appearing 'something'.

'Anticipation' of this future rule of God has come in Jesus, "a power determining the present" [*TKG*, 133]. Language, however, such as that this is "only the anticipatory glimmer of its coming", might imply that the present form of the kingdom's coming in Christ is being devalued. This might be further supported by Pannenberg's description of Jesus' having pointed away from himself "to the coming Reign of God that he proclaimed, insofar as it was the future of *another*" [*TKG*, 134, my emphasis]. However, a different perspective on this discourse is created by the fact that Pannenberg speaks of Jesus' resurrection "as the irruption of the consummation of history, which for us is still to come [and "is so conspicuously absent at present"] but in Jesus has already happened".[59]

Consequently, the concepts of the 'anticipation' and 'appearance' of the Future in Jesus may provide Barth with a clearer picture of the christologically particularist form of the kingdom's coming in Christ *pro*

---

[59] Pannenberg (1977), *Faith and Reality*, trans. John Maxwell, Search Press, London, 77; 1970, 32.

nos while maintaining that only therein may one perceive the 'appearance' of the 'anticipation' of that Future rule of God *in nobis*.

As the next chapter shall indicate, the concept of 'anticipating' the Future is particularly vital to Barth's presentation of Christian hope in responsible action.

Chapter 7

Hope's Performance in Anticipating the Coming Dawn
(*CD*, IV.3, IV.4, *CL*)

Introduction

Chapter 6 argued that eschatological provisionality, or penultimacy, is crucial to Barth's account of redemption and to one's experience of the present. Theological time is eschatologically structured, in that it is the provisional time of the great 'Not Yet', a time between Easter and the Consummation. The Christian's experience and understanding of time is generated by Christ's having come (Easter), secured and strengthened by Christ's contemporaneous presence (Pentecost), and is geared toward creation's *telos* in Christ's Future manifestation (Consummation). Thus, the light of Easter's 'already' floods the present, providing a dim, but nevertheless real, glimpse into the "absolute future" since eschatology is christologically regulated talk about the history's divinely elected teleology [*CD*, IV.3.2, 488]. Therefore, the Christian

> Necessarily ... live[s] absolutely from the inauguration and absolutely towards the consummation of His prophecy [*CD*, IV.3.1, 343].

For Barth, therefore, awareness of theological temporality is inclusive and all-determining, creating the form and character of consciousnesses of temporality's meaning, direction and purpose.

It is this theological consciousness that generates Christian hope. The Christian hopes for the Future of Christ *in nobis*; and this particular content determines not only the shape that Christian hope has, but also the form of hope's active expression in one's life lived with faith in and love for this coming One.

Explaining the nature of that hope is this chapter's interest. The contention is that, deriving from his treatment of the Easter victory *pro nobis* and the proleptic hope for Future victory *in nobis*, Christian hope is assured and confident according to Barth. Moreover, given that God has allotted time for Christian existence and mission, hope is active in its movement of personal, social, and political critique and transformation.

Hope's Basis and Security in the Concrete Particularity of Jesus Christ

Chapters 3, 5 and 6 have indicated how Barth rejects hopes of both humanly constructed futures and the human race's discernible progress, as eschatological and ultimate. Characterising them as "optimistic ... expectation[s] of man" Barth suggests that they are unrealistically forgetful of the sinful nature of all human agency, and "the resisting element in man" [*CD*, IV.3.1, 264]. This is why he speaks of the "ambiguity" of these futures, and of their "fluctuating conjectures rather than certainties". Human agency, even when its aim appears to be obedient to the divine command, is so pervaded by sin that its constructed futures remain inextricably caught in the web of the 'old'. Ruled out, therefore, is the self-delusion of an already redeemed ecclesial state and "the mischievous ecclesiastical optimism" of adducing the ultimate, eschatological, victory from "even the best moments of its [the church's] history" [*CD*, IV.3.1, 264]. In relation to "what is regarded [in these] as light", "the darkness [appears] as a power which seems to be equal if not superior" [*CD*, IV.3.1, 264].

Unless sustained by strongly optimistic accounts of humanly, or evolutionary creativities, one could argue that an 'open' future is not necessarily creative of hope. The future, as that constructed out of the possibilities and latent potentialities of the present, can be just as dark a place as the present and past. Barth recognises this in terms of the fear of death, "the bitter Too Late", that awaits even the Christian [*CD*, IV.3.2, 927]. He further speaks of "a dark future full of conflicting possibilities" before which can occur "a divided expectation fluctuating between confidence and uncertainty" [*CD*, IV.3.2, 928].

The distinctive Christian hope for the *Eschaton* is acutely contrasted with these humanly projected hopes. Particularly so since, as Webster claims,

> What the Christian community has to say theologically about
> hope is inseparable from that community's renewed attention
> to and inhabitation of its distinctive linguistic, intellectual and
> ethical practices as the community is brought into being by,

sustained by and wholly referred to Jesus Christ, its origin and goal.[1]

Firstly, therefore, Barth rejects the illusory optimism of the self-grounding of hope in one's own creative potentialities. Hope, if self-grounded, cannot guarantee itself to be anything more than an arbitrary projection leading "to illusory results" [*CD*, IV.3.2, 914]. In contrast, Christian hope's true Reference is not in itself, and consequently as Reist argues is distinguished

> from mere religious hopefulness, or personal wishful thinking, or melancholy resignation, or political projections and programs based on an historical *élan vital* by which society might thrust itself revolutionary into the future.[2]

Christian hope, and also the eschatological assertions from which it takes its rise, is defined realistically by its being rooted in christological soil. Indeed, since hope's realistic *content* is Christ, Barth will not, therefore, begin eschatological deliberations with questions of hope at all.

> Eschatology can do nothing more than display and develop in a quite definite way how ... [it] is meant as a confession of the promise given to man, of the hope set up before him

in Christ [*C*, 162]. Hope rests, in other words, on faith in the Word incarnate, the Barth of 1926 declared.[3]   From an account of the eschatological direction of Easter, Barth declares, *Christus ist unsere hoffnung* [*C*, German, 106]. Therefore, hope is created and determined by the eschatological commencement of Christ's *parousia* on its way to its consummation [*CD*, IV.3.2, 919]. It has "its final and decisive basis [*Grund*]" in Easter, its external basis "in the fact the prophetic action of ... Christ ... while it is complete in itself, is only moving towards its fulfilment [*Vollendung*]", and its *telos* in the promise that this *Vollendung* will not be

> an amplification or transcending of its [Easter's] content or declaration [*nicht einer Ergänzung oder Überbietung ihres Inhalts, ihrer Aussage*], which is neither necessary nor possible, but to a supremely radical alteration and extension

---

[1] Webster, 1994, 36.

[2] Reist, 1987, 196.

[3] Barth, 1959, 14.

[*höchst grundsätzlichen Veränderung und Erweiterung*] of
the mode and manner and form of its occurrence.[4]

The *Eschaton*, therefore, will not be a second reality utterly
distinct from the Easter and Pentecost forms of Christ's *parousia*, and
therein potentially exposed to the suspicion of being merely ideal. On the
contrary, it will be the coming of the One who here and now still
encounters us in concealment but there and then will make himself both
clearly knowable and universally known without concealment.

Consequently, Barth speaks of our time as being determined,
shaped, and directed by the eschatological horizon; in other words, by our
awareness of Christ as *Eschaton* [*CD*, IV.3.1, 334f.].

Firstly, time is not empty or *remoto Christo* since its significance
is determined by its having come from Easter-time.

Secondly, history is given a dynamic teleology of moving directly
to Christ's universal revelation.

Thirdly, in contrast to characterisations of it as an escapist denial
of life, Christian hope actually affects "our whole life" in the sense that the
Consummation ultimately completes this life [*DO*, 154].

Fourthly, because of Christian hope's *Grund* in Christ's Easter
victory, hope for his universal manifestation of God's glory has *absolute*
confidence. It has "a certainty about our goal, which surpasses all other
certainty", for it is an "absolutely unequivocal, unbroken and therefore
certain hope".[5] Barth maintains that Christian hope cannot be ambivalent
or hesitant about this Future since "the Subject of expectation, i.e., the One
expected," is not a human projection [*CD*, IV.3.2, 908]. As such, Christian
hope's confidence operates as a counter-factual, "*believed*, in death's
'despite' because of ... the witness of the risen Jesus Christ" [*DO*, 154f.].

However, is the absoluteness of this form of discourse forgetful of
the fact that hope remains a *human* work, albeit grounded in and sustained
by Christ, and therefore that it cannot achieve any absoluteness of certainty
in eschatologically provisional temporality? Barth does partially refine the
rather loose language of absoluteness and certainty by claiming that the
practice of hope is threatened by "all the present elements which contradict
it", and speaks of it as negotiating a "perilous passage" [*CD*, IV.3.2, 917].
Moreover, given the nature of eschatological provisionality in Barth's

---

[4] *CD*, IV.3.2, 903; *KD*, IV.3.1, 1036.

[5] *DO*, 132; *CD*, IV.3.2, 909.

writings, the potentialities of sin and evil (albeit, absurd and irrational) necessitate a description of a much less direct and optimistic hope.

It is in this context that Barth claims that there is no "sense in trying to leap over this barrier with the confident mien of a Christian world conqueror" [*CD*, IV.3.2, 918]. The thing that the Christian has to do is hope for the promise's fulfilment.

> He hopes for it in face of this other aspect of the
> insurmountable barrier placed around his Christian existence,
> in face of the second riddle by which he finds himself
> confronted. The only thing is that he must use this freedom to
> hope [*CD*, IV.3.2, 920].

Nevertheless, for Barth there is no doubt of the outcome of the conflict between Christ's prophetic work and the resisting forces [*CD*, IV.3.1, 214, 328]. The Christian exists, thereby, in "a hope which overcomes fear", "already" living "in the power of the kingdom of God ... already on the new [earth], and ... under the new [heaven]" [*CD*, IV.3.1, 340]. This is a *practical certainty* in which one gives oneself to one's Future in God, something that differs in kind from the cognitive forms of scientific or logical certainties. It is a hope that gives the church

> a confident expectancy of the end, and strengthens it in its
> service and struggle in the world, enables it to bear patiently
> the sufferings of this age, keeps it from all false activism and
> confirms it in sober activity day by day [*FGG*, 61].

In this expectation and movement towards their Future, as lit by the resurrection's glory, Christians believe that their present sufferings are not absolute. Moreover, the Christian has no fear or anxiety over her own personal future, expecting not twilight or shadow, but "good and salvation" and the judgment of grace [*CD*, IV.3.2, 908]. This is because the Future expected is the gracious God, "the God towards whom he can go [wholly and] ... only with confidence".

In the period characterised by temporal provisionality Christian hope is christologically and pneumatologically supported and sustained. In leading creation to its goal, in Christ's prophetic work, the Spirit is the "sure promise" and certainty of the final *parousia*, the world's Future redemptive fulfilment, and our participation in eternal life [*CD*, IV.3.1, 351].

Moreover, in the Spirit the Easter-event does not remain either a remembered past or a purely awaited Future, but rather the Risen One becomes contemporaneously present in the second form of his *parousia*.[6] In III.2, this pneumatological presence had led Barth to dispute the conception of an identifiable 'delay' of the *parousia* in the New Testament [*CD*, III.2, 497]. Subsequently, he comes to criticise any disparaging of the Christians' present in favour of any past or future, since the second form of the *parousia* is as much Christ's direct and personal coming than the other two forms [*CD*, IV.3.1, 356f.].

The Christian life, therefore, is not a purely futural event, as Cushman maintains is the case in Barth's thinking.[7] Rather it begins with the recollection of Easter and moves towards its completion in the Consummation, living in that movement in anticipation of the eschatological fulfilment. In the present, the Christian life "is life lived with Him ... in the fellowship of faith in Him, of love for Him and of hope in Him" [*CD*, IV.3.1, 305f.]. Present sufferings and groanings, therefore, should not cause Christians "to complain of an inadequacy of the [presence of the] future", since in the Spirit we anticipate the final revelation [*CD*, IV.3.1, 359]. Christ, in the Spirit, continues with and assists Christians, continually permitting, commanding and helping

> them to become and be Christians step by step on this allotted way to the indicated goal, bestowing upon them in the twofold form and strength of His promise the gifts and lights and powers which they need for this purpose. He makes them Christians, and arms them to exist as such [*CD*, IV.3.1, 353].

Utilising the Pauline imagery, Barth claims that grace creates "fruits" in Christians' lives and actions, and these become recognised as "important indications of the future". They

> are provisional, little fulfilments, anticipatory and indicatory of the great, comprehensive and definitive fulfilment to be expected in that future revelation [*CD*, IV.3.2, 644].

However, Barth issues a warning. Important as they are, these "isolated, fluctuating and variable indications of the existential

---

[6] Barth rejects both the Lutheran doctrine of Christ's ubiquitous humanity in favour of Christ's circumscription [*CD*, IV.3.1, 357]; and the Nestorian-sounding Zwinglianism, that Christ is only present in his deity while his humanity is circumscribed [*CD*, IV.3.1, 357f.].

[7] Cushman, 167.

determination" cannot be given centre-stage in hope's consciousness, as if they are the focal point from which hope is generated, shaped and directed. That place is reserved for, and here the christological character of Christian hope comes into focus,

> the fact that the Christian in affliction is a man who is absolutely secured by the goal appointed for him in Christ [*CD*, IV.3.2, 645].

Moreover, these intimations of the Future are removed from any central point in the construction of Christian hope for a second reason. Barth is careful not to de-eschatologise time by identifying Christ's contemporaneity with the consummation, as if the eschatological presence could be read directly and clearly off the existence of the "fruits" of the Spirit and the church's character [*CD*, III.2, 510f.]. Our time remains "also determined by the fact that" the Consummation remains temporally "Not Yet" [*CD*, IV.3.2, 904]. Barth is emphatic that

> It is only in the imagination of a non-Christian and only too human arrogance and folly that the Christian can try to leap over these limits, and in so doing he will always land on his feet, or more probably his back, on this side of the barrier. For the limit set to Christian existence can be removed only with the coming of Jesus Christ Himself to complete His revelation [*CD*, IV.3.2, 904].

Time for Hope's Prophetic Action

Time for the Community, Mission and Repentance

Explaining the reason for evil's continuing existence leads Barth into claiming that the present's "not yet" is not due to the presence of any power of "the defeated enemy", since that has been negated. Rather, it

> has its basis in the fact that it is the good will of Jesus Christ Himself to be not yet at the goal but still on the way, so that the rest of creation has no option but to participate in and adapt itself to His situation [*CD*, IV.3.1, 329f.].

This discourse about Christ's freedom is clarified by referring to time for the community, mission and repentance.

Our day, Barth argues, is a day of mission to non-Christians, whose existence is a reminder of the darkness which resists Christ. It is for their sake that his prophetic work must go forward, since their conversion and faith and freedom is its goal. Recognising that Christ is also their hope, mission is the necessary expression of Christians' christological solidarity with non-Christians, since through it the Christian community perceives that its existence is only that of "the provisional representation of the calling of all humanity and indeed of all creatures as it has taken place in Him" [*CD*, IV.3.2, 681]. Hence, the Holy Spirit sends this summoned people "among the peoples as His own people" in order

> to make known to the whole world that the covenant between God and man concluded in Him is the first and final meaning of its history, and that His future manifestation is already here and now its great, effective and living hope [*CD*, IV.3.2, 681].

Barth emphasises that Christ "does not really need any representatives" in order to fulfil his prophetic task [*CD*, IV.3.1, 350]. Nevertheless, these human voices, with all their inherent fragileness, are freely chosen and summoned to serve this task, although neither Christ is bound to them in some mechanistic sacramental fashion nor can these actions contribute to Christ's completed Priestly and Kingly works.

Our day, then, firstly, is the day when Christians are not just passive objects of his work but are also given time to be "independently active and free subjects" in "this harvest", called and equipped to be subjects in Christ's service of witness, however clumsily or softly they may do so [*CD*, IV.3.1, 332]. Smitten by the apparently dominant darkness of the unredeemed and unperfected state of the world in its present form, they become dedicated to Christ's cause against that darkness. Even in this darkness, therefore, one may dare to hope that Christ's voice may be heard.

Introduced into this particular discussion is the fact that Christ, in "His gracious, merciful and patient will", is faithful "to His covenant-partner" [*CD*, IV.3.1, 333]. In a manner that invokes a very different image of the divine agency from those accounts suggesting an eternal monologue, Barth claims that God in Christ "takes the creature or man so seriously" that he enables him to freely witness. Reiterated is the prominent theme that God's activity towards humanity is unlike "the automatic functioning of a machine", the *potentia* of "a blind, brute power working causally and mechanically" [*CD*, IV.3.2, 486, 528]. God's active power, here, is emphatically rather *potestas*, "the liberating power of His

Word which is opposed to all compulsion and eliminates and discards it"
[*CD*, IV.3.2, 529].[8] It both "awaken[s] him to faith rooted in that free
recognition", through the Spirit's persuasion, and summons him to the free
and spontaneous service of witnessing to the reconciliation-event [*CD*,
IV.3.2, 529].   Although Barth does claim that God has the right over
humans of an owner to his property, this potentially authoritarian form of
discourse is clarified when he describes the possession non-competitively.
In other words, humanity retains its freedom and individuality as God's
covenant-partner for whom God condescendingly offers, claims and awaits
a response. In so doing, humanity becomes truly human [*CD*, IV.3.2, 942].

> There is a true subjection to Him. But this does not consist in
> his being crushed and trampled underfoot. It consists in the
> opening of his eyes, in the acquiring of the courage, exalted
> by Kant as the essence of true enlightenment, to use his own
> understanding, in finding himself placed on his own feet and
> set in motion on his own path [*CD*, IV.3.2, 529].

Secondly, time is given so that Christ's glory may be manifested in
his prophetic work; in other words, that falsehood may be transformed into
truth, and non-Christians may be called into the Christian community [*CD*,
IV.3.1, 360f.]. Barth, therefore, understands the sighing of the 'still' and
'not yet' not as primarily negative and burdensome, but rather as a specific
form of the greatness of God's gracious and pitying and patient love for his
creatures. By willing creatures' ultimate salvation and not destruction,
there is allotted this

> time by which the patience of God is allowed as room for
> repentance to the old man and so also to the Church [*C*,
> 120f.].

A Practical Hope

It has been argued above that, according to Barth, time is only on its way
to its Future, and that that Future has a particular Name. Therein is opened
up the necessary dimension of Christian hope, a hope for redemption in
Christ which has its basis in the events of the foundational Easter and in
our Easter-memory, its sustenance in Pentecost, and its *telos* in the
Consummation.
    Barth's subsequent account of hope differs markedly from certain
late nineteenth-century caricatures of hope in several respects. Firstly,

---

[8] See *CD*, IV.3.2, 528 on the compulsion exerted by human lords.

Christian hope is distinguished from all forms of illusory optimisms by having its content in the 'Real': Christ's past, present and future coming.

Secondly, the universality of that Future entails that hope's object is not a compensatory world for the hoping individual. In contrast to all forms of individualism, for instance, Barth presents what Matheney names a "social ontology" in which human beings are conceived existing in an intersubjective space as *Mitmenschlichkeit,* or "co-humanity" [*CD,* III.2, 222-285].[9] Easter indicates that the Consummation is less the believer's own redemption than the *telos* of *all.* In hope one anticipates "the liberation of all men", and indeed even the cosmos [*CD,* IV.3.2, 675]. Hence, Barth speaks of the "public ministry", responsibility, and hope for others that Christians have. They are provisional representatives of Christ to the world and vice versa.

Thirdly, whereas the caricatures of hope attribute to Christianity a form of life-denial, Barth rejects as unsatisfying the claim that Christians

> recognise, affirm and grasp within the world the possibility of their own non-worldly being, and therefore transcend and leave behind the world even as they still exist within it, and to this degree improperly [*CD,* IV.3.2, 558].

Barth's 'holistic' eschatology necessitates the perspective that the redemption is precisely the end, goal, and fulfilment of *this* world [see *CD,* IV.3.2, 937].

Fourthly, and finally, Barth's treatment of hope differs significantly from the Marxian impression of religious belief's function as escape from the realities of this world, and which therefore leaves the structures of this world untransformed by human agency.

It has already been argued that Barth's theology stands in the service of, and with an eye to, the life and activity of human beings.[10] Rhetorically he asks,

---

[9] Matheney, 101.

[10] Although this had been noticed earlier by Oden, only recently has its significance been taken seriously, particularly by Webster (1995), Biggar (1993), Matheney, Hunsinger (1976), and a number of other scholars in relation to theologico-political engagements: e.g., Bettis, 1976, 159-179; Gollwitzer, 97; W. Waite Willis, 134.

Can we ask God for something which we are not prepared to
bring about, so far as it lies within the bounds of our
possibility?[11]

Hence, in Barth's eschatological scheme Christian hope has a
necessary public and ethical expression in contrast to any encouragement
to passively wait for that Future to arrive, and therein it also critically
interrupts any secular moves towards the privatisation of religion [*CD*,
IV.3.2, 644]. That is why the editor of the collection *Against the Stream*,
Ronald Gregor Smith, is able to state that Barth's "theology is existentially
involved in the tragedies and the aspirations of our time".[12]
Barth recognises that a number of versions of eschatology, and the
hope that it produces, do precisely promote and sustain such an ethical
passivity [*CD*, IV.3.2, 936]. This, he attributes, to "the rigid [and
exclusive] orientation of the Christian on what is finally expected", which
in its contradiction with the perceived present promotes a pessimism over
the present state of things [*CD*, IV.3.2, 935]. In other words, because this
pessimism perceives "what is now visible in time, on this side of that goal
and horizon, as ... something unpleasant", it results in the possible failure

to do what might be done on the ground that it is meaningless
and even dangerous. He might refuse to have anything to do
with the world in its present form or history, resigning in face
of it. Hope as the total but also exclusive expectation of the
one great, eternal and definitive thing would thus extinguish
every small, temporal and provisional expectation [*CD*,
IV.3.2, 935].

Barth dismisses this version of hope as "a pious illusion", and an
"attempt [which] is in fact an impossible one at its very root" [*CD*, IV.3.2,
936]. Even Christian petitioning of God itself implies a command to do
something ourselves. It summons us to a corresponding use of our
freedom, and supplies a "burden" and "imposed ... task" in which the
Christian has no option but to participate joyously.[13] The Christian,
therein, is commanded to adopt an active responsibility, zealous for God's
honour and the hallowing of his Name [*CL*, 169f.]. Indeed, Barth imposes
that a person

---

[11] Barth, 1939, 79.
[12] Ronald Gregor Smith, 'Editor's Foreword', in Barth, 1954, 7-11 (10).
[13] *CD*, IV.3.1, 344f.; *CL*, 168.

is a Christian only to the extent that he is obedient to his calling to be a witness and messenger of Jesus Christ [*CD*, IV.3.1, 344].

Barth, therefore, advocates a hope that is necessarily bound up with the penultimate hopes that "too rigidly eschatological versions of Christianity" have forfeited.[14] Hope is "not a flight into the Beyond" which leaves this life unaffected, and becomes an "idle contemplation" of some remote future.[15] Webster correctly depicts Barth's account of hope as not

> some eschatological suppression of the ethical; rather it involves a description of the world as a reality whose situation has been so transfigured by God's act in Jesus Christ that hopeful human action is both possible and necessary.[16]

In fact, Barth goes so far as to proclaim that "Eschatology, rightly understood, is the most practical thing that can be thought" [*DO*, 154].

As will be detailed later, the centre of Barth's ethical project, particularly in the *CL*, is a delineation of the kinds of human responsibility that follow from, and are shaped by, an understanding of the nature and content of eschatological assertions - or, rather, the christological object of hope. Moreover, the consciousness of the nature and limits of human agency will need to be clarified since humanity serves as Christ's "afflicted but well-equipped witness", as a herald, but not agent, of the realisation of the Absolute Future [*CD*, IV.3.2, 481, 606].

Hope's Interrogative and Transformative Performance

An Occasional Hope? The Actualism of the Divine Command Paralleling Barth's rejection of natural theology is his repudiation of what he terms a general, naturalistic ethics, based on timeless truths of 'natural' or rational foundations. These imprison the free God in a 'natural' framework by codifying ethics into a humanly controllable and timeless set of ethical rules [see *CL*, 4]. In contrast to this move, Barth advocates a *theological* ethics of the divine command, presenting it as

---

[14] See, e.g., *CD*, IV.3.2, 937.
[15] *DO*, 154; *CD*, IV.3.2, 938.
[16] Webster, 1994, 38.

the specific content of what is always a special event between
God and man in its historical reality [*CL*, 4f.].

The divine command that takes place in God's gracious freedom,
Barth stresses, is not "a norm which we have thought out for ourselves".
Nor is it a "mere theory, or vision, or moral ideal", but instead the divine
command is "the truth of the reality of the work and activity of God" [*CD*,
II.2, 666; I.2, 866]. As Lovin recognises, it is because of this that "God's
persistent intentions toward the world" cannot be traced "in general
terms".[17] For the same reason, Barth is even reluctant to speak of the
Christian life through language depicting necessary continuation or
progress, preferring instead to focus on the continual freshness of the
Spirit's presence and work, something that provokes complaints from
Hauerwas.[18]

This stress on the *act* of divine command, however, has led to a
complaint that Barth exhibits an ethical 'occasionalism' (the occasional
character of divine commands with no logically predictable connections
between the various instances of command). This often doubles up as a
charge of an irrational failure to provide rules or strict guidelines. The
supposed logic of Barth's position appears as follows:

1. ethical action is guided only in obedience to one's hearing of
God's command;
2. the latter comes as an event only in the specific situation and
moment;
3. this cannot be expressed by any general rule, thereby providing no
connection between situations;
Conclusion: therefore, Barth fails to provide ethics with any means
of logical deliberation.[19]

One's eye is here cast back to Chapter 2's identification of the
Barthian problematic described by Roberts and Moltmann: that of the
human's being immediately encountered by God in the eschatological
Moment. God encounters the human subject immediately so that the latter

---

[17] Robert W. Lovin (1984), *Christian Faith and Public Choices: The Social Ethics of
Barth, Brunner, and Bonhoeffer*, Fortress Press, Philadelphia, 42.
[18] See Stanley Hauerwas (1988), 'On Honour: By Way of Comparison of Barth and
Trollope', in Biggar, 145-169 (149).
[19] So Robert E. Willis (1970), 'Some Difficulties in Barth's Development of Special
Ethics', *Religious Studies* vol. 6, 147-155 (149f., 151f.); Lovin, 41f.; René de Visme
Williamson (1976), *Politics and Protestant Theology: An Interpretation of Tillich, Barth,
Bonhoeffer, and Brunner*, Louisiana State University Press, 62; Hugo Meynell (1965),
Grace Versus Nature: Studies in Karl Barth's Church Dogmatics, Sheed and Ward,
London and Melbourne, 185.

perceives the essence of the command. However, the fact that the believer hears and correctly interprets the command, in the Moment of the eschatological *Ereignis*, is acknowledged by Gustafson to be an unwarranted Barthian "confidence in the objectivity of a particular command of God that can be heard", and an over-certainty that there are no genuine ethical dilemmas.[20]

Because of the complexity of human behavioural options and even their underlying motivations, it is asserted by Robert Willis, for example, that there needs to be moral guidance which is precise and defined.[21] By refusing to provide this, Barth's occasionalistic and actualistic "eschatological" ethics (Lovin) or "situation ethics" (R.E. Willis) appears to deny that there is any basis for such ethical guidance in the present.[22] According to Biggar, the only type of ethical reflection that Barth permits is that of self-examination in order to ascertain whether or not one is ready to encounter the next divine command.[23] Consequently, it is asserted that "for all its theological integrity, Barth's position is impossible for a public ethics".[24]

To assert from this that Barth's theology is not politically relevant is not, however, to claim with Reinhold Niebuhr that it is not politically *interested*.[25] For Barth, there are no purely autonomously existing religious and secular spheres [*CD*, IV.3.2, 687]. Rather, all forms of living are done under the eye of the "Lord, the King of Israel who is also the King of the world" [*CD*, IV.3.2, 686]. The claim is more serious than that, attributing to Barth an actualistic theology that can have no proper criteriological function.

The Eschatological 'Criterion' for Ethical Agency The actualistic motif is prominent in Barth's writings, thereby frequently obscuring other themes and emphases. Hunsinger particularly discovers this over-emphasis in Barth's politically charged essay, 'The Christian Community and the Civil Community'. Especially in this essay, but not exclusively here, Hunsinger claims that

---

[20] James M. Gustafson (1984), *Ethics from a Theocentric Perspective, Volume II. Ethics and Theology*, Chicago, 33.
[21] Willis, 1971, 183.
[22] Lovin, 41f.; Willis, 1971, 183.
[23] Biggar, 1993, 18f.
[24] Lovin, 42.
[25] Niebuhr, 1959, 184, 186.

> Barth failed to make sufficiently explicit the ethical
> foundations for political decisions in the church. Although
> he certainly exemplified the content of such decisions, he did
> not fully articulate their basis.[26]

Barth frequently, therefore, appears to espouse an ethical
occasionalism of the momentary, but immediate, divine command, and
thereby fosters "the misimpression that his political [and by extension,
ethical,] decisions were arbitrary".[27]

However, in emphatically rejecting the "obscure ethics of the
kairos in general", Barth implicitly distinguishes his ethics from that of the
purely occasionalistic, eschatologically immediate, type attributed to him
by Robert Willis *et al*. [*CL*, 5]. Primarily, the event of encounter, as the
constituting of one's commanding and hearing, is not that of Christ's
contemporaneous encountering of the Christian. Rather, Barth pre-
eminently and primarily refers to the incarnate-event, that from which
hope is generated and directed, as the place in which God has commanded
and humanity has heard, a dual movement that corresponds to the structure
of reconciliation in IV.1 and 2: the Son's way into the far country (divine
commanding) and the Son's homecoming (human hearing).

> Who the commanding God is and who responsible [and
> hearing] man is ... is not hidden from us but is revealed and
> may be known in the one Jesus Christ: God *and* man [*CL*, 5].

Special ethics' "task is to expound *this kairos* ... of the event
between God and man" in Christ, and not to illegitimately abstract or
generalise about the divine command in a region apart from this particular
eschatological history [*CL*, 5]. Moreover, a form of continuity of the
commands is provided also by the fact that God is the non-capricious One
who is "absolutely reliable ... [and] faithful to himself, and therefore to
creation and man" [*CL*, 18].

What surfaces here, albeit not completely submerged elsewhere, is
an inexhaustive christological directing of the human actor, and in this
movement relative "lines emerge ... which are at least distinctive to the
event" [*CL*, 7]. Barth's stated intention is "to steer a course between that
Scylla [of legalism] and this Charybdis [of subjectivist situationalism]"
[*CL*, 5]. Special ethics at once, then, excludes foreclosing fresh forms of
hearing the divine command, while yet still providing instructional

---

[26] Hunsinger (1978), 'Karl Barth and Radical Politics: Some Further Considerations',
Studies in Religion vol. 7, 167-191 (177).
[27] Ibid., 180.

preparation for them, or rather a training in being able to recognise the divine voice [see *CL* 5]. This it does by the divine-human encounter in Christ functioning as criteria, or standards, for human activity: criteria which indicate concrete imperatives midway between absolutely binding principles and mere opinions [see *FCF*, 447]. Herein Barth is furnished with an open form of 'normative ethics' which is learned in the risen Christ's power, through the scriptures, and in the context of the *ecclesia*. Moral, or obedient, character is formed in this ecclesial 'space', a location that helps "to form us into the kind of people who are able to hear the voice of God".[28] For example, it is in this context that Barth speaks of Christ as "exemplar" [e.g., *CL*, 63f.], and of the "normative description in the imperatives of the Sermon on the Mount or the admonitions of the apostolic Epistles" [*CD*, IV.3.2, 558f.].[29] In other words, the command is concrete in Christ's obedience on which ours' is modelled.[30]

Contrary to Hauerwas' critique, then, according to Barth the life-history of the disciple is portrayed as possessing some form of continuity rather than as a collection of moments [*CL*, 94], and this continuity can even include significant progress without possessing *guarantee* of development [*CD*, IV.4, 198, 203]. The image of the good seed which is constantly threatened goes some way to suggesting what Barth has in mind here [*CD*, IV.4, 39].

This becoming what/who we are in Christ through obedience is a secondary (but no less important) implication of discourse of the divine command, and entails that the command is concrete and not abstract. Matheney declares that

> Very early in his career, Barth was convinced that a proper construal of the scriptural understanding of divine-human relationality could be used as a parable or model to provide a criterion and a point of reference that would set limits and furnish guidelines for human ethical agency.[31]

---

[28] Biggar, 1993, 145.

[29] Biggar, however, is incorrect to argue that this theme is only occasionally, and therefore inconsistently, present in Barth [1993, 25].

[30] See Hunsinger, 1978, 171; Bettis, 1976, 170; John S. Reist, Jr. (1983), 'Barthian Ostraca: Ethical and Epistolary Fragments', *Journal of Religion* vol. 63, 281-289 (282).

[31] Matheney, 5.

Such a characterisation, however, does not intend that eschatological assertions are purely formal regulative ideals or principles in which one may be chosen or renounced in favour of another. Nor are they like a mere dream from which a new vision for a particular future is inspired (human dreams so often turn to nightmares, as the Soviet Union's history could testify).

Nevertheless, eschatology's criteriological function does parallel this form of regulative ideals in two ways. Firstly, as will be discussed below, the eschatological goal is *humanly unrealisable*; and secondly, and more importantly for present concerns, the eschatological horizon serves to generate and shape human practice.[32] The kingdom exists as something that (through the memory of Easter, participation in Pentecost and expectation of the Consummation) is context-creating and therefore really and bindingly constitutive of human identity. As such, it is practice-making through its determining of the nature of human agency; and it also provides a motivating force that enables bold commitment in one's creative responsibility for the world.

Hope in Christ, by bringing existence into "a light which makes everything appear in a new light", re-designs the shape of the human imagination; incites the dreaming of new dreams, which were previously beyond the dreamer's horizon; provokes desire for their, albeit provisional, realisation; and ignites and directs human planning for, and acting in, ways in which to make human life in the world human.[33] As Barth articulates, "It thus demands and creates freedom for human thought and volition in a new dimension", and in this way "that future already determines and shapes the present of the Christian in affliction".[34]

Hence, Rahner argues that one's fundamental nescience of "the material *content*" of the Future does not entail a stumbling around in the dark, but rather the eschatological criteria enable one to undertake an "enlightened yet daring decision of faith where all is open but dark" [*TI*, 6:64; 4:334].[35]

---

[32] On the nature of regulative ideals, see Dorothy Emmet (1994), *The Role of the Unrealisable: A Study in Regulative Ideals*, St. Martin's Press, New York, especially chs. 1, 2.

[33] Citation from Jüngel, 1989, 172.

[34] *CL*, 235; *CD*, IV.3.2, 644.

[35] John Milbank's assessment that Rahner's future tends to become "the ineffable goal or an endless aspiration", is one-sided [Milbank (1990), *Theology and Social Theory*, Basil Blackwell, Oxford, 223]. Moreover, Phan misses this criteriology when claiming that Rahner's stress on ecclesiastical limitations in issuing concrete proposals for socio-political action may unwittingly have a paralysing effect on Christian agency [199].

Revolution, Renewal and Renovation: The Nature of Human Agency
Barth's careful distinction between this ethical 'criterion', with its guiding
of hope into the Future, and a blueprint for clear specification and control
of the Future is theologically important. It designates not only the shape
but also the environment, nature and limitations of human agency. As
Jüngel declares,

> we are not ... simply agents; we are not just the *authors* of our
> biography. We are also those who are acted upon; we are
> also a text written by the hand of another.[36]

It will be argued below that Barth places human agency strictly
within a framework of the asymmetry of the divine-human relations; and
the analogous nature of ethically 'good' human action; which, in turn,
determines the character of that activity.

As has been argued in Chapter 6, according to Barth God does not
need our co-operating activity, especially in Christ's Priestly and Kingly
ministries. But "In a distinctive overflowing of divine grace" [*CD*, IV.3.2,
608], he has freely willed not

> to tread without us, as He might have done, the path which
> He has entered in [prophetic] prosecution of His cause in the
> world [*CD*, IV.3.2, 656f.].

> And so even here and now He wills to rely on, to make
> common cause and to compromise Himself with these
> curious saints called Christians by calling them as the Lord to
> His service [*CD*, IV.3.2, 656].

Barth, on the other hand, is profoundly aware of the limitations of
this human action, since he appreciates the fragility and hubristic nature of
human agency, and also the eschatological reservation (*Vorbehalt*) under
which all human agency stands. Humans, even if their hope is in God in
Christ, remain human in their witness; and, as such, when this recognition
is combined with the necessary perception of human finitude, Barth
cogently argues that humans remain sinful beings. Consequently, his
rhetoric portrays the provisional, relative, vulnerable and tentative human
movement to the future as being taken in "little steps", although that

---

[36] Jüngel, 2:121.

presentation does not intentionally dilute the required urgency and courage of human action, made through hope in Christ [*CL*, 172].

Moreover, the overthrow of this regime, and the removal of its contradiction to its true being in Christ, cannot be the affair of creaturely action.[37] Barth is emphatic that eschatological assertions refer to the sole agency of God himself in creating the Absolute Future [see *CL*, 170]. That is what is signified by the passive sense of the human invocation (*Anrufung*) "*Thy* kingdom come" [*CL*, 171]. Subsequently, there may be change this side of the final Consummation, but that will not be the total, universal, and definitive eschatological change.

And yet, Christian hope must risk venturing forth, "however softly or clumsily", with a sense of courage, although simultaneously retaining the sense of the provisionality, relativity and modesty of its action [*CD*, IV.3.1, 366]. These prayers for the coming of God's kingdom stimulate the Christian into accepting the provisional role of witnessing to the eschatological honouring of the divine Name, and that a witness occurring in all forms of de-demonising the present's ignorance and disobedience of its true being. She thereby involves herself in the human struggle for a properly "human [and] not divine righteousness" [*CL*, 264].

Thus Barth distinctly and clearly qualifies the nature of this activity and places it in its own order and context, or the "moral space" of human existence in Christ, to use Webster's description.[38] Recognising that the term "co-operating subject" could misleadingly imply synergism, Barth qualifies it by claiming that although the human being is such a subject "he is in no sense an independent promoter of the kingdom of God" [*CD*, IV.3.2, 599]. His preference is for the terms 'service' and 'ministry' (IV.3), and 'vocation' (*CL*), since they indicate the order of "the fellowship of action between Christ and Christians", "with a clear differentiation of function" and human subordination to Christ [*CD*, IV.3.2, 601]. These terms also maintain a distinction between creatures' passive participation in Christ's reconciliatory work, but active incorporation into his prophetic work. Moreover, they resonate with the theme of human 'obedience' (*Geharsamkeit*) to the divine command, a concept that forces one away from thoughts of humanly constructing the eschatological Future since what constitutes 'good' human action is a *faithful following* of the prior acting of God [*CD*, IV.3.2, 606f.]. The concept of 'correspondence' (*Entsprechung*) similarly implies this obedient *Nachhandeln*, since it presents human activity as obediently 'reacting' to the prior divine activity

---

[37] See *CD*, IV.3.2, 920; *CL*, 171, 174.

[38] Webster, 1995, 37.

[see *CL*, 32]. Human obedience takes the form of a "corresponding, willing, acting and doing on man's part" [*CL*, 156].

And yet the concept of 'correspondence', as Barth uses it, is filled with an even greater significance, specifically portraying an analogous movement between the human and divine acts.[39] This concept particularly prevents one's recognition of the eschatological reservation over all creaturely activity from having a paralysing effect on one's agency. Because the Christian expects corresponding "indications of the ultimate"

> he will not sit down waiting for something to come and snatch him away, but will manfully go forward hoping for the concrete help needed to enable him to do so [*CD*, IV.3.2, 938f.].

This discussion has pronounced significance for Barth's treatment of the relation of hope and ethics. Consequently, Barth argues that

> Just because the Christian hopes for the ultimate and definitive, he also hopes for the temporal and provisional ... for the little lights, which may come and go, but which will not come and go in vain, since as a temporary illumination they will help him to look and move more properly towards that which they can only indicate, but which in their time they can in fact indicate [*CD*, IV.3.2, 938].

Analogy, as Jüngel notes, preserves the divine-human difference, while emphasising

> as strongly as possible their partnership. In a human way, the human person has to act humanly and in no way divinely. But the goodness of such human action consists in the fact that even in its humanity [it] is similar, parallel and analogous to the act of God himself.[40]

---

[39] See, e.g., *CD*, IV.3.2, 938; *CL*, 169, 171, 175, 201ff.; John Webster (1994), 'Justification, Analogy and Action. Passivity and Activity in Jüngel's Anthropology', in *The Possibilities of Theology: Studies in the Theology of Eberhard Jüngel in his Sixtieth Year*, ed. John Webster, T&T Clark, Edinburgh, 106-142; Webster, 1991, 4-18.

[40] Jüngel, 1989, 159.

'Good' human action, therefore, is that which is a mirroring repetition of God's activity in Christ [*CL*, 41, 181]. Human agency, when obedient to the divine imperative, is a "kingdom-like" action, "a modest but clear analogue" which creates earthly "parables" of, and analogies and witnesses to, the kingdom [*CL*, 26, 175]. Barth even speaks of the church as, in some sense, a provisional representation of the *Eschaton* [*CD*, IV.3.1, 319f.]. He goes as far as to contend that

> we cannot avoid a statement which Protestantism has far too
> hastily and heedlessly contested - that the kingdom of God is
> the community [*CD*, IV.2, 656].

This positive dimension of human agency contradicts Williamson's reading that Barth's negativism over social and political action "denies humanity of political and social goals".[41]

Barth does clarify this by once again recalling the eschatological reservation, and further claiming that the statement cannot be reversed. The community is not the kingdom completed, since Christ *alone* is. Nevertheless, he speaks of the Christian community in terms corresponding to his discussion of parable (*Gleichnis*) [*CD*, IV.2, 655-9].

However, Barth's talk of the relation between God and the church and world tends toward an emphasising of their difference. In fact, in IV.3 and IV.4 Barth appears to refuse to provide any concrete examples of "parables" of the kingdom, or its noetic equivalents (the "little lights" or "true words"), despite the great detail in which he sets out his criteria for the possibility of truth found *extra muros ecclesiae* [see *CD*, IV.3.1, 135].

> All such phenomena [that could be advanced for this
> standing] are doubtful and contestable. What is not doubtful
> and contestable is the prophecy of the Lord Jesus Christ and
> its almighty power to bring forth such true words even *extra
> muros ecclesiae* and to attest itself through them. This and
> this alone is the matter to be treated [*CD*, IV.3.1, 135].

This claim that such phenomena are not "the matter to be treated" appears to be logically suspect. A theology that does not discuss the phenomena of witnesses to the divine Word, even those *extra muros ecclesiae*, is a docetic one that floats free of the contextuality of one's hearing of that Word. Barth recognises this pedagogy in his discussions of scripture and *ecclesia*, for instance. Moreover, if a supporting justification for Barth's policy is to be found in the ambiguity of perception one can

---

[41] Williamson, 63.

only, by analogy, remind Barth of the theme of the necessity of human agency in spite of its inherent fallibility and hubris. Further, earlier Barth had actually suggested a concrete instance of a 'parable': that of Mozartian music.[42]

Geoff Thompson has raised questions about what Barth was doing in his reflections on Mozart, claiming that the Mozart texts draw a distinction between 'parable' and 'Gospel', whereas in §69.2 of IV.3 *Gleichnis* "is synonymous with Gospel".[43] Consequently, Thompson asserts that Barth was primarily interested in Mozart's capacity to listen to and hear creation and not in his ability to "reveal". In response to this suggestion, however, a number of points should be made:

1. Barth appears to claim for Mozart a special divine inspiration.[44] Therefore, the resultant music would be an inspired witness.
2. In practice, Barth's high regard for Mozart's music sets the composer almost on the plane of theological sainthood, raising theological questions about creation itself. He even, albeit slightly tongue-in-cheek, in 1968 suggested that Mozart be beatified if not canonised.[45]
3. Why would Barth use a key term, such as *Gleichnis*, in such a contrary way in a short time-period (1956-9)?

Barth's iconoclastic suspicion of all identifications of the human with the divine is certainly an invaluable critical device. But a weakness in his theological presentation is nevertheless suggested, one which has led a number of scholars to ascertain, albeit contrary to his intentions, an almost hermetically sealed approach to theological method which fails to seriously eavesdrop on the world. For example, Ford complains of Barth's anthropological "impoverishment" in his "alienation from the natural sciences".[46]

---

[42] See Barth, 1969, 71f.; Barth (1956), *Wolfgang Amadeus Mozart*, Zollikon-Zürich, 57.

[43] Geoff Thompson (1995), "'... As Open to the world as any theologian could be ...'"? Karl Barth's Account of Extra Ecclesial Truth and its Value to Christianity's Encounter with Other Religious Traditions', unpublished Ph.D Thesis, Cambridge, Appendix C.

[44] Barth, 1956, 27.

[45] Cited in Eberhard Busch (1976), *Karl Barth: His Life from Letters and Autobiographical Texts*, trans. John Bowden, SCM Press, London, 493; cf. *CD*, III.3, 299.

[46] Ford, 1981, 172, 171.

Nevertheless, through this scheme of the analogy of divine and human agencies Barth delineates human agency, in its venturing under the Word's guidance, as responsible for the world's modest renewing and transforming [*CL*, 194f.]. For although human steps will always be unlike God's activity because of both human finitude and sin, and therefore not responsible for the eschatological transformation, they also run in parallel to it [*CL*, 175, 205]. In a passage which not only positions language of 'revolution' in a theological and eschatological context, but also suggests one form of overlap between reflections on sin and the *hubris* of tragic literature, Barth claims that

> It is not man, or any one man, who can make the break with these given factors and orders and historical forces. What man does of himself may take the form of an attempted repudiation but it will always serve to confirm and strengthen them, continually evoking new forms of their rule. ... It is the kingdom, the revolution, of God which breaks, which has already broken them [*CD*, IV.2, 544].

"That," Gollwitzer recognises, "is incomparably more skeptical than what the Safenwil pastor used to say about human revolutions."[47] Gollwitzer is incorrect, however, to further claim that this "is meant to sober but not to hinder 'little revolutions'". It is rather to sober human agency and thereby prevent it from overestimating its importance in revolutionary terms altogether. Thus Barth draws no qualitative distinction between his rejection of revolutionary and reactionary attitudes [*CD*, IV.3.2, 717]. Revolutions are after all generally forgetful of not only hubris but also the fact that God's Kingdom is assertively and positively, as well as critically, related to this world.

Hope for Society Also: Political and Social Liberation   The form of imaginative proposals for the shape of human activity, that Barth creates out of his eschatological vision, depends on actual concrete circumstances. Nevertheless, two general guidelines are locatable within his ethical scheme. These are very broadly defined as hope's negative, interrogative and critical function; and its positive and transformative function. One may summarise these as hope's engagement in liberating humanity from all forms of dehumanising bondage, of acting in those areas of life in which we need not suffer, and of participating in God's "dedemonising" of the world [*CL*, 218]. Or as Tracy argues,

---

47 Gollwitzer, 91.

Christian salvation is not exhausted by any program of political liberation, to be sure, but Christian salvation cannot be divorced from the struggle for total human liberation - individual, social, political and religious.[48]

1. Hope's critical performance

Given Barth's understanding of creation and eschatology, of human nature as sinful, and of the freedom of God in his act, eschatology becomes "the rude incursion of God's kingdom", and "the intervention of God" [*CL*, 16, 246]. Drawing heavily from the New Testament's contrast between the eschatological 'new' and the sinful 'old', Barth declares that Christ is the *novum* who stands in radical discontinuity with the still extant 'old' life [see *FGG*, 61f.]. The eschatological horizon becomes, in Jüngel's description, a "critical comparative" and interrogation by creating a critically dynamic vision of the Real from which Christians are not only implicated in this present's sinfulness, but are also placed in solidarity with God against it.[49] The Christian is forbidden to accept the present's sinfulness (either through assimilation or despair's escape), and impelled instead to recognise it as something "already judged, removed and outmoded by the coming and secret presence of the kingdom" [*CD*, IV.3.2, 717]. Eschatology then, when correctly interpreted, operates within the public sphere as a critique of the existing states of affairs. This "new reality of world history" enables the Christian

to see things very differently in practice, to participate in world history very differently in its own attitude and action, than is the case with those who do not yet have knowledge of this new reality.... It thus anticipates the appearance of that which already is but is not yet manifested [*CD*, IV.3.2, 716].

Things, therefore, cannot be left as they are [*CL*, 157, 165]. As a result of the divine reconciliatory activity, in which God in Christ bore and destroyed the pain of sin's division of humanity from himself, there comes a corresponding willing and acting on humanity's part. Consequently, hope produces a provisional resistance-movement, or counter-movement (*Gegensbewegung*), and therein "a prophetic existence" and "rebellion" is

---

[48] Tracy, 1994, 72. Cf. Barth, 1963, 20.

[49] Jüngel, 1989, 183; cf. *CD*, IV.3.2, 557; *CL*, 3.

created for a Christian life and practice that swims against the stream.[50]
The Christian, seeing beyond the present's existence to sin's conquest and
removal, has to fight against the darkness on the presupposition that it
stands in dreadful juxtaposition to the Light, and as such becomes

> More restless than the most restless, more urgent than the
> most urgent revolutionaries in his immediate or more distant
> circle [*CD*, IV.4, 201].

Several forms of the manifestation of this counter-factual are
ascertainable in IV.4 and *CL*. Firstly, it is a movement against the
dishonouring of God's Name in the absurd continuation of human
disobedience to, and the corresponding ignorance of, God. In this context,
Barth's eschatology becomes an iconoclastic interrogation of those moves
in which humanity creates her various self-imaged gods, and subsequently
justifies herself and her activity before them. It is emphasised that

> man proves himself to be a liar in whose thinking, speech and
> conduct ... [is revealed] an attempt to claim God by and for
> himself ... - a perversion in which he can only destroy
> himself and finally perish [*CD*, IV.3.1, 368].

Secondly, although Christian hope reminds one of one's political
responsibility, the eschatological counter-factual interrogates and critiques
the self-understanding of political activity. It must remind politics both of
its limitations and direct it to its properly theological grounding in the
humanity of God in Christ.[51]

> It must remind the State that the true kingdom, the kingdom
> without end, is the kingdom of God, which is founded in
> Christ [*FGG*, 74].

Christian hope, even if it cannot delineate any concrete final plan
of its own, renders every intramundane hope contingent and relative. This
it does by exposing as idolatrous and ideological any promotion of
necessarily partial and particular human calculations into the category of
finality and absoluteness, a move that is characteristic of all political
totalitarianisms.[52] It was this perspective, for example, that originally led

---

[50] *CD*, IV.3.2, 939; *CL*, 174.

[51] On Christians' responsibility to pray and work for the State, see *FGG*, 81.

[52] See Moltmann (1984), *On Human Dignity: Political Theology and Ethics*, trans. M.
Douglas Meeks, SCM Press, London, 79-96 (85).

Barth to critique the Religious Socialism of Ragaz, Kutter and the younger Blumhardt, with their "identification" of their movement and God's kingdom [see *CD*, II.1, 634].

But far from perceiving this as a cause of despair, Barth celebrates this perspective as a necessary and humbling demarcation of all human planning, as well as a liberation from the stultifying need to create absolutes. We are enlightened about ourselves, about our illusions of controllability and realisability. But we are also informed of our true possibilities of change. Hence, hope promotes a passion for the *humanly possible* in our time, and of an honest and resolute engagement in the prophetic conflict without being required either to be utterly victorious or create the kingdom [*CD*, IV.3.2, 920]. Christian hope is thereby kept "from all false activism" and is confirmed and strengthened "in sober activity day by day" [*FGG*, 61f.].

Thirdly, and more particularly, Christian hope maintains a responsibility to stimulate resistance to those dreams and nightmares in which various human projects, policies, agencies and structures in which humans are dehumanised and oppressed. One concrete expression of this protest is Barth's rejection of capitalism's inhumaneness, with its principles of competition (leading to alienation), and exploitation (leading to reification). According to Barth, both derive from an idolatrous "lust for possessions", and "for an artificially extended area of power over human beings and things" [*CD*, III.4, 538]. Another concrete expression could be expressed through Gorringe's suggestion that "From first to last ... [Barth's] work is 'against hegemony'", where hegemony takes the form of 'structural evils' and societal forces within which human freedom and control is lost.[53] Herein Gorringe cites *CL*'s depiction of "the lordless powers" as

> The hidden wirepullers in man's great and small enterprises
> .... It is not really people who do things, whether leaders or
> the masses. Through mankind's fault, things are invisibly
> done without and above man [*CL*, 216].

Finally, in criticising eschatologies that fail to have any hope for the present, and therein conservatively (and quietistically?) submit present existence to the power of lordless forces, Barth's reflections stimulate

---

[53] Gorringe, *Karl Barth*, 1.

resistance to nihilistic despair, and encourage the development of hope for society through Christ since in him this world has a Future.

2. Hope's transformative performance

Barth's eschatological vision operates as a stimulus to and a determining of the 'humanising' of the present, as far as that is possible. As Pannenberg declares, this form of critical engagement

> clears the stage for a realistic involvement with ... [the world's] struggles, without admitting illusions of obtaining ultimate solutions.[54]

From the perspective created for Christian hope by the Crucified's having been resurrected and his, as yet, Future consummating manifestation, Barth rejects both the optimism that the "old form" is capable of "true and radical improvement", and

> the scepticism of those who in view of the impossibility of perfecting the old form think that they are compelled to doubt the possibility of a new form [*CD*, IV.3.2, 717].

Although, as Pannenberg argues, human agency contains no possibility of achieving ultimacy, it, nevertheless, needs to strive for bettering the conditions of life since natural and social evils can at least be mitigated.[55]

Barth conceives of human agency, included within Christ's Prophetic work, primarily in terms of mission. The purpose of Christian vocation is identified as being,

> with some degree of urgency to save human souls, to show men the way of redemption, to cause them to become Christians for the sake of their personal salvation and the experience of salvation [*CD*, IV.3.2, 563].

Although Barth would have raised an eyebrow to the claim that humans can themselves create anything "new", Brunner encapsulates the heart of Barth's account: "Before man can really create something new, he must himself be renewed."[56]

---

[54] Pannenberg, 1984, 124.

[55] See Pannenberg, 1998, 180.

[56] Brunner, 1954, 62.

However, Barth also recognises the social and political situatedness of all human life and activity. Hope is active, then, in a reordering not only of immediate individual relationships in justice, liberation, and compassion, but also the larger patterns of relationships that determine whether they can live humanly or are brutalised.

Expressing the structural implications of sin is Barth's treatment of the "lordless forces" as "not just the supports but the motors of society" [*CL*, 216]. Moreover, Barth ascertains that one of the state's functions is the securing and preserving of a space for the exercise of "individual freedom".[57]

So Barth announces, after speaking of Christian life and service flowing from Christ's victory, that

> In this confidence the Church helps within the frame of the
> humanly possible to overcome the sufferings and cares of the
> world and to replace the worse by the better ... [although, in
> its waiting, it] knows that all human endeavour is provisional
> and imperfect [*FGG*, 62].

Recognising this leads immediately to the questions of the nature of Barth's relation to socialism, prominent post-Marquardt, since it is claimed that Barth's understanding of the redeemed society follows a socialist vision.[58] So although the Barth of 1941 had become less enthusiastic to democracy as it had developed in the west, a somewhat contrasting mood to his 1938 preference of it to tyranny and injustice, Butler is right to note that in political, economic and social terms, Barth's own hopes for the extension of freedom lie, broadly one must add, in the direction of democracy and socialism.[59] In the 1950s Barth was still able to proclaim that

> The one God in Jesus Christ, who became our brother, is
> closer to the democratic idea. ... In Jesus Christ we are all
> brothers; this is the point that tends toward democracy.

---

[57] Barth, 1954, 80; cf. *CD*, III.2, 721; III.4, 545. That the whole scheme of 'liberation' was Barth's concern was already suggested in *CD*, I.1, xiii.

[58] So Robert E. Hood (1985), *Contemporary Political Orders and Christ: Karl Barth's Christology and Political Praxis*, Pickwick Publications, Allison Park, Pensylvannia, 174f.

[59] Gerald A. Butler (1974), 'Karl Barth and Political Theology', *SJT* vol. 27, 441-458 (447); cf. Barth, 1939, 80.

> Democracy is not in the middle between anarchy and
> tyranny, but is *above* both, above this dichotomy.[60]

Similarly, Bentley indicates that Barth does not abandon Marx but rather continues to regard historical materialism as "a necessary historical weapon and an apologetic and polemical ally" against defects in Christianity in particular [*CD*, III.2, 387].[61] Marx helps Barth to critique: firstly, the church's tending toward "the side of the 'ruling classes'" [*CD*, III.2, 389]; secondly, its having "shown a culpable indifference towards the problems of matter, of bodily life, and therefore of contemporary economics" and praxis [*CD*, III.2, 389]; and thirdly, nineteenth-century Christian individualism [see *CD*, IV.3.2, 569, 893]. Moreover, as late as 1959, Barth refuses to minimise his appreciation for the politically corrective work of the men of the Religious Socialist Movement [*CD*, IV.3.1, 29]. Gollwitzer's claim, then, that this emphasis in the *Römerbriefe* was suppressed in IV.3 by the limitation of the future "to the future of man" may be seen as inaccurate.[62] Here Gollwitzer fails to notice the continuation of ethically socialist-sounding statements in IV.4 and *CL*.

In recognising this, however, one needs to remember that from *2Ro* onwards Barth was highly critical of Socialism and its religious forms, something which Marquardt bypasses too readily. Admitting this does not constitute a negative pre-judgment over whether Barth's early theology was forged out of socialist interaction, as Marquardt and Gollwitzer claim, particularly in relation to his conception of eschatology in "material, universal, and social terms".[63] Nevertheless, it does significantly qualify statements such as Hunsinger's, that "Karl Barth was a socialist" moving "from praxis to theology as well as from theology to praxis".[64] In *2Ro*, Barth even asks whether an idol could even be made of the world's oppressed, and rejected is the apparent immorality of Marxism in favour of a return to Kant [*2Ro*, 464, 468]. This is why Gollwitzer claims that Barth was only rather superficially, and therefore insufficiently, influenced by Marxism, particularly in relation to the political economy.[65] It would

---

[60] Barth, 1963, 81.

[61] James Bentley (1973), 'Karl Barth as a Christian Socialist', *Theology* vol. 76, 349-356 (352).

[62] Gollwitzer, 94.

[63] Citation from Gollwitzer, 93.

[64] Hunsinger, 1976, 224.

[65] Gollwitzer, 102f.

seem, then, unwise to describe the later Barth as legitimating a purely "a radical political ethics", as Bettis believes.[66]

Baranowski argues that Barth was much less politically militant than Marquardt imagines, and also too theological and· unengaged in socialist politics to achieve the unity of theory and political 'praxis'.[67] While this erroneously implies a disjunction of the theological and ethical, Baranowski has at least indicated the difficulty of understanding Barth as a *radical political activist*. Rather Barth is driven to engage freely with political thought and practice, depending on the circumstances, in various ways out of obedience to his understanding of Gospel's ethical requirements. Indeed, as Baranowski recognises, Barth turned aside from those occupations common to socialist intellectuals such as journalism and parliamentarianism in order to pursue theology (albeit, one would add, one which has ethical and political significance). This Gollwitzer names as "the bourgeois slant even to a theology anti-bourgeois in tendency".[68] One, on the other hand, needs to temper such claims with the recognition that Barth's shying away from political engagement in the 1920s was more for pragmatic reasons than anything else. For example, Gorringe draws attention to the fact that Barth, as a foreigner in Germany, felt himself constrained in matters of national politics, and was indeed advised to be restrained by Martin Rade.[69]

Nevertheless, although he avoids any programmatic socialist platform, Barth admits many areas of overlap in the Christian's eschatologically inspired vision, and the socialist imagination: particularly those of peace and justice. Several possible analogies are listed:

1. serving people rather than abstract principles;
2. a constitutional state protecting all people equally;
3. social justice, i.e., helping the poor and oppressed;
4. a balancing of individual and community interests;
5. equality of freedom and responsibility for all adult citizens;
6. the separation of powers;
7. opposition to secret policies and diplomacy;

---

[66] Bettis, 1976, 161.

[67] Shelley Baranowski (1981), 'The primacy of theology: Karl Barth and Socialism', *Studies on Religion* vol. 10, 451-461 (452).

[68] Gollwitzer, 106. Cf. Hunsinger (1983), 'Karl Barth and Liberation Theology', *Journal of Religion* vol. 63, 247-263 (260).

[69] Gorringe, 15.

    8. freedom of speech;
    9. rules to be seen as people's servants, rather than their lords;
    10. an awareness of world-wide, as well as parochial, interests;
    11. and violence's use only as a last resort.[70]

This degree of overlap leads Barth to refuse any simplistic comparison of Stalinist crimes with those of the Nazis, without implying Barthian double standards. Not only does he refuse to indulge in western self-satisfaction and anti-Communist hysteria, he perceives the Soviets as at least tackling, "albeit with very dirty and bloody hands ... in a way that rightly shocks us", "the social problem".[71]

Nevertheless, these thematic overlaps cannot become normative *sources* of theology, but rather remain legitimate social and political *consequences* of reflection on theology's proper content.

> The Christian community both can and should espouse the cause of this or that branch of social progress or even socialism in the form most helpful at a specific time and in a specific situation. But its decisive word cannot consist only in the proclamation of social progress or Socialism. It can consist only in the proclamation of the revolution of God against 'all ungodliness and unrighteousness of man' (Romans 1:18) [*CD*, III.4, 545].

Hunsinger correctly points out against Marquardt that Barth's socialism was "pragmatic" and periodic, being conditioned by theological presuppositions. Depending on the situation, Barth sided with reformist Social Democrats or with radical left-wing socialists.[72] Political activism is a witness to, and not a clear mirror of, God's final eschatological resolution. In certain contexts, it expresses well God's love for the world, without qualitative distinction or inequality between fellow human beings. It was precisely that vision which, in the midst of the Safenwil misery of the women who contracted abdominal disease through factory conditions, caused the young pastor to become a social reformer. Barth admits that the crucified Jesus is the partisan of the poor and is victimised because of his desire for justice.[73] Consequently, for example, out of love for their fellow-humanity, Christians are responsible

---

[70] Barth (1960), *Community, State and Church*, ed. Will Herberg, Doubleday Anchor Books, New York, 148-189.

[71] Barth, 1954, 123. See *CD*, IV.1, 504; 1969, 63.

[72] Hunsinger, 1976, 185, 187.

[73] See, *CD*, IV.2, 179f.; Barth, 1954, 241-246.

for the preservation and renewal, the deepening and
extending, of the divinely ordained human safeguards of
human rights, human freedom, and human peace on earth
[*CL*, 205].

Such a recognition of Barth's theological politics particularly
obviates Rosato's reading that Barth's eschatology is unconcerned

for the hungers and longing of Christians and of all mankind
for a more just social order [*SL*, 170].

More appropriate than Rosato's perspective here is that of
Hunsinger when he declares that

This thoroughgoing political involvement [and theological
engagement in politics] means that it is fundamentally false
to portray Barth as a theologian who did his thinking in
monkish isolation from the world.[74]

Another thing that these recognitions of the overlap between the
imagination shaped by Christian hope and what is considered to be
'ordinary, everday reality', do is remind that Barth was not, contrary to
many popular readings of his project, in the business of rejecting the
present, its structures, values, etc. wholescale. Perhaps one could say that
he was certainly sceptical of their 'ultimate' value since all structures, and
even one's interpretations of their significance, are infused with sin, and
therefore limited. Nevertheless, Barth delineates a positive role for the
state and its connection with the church.[75]

Conclusion

Barth's account of hope could be summarised as a realistically critical
dialectic hope.[76]

---

[74] Hunsinger, 1976, 224.

[75] See Barth, 1954, 15-50.

[76] The echo of McCormack's study is unintentional, especially since the content of these
terms are here somewhat refilled.

There are two senses in which it may be termed 'realistic'. On the one hand, Christian hope is, in terms of its divine Object, generated and constituted by encounter with the Real in Christ. On the other, in terms of its human subject, hope retains an appropriate sense of the limitations of what is humanly possible, in the light of the divine 'revolution' in Christ.

Its 'critical' nature lies in the fact that the pronounced eschatological reservation on all creaturely existing and acting creates a sense of provisionality, penultimacy, and even hubristic fragility. And yet, this iconoclastic interrogative serves to direct hope into provisional activity for the healing liberation, and therein the de-demonising, of contemporary existence. If as Tracy exhorts, deliberately echoing Marx, that "the point is not to interpret the world but to change it", then Barth could wholeheartedly agree, as long, of course, that the term 'change' be clarified to prevent any immodest claiming of eschatological transformation and finality by human agency.[77] In encounter with the Father of Jesus Christ we are denied our delusions and pressed to engage in the healing of this world.

In this sense, then, Christian existence and activity is, all in all, indispensable as an antidote to society, doing modestly that which is in the general and public interest [*CL*, 101f.]. Christians, Barth almost idealistically and loosely asserts, have an influential impact on the world.

Finally describing Barth's version of hope as 'dialectical' courts misapprehension, especially since it is frequently, albeit erroneously, supposed that the *CD* suppress Barth's earlier dialectical theology. It is true that Barth's later style becomes presentationally more self-assured than that of his 1916-1921 period, no doubt an expression of the development of his christocentric style. Nevertheless, Chapter 4's reflections on Barth's understanding of revelational veiling and unveiling indicate that dialectic retains an important role in *CD*. Frequently, one element in Barth's theology can be so countered by another as to necessitate a corrected revision of his earlier statement. An example of this is the readjustment that needs to be made to his presentation of eschatological actuality, in the vicarious eschatological humanity of Jesus Christ, by his perspective of eschatological provisionality, which itself intends to prevent any premature conceptual closure. Barth's is a theology, at least in principle, aware of attempting to feel its way in the dark.

So his hope, on the one hand, is supremely confident and certain of its place in the eschatological agency of God. And yet, on the other, he is recognisably aware of its fragility. It is a human, and therefore a finite

---

[77] Tracy, 1987, 114.

hope. As such it is subject to all the possible temptations that draw it toward pessimistic frustration and optimistic ideology. Even the Christian version of hope itself has to stand under iconoclastic interrogation and continual re-forging in humble repentance. That is why the post-Safenwil Barth remains allergic to any identifications of human and divine agencies, an allergy that has unfairly come to be frequently perceived to be the distinguishing mark of his theological project. Therefore, it is significant that Barth's description of Mozart's music as a 'parable' of the kingdom is not repeated in IV.3 and IV.4, in which Barth's suspicions of any such identifications is accentuated.

Barth has learnt to describe that the Christian recognises that time moves from its Friday to its Sunday, wholly expecting that Sunday will dawn because of what one knows of the trajectory of the original Easter weekend. Thus, Christians are

> very conscious that it [the future] will be a dark and cloudy future. They know the hazards of the way they will tread. They recognise that they are no match for them.... [However, the act of baptism] is the overcoming of all worry about this future and hence the act of the most calm, assured and cheerful hope in which they take this first step of the Christian life [*CD*, IV.4, 209f.].

Barth's account of Christian hope, therefore, moves unsteadily between, and indeed beyond, human optimisms and pessimisms. It does not claim to know the Future's details, and certainly not the exact shape of our intramundane futures. What it does know is that it has faith and hope in the One who has promised to fully manifest the world's reconciliation in his redemptive presence. This not only generates hope, but also constitutively provides it with its direction and sustenance, and indeed stimulates the critical and liberating practice of Christian hope in the present.

These indications of hope's fragility and potentially hubristic activity, in particular raise the question of the application of themes from tragedy to Christian hope, and it is with this that this study will close.

Chapter 8

Conclusion: Faintly Detecting Edgar's Voice in Barth

Introduction

Chapter 7 in particular, contended that Barth's account of Christian hope appears to be significantly different from that form of Christian hope portrayed by Steiner as an optimistic escape from the tragic vision (see Chapter 1). This is so in three senses. Firstly, Barth's version is more fragile and revisionary than those hopes that are created by optimistically 'predictive' or 'assertive' approaches, with the latter escaping, as they do, all manner of contingency through their knowledge of future compensation. Drawing on Steiner's metaphor of temporality's 'Sabbatarian' character in a way that undermines the reading of Barth's de-temporalising of eschatology, one could claim that Barth remembers that the brokenness and despair of Friday lies behind, and Sunday lies ahead (although it has come for Christ), giving some light to the "long day's journey of the Saturday" [*RP*, 232].

For the disciples, of course, Saturday was the period of reflection on the messianic movement's failure, and for Jesus it was the day of the desolate silence of the passivity of death. However, for those whose temporal location permits a looking back to Jesus' Easter Sunday, the situation is very different.

> Saturday is all those days through which we live or suffer, strive to make something of ourselves or just hang on, endure, from Friday towards Sunday. Saturday, in other words, is every day in every place, all times and seasons of our human hope and patience.[1]

Secondly, any hope that attempts to escape earthly contextuality, through either surmounting its limitations or pessimistic hopelessness for this world, denies its proper, and indeed only, habitat.

---

[1] Lash, 1990, 114.

Thirdly, Barth's portrait of human subjectivity is not modelled on the lines of mere spectatorial involvement in developing one's 'history'. His eschatological style is less that of confident prediction about the shape of the future, than a risking of an iconoclastic interrogation of prevailing attitudes and tendencies, thereby hazarding itself in the provisional process of worldly healing.[2]

Therefore, eschatological assertions take their cue less from a desire to provide the narcotic of a secure 'way *out*' than an unavoidable risky pilgrimage *through*, and engagement *with*, the pressures, strains, and futilities of our unlit and unwritten futures.

By way of grounding this insight into hope's critically active performing, Chapter 6 responded to readings of Barth in terms of a purely cognitive form of eschatological provisionality. It was suggested that in Barth's eschatology the Future is creative not only in the sense of generating and patterning present activity, but also in the sense of being the eschatological *fulfilment* of our becoming and *transformation* into *being*-in-communion with God in Christ. Talk of a 'realised eschatology' in Barth is only misplaced, but is crucially so, in overlooking the *particularity* of that eschatological realisation in Christ (Chapters 4 and 5 traced Barth's developing christological approach to eschatological assertions). Consequently, the world awaits its definitive and transformative future manifestation in him.

There is in Barth, therefore, the retention of an 'open' future, if this refers to contingent earthly futures. The eschatological Future, by contrast, is christologically determined and therefore 'filled', although its shape and *details* remain unknown to Christian hope, and indeed, even 'unwritten' as yet. It is in this thematic context that Barth's statement about the Christian expectation of the End "in whatever form it comes" may be understood [*CD*, IV.3.2, 927f.]. Moreover, it is because of this element of the nescience that pervades all proper theologically ordered future-talk, as will be described below, that Barth rejects the doctrine of *apokatastasis*.

Nevertheless, Barth's presentation of hope retains elements that can appear unwelcoming to 'the tragic' element within eschatological provisionality, and therefore certain tensions are here created with his

---

[2] On hope's interrogative mood, see Nicholas Lash (1981), *A Matter of Hope: A Theologian's Reflections on the Thought of Karl Marx*, Darton, Longman and Todd, London, ch. 13., 269f.; Lash (1986), *Theology on the Way to Emmaus*, SCM Press, London, 208.

fallibalistic approach to hope. The general problem lies in his rhetorical over-use of certain triumphal categories. However, this problem is prevented from relatively easy correction by the nature of Barth's unqualified use of 'correspondence' in depicting the relation of the divine and human agencies; and, further, by his rejection of sacramental categories. This involves Barth in almost sounding like Shakespeare's Edgar. In other words, Barth unwittingly appears oblivious to the surrounding catastrophe. In a similar way to Edgar, Barth could praise the divine justice and control, although in the latter's theology this divine teleology is not visible anywhere else than in the Easter-event, and hence the *intention* is not to elude life's miseries.

Frei, for example, claims that "the one form of the imagination of which he really had little sympathy was the tragic".[3] Moving a little further, but less satisfactorily, than this is Torrance's claim that for Barth "The Christian is the only one with a genuine message of hope and is the true optimist".[4] One would need to ask questions about Torrance's operation with a model only involving the antithetical relations of despair and hope's optimism. Nevertheless, there is a sense in which these comments are true to Barth's sensibility, especially in relation to much of his rhetorical style. What is required for his presentation, then, is a certain set of qualifications and corrections. However, the reading of Barth argued for through this study has contented that there is another sense, and indeed a very vital and more prominent one, in which Barth is profoundly aware of the tragic struggle of God and humanity with sin, and even the threat of damnation.

A Potentially Tragic Outcome?

Barth and the Possibility of Eternal Damnation

As has been argued earlier, election is not a divine decision in a remote eternal *past*, which accomplishes its work irrespective of the contemporaneity of the divine and human decisions. The pneumatological significance of the salvific work of the trinitarian God entails that "Baptism with the Holy Spirit is effective, causative, even creative action on man and in man" [*CD*, IV.4, 34]. It is for this reason that Barth speaks of the Spirit's "calling" as the "objective difference" (*die objective Unterscheidung*) which "corresponds objectively" (*entspricht objektiv*) to

---

[3] Hans Frei (1993), 'Karl Barth: Theologian', 167-176 (175).

[4] Torrance, 1990, 6.

the being of the elect in Christ.[5] It is the means by which "their election is accomplished in their life" (*zur Vollstreckung ihrer Erwählung in ihrem Leben*).[6] Although he has been significant in drawing attention to this contemporaneity of the divine decision, and indicating how this theologically trinitarian perspective is the reason why Barth does not 'logically' and 'eventually' succumb to a doctrine of the *apokatastasis*, Colwell's discourse on the contemporaneity can nevertheless all too easily lean towards an actualistic style of election, the like of which pervades *GD*, §18. His account appears to underestimate the sense of election's *pastness* and *completion* since it is the election of the particular and vicariously existing man, Jesus Christ. It is here, in pressing this *particularity* that Barth is able both to argue for sin's 'impossibleness' (hence Barth's hope for universal salvation) and 'possibility' (the seriousness of the threat of hell).

Barth's discussion of sin reflects primarily upon its absurdity and irrationality. Despite the eminent attractiveness of an infinitely rich and gracious God, sin absurdly retains a persuasive hold over creation as the world, on the whole, as yet continues on its wicked way. Relevant here is Barth's reference to the Johannine image of the darkness being loved more than the light by humanity [*CD*, IV.3.1, 251].

Pressing this story further could render suggestive possibilities for a much more un-optimistic form of hope. Indeed, such tragic potentialities find their occasional eschatological expression in Barth's statements that imply the possibility of ultimate damnation. Themes of conditional immortality and the void's nothingness suggest that, had he discussed such an issue, Barth could have been amenable to some form of 'annihilationism', although, of course, this would have to be qualified through reference to the further theme of nescience of the details of the shape of the future. A creature existing without God (what could be termed 'hell' or 'damnation') is a contradiction in terms. So, for example, he claims that by falsehood humanity "can only destroy himself and finally perish" [*CD*, IV.3.1, 368]. This falsehood places the sinner under the threat of being nailed to her lie, operating as the portion which she herself has chosen [*CD*, IV.3.1, 462]. Naturally, we cannot change the truth into untruth. But in calling it untruth we set ourselves in the shadow of the sinner who is dead in Christ, and therein on the steep slope at the end of

---

[5] *CD*, II.2, 345; *KD*, II.2, 380.

[6] *CD*, II.2, 348; *KD*, II.2, 383.

which there is not merely the *threat* of damnation and God's naked and destructive wrath [*CD*, IV.3.1, 464ff.]. This "may be only an attempt ... which finally proves impracticable", but it

> has its consequences in which the future chosen by the man who lies, even though not yet present, is directly enough delineated and proclaimed [*CD*, IV.3.1, 466].

As such, humanity in practice is "moving to ... condemnation and perdition ... [through implicating] himself in a lost and false situation" [*CD*, IV.3.1, 466]. Fortunately, however, this actual condemnation, which would be an echo of Christ's having been divinely rejected vicariously on our behalf, has not fallen. God still gives humanity time for repentance and obedience, and "has not yet allowed [it] to pursue its contradiction to the bitter end" [*CD*, IV.3.2, 687]. But, it remains God's prerogative as to whether or when he will take seriously this insane desire [*CD*, IV.3.1, 465f.]. Hence, the threat and danger are very real, and there is no human guarantee that they will not finally be executed. This would entail

> God's acquiescence in the cheerless disintegration of man's existence and situation. It implies His allowing man to glide headlong down that slope and finally to be lost. ... It is to have to be finally what we wish to be when we change truth into untruth and live in and by this untruth [*CD*, IV.3.1, 473].

Hence, in *C*, for instance, Barth articulates this movement toward damnation by referring to a human rejecting of the positive decision (*bedeutet Entscheidung*) for God.[7] Of course, in the 1940s he would come to add to such a statement that this is an absurd rejection of humanity's true and real being for God in the person of Jesus Christ (since it is in him that our being is defined). Hence, the idea that the actual decisions of actual people can echo Christ's having been condemned, remains present in Barth's writings [see *CD*, II.2, 322].

In relation to damnation, Barth's account appears, then, to be that the trinitarian God, in his loving freedom, *permits* human beings to pursue their disintegration. On saying this, however, one needs to be careful of attributing arbitrariness to Barth's conception of this freedom, as Bettis does when rightly refusing to define God's love *externally*.[8] God's love chooses, and is consistently faithful to, an object *ad extra*, and therefore faithfully loves it.

---

[7] *C*, 172; German, 148.

[8] Bettis, 1967, 428.

What is emerging here is that Barth is one who does not disregard the eschatological importance of themes of rejection and hell, in other words, themes that can encourage, or at least not undermine, the active envisaging of the place of the tragic in Christian eschatological discourse.

Hope for the Future of All

Earlier, in Chapter 7, it was noted that Barth does not provide any concrete examples of earthly analogies and parables of the kingdom, although he emphatically admits their potential existence, primarily because they are not "the matter to be treated" (also, Barth recognises the difficulty of human locations of the divine speaking *extra muros ecclesiae*) [*CD*, IV.3.1, 135]. Similarly, although he speaks of sin and damnation, it is clear, however, that Barth's primary interest lies elsewhere. To entertain any thought of ultimate condemnation for anyone, while time continues, is to forget the hope that springs from *Christ's victory*.

> It is not only out of kindness, out of good nature, that the Creed does not mention hell and eternal death. But the Creed discusses only the things which are the object of the faith. We do not have to believe in hell and in eternal death [*FC*, 145].

The premature belief in an already populated hell, which Lash indicates was not part of the original fabric of the rejection of the tradition of the *apokastastasis*, is rendered unchristian because its hope has become lost in the mist of despair over the present.[9] Barth suggests an

> openness to the possibility that in Jesus Christ there is contained much more than we might expect and therefore the supremely unexpected withdrawal of that final threat, i.e., that in the truth of this reality there might be contained the super-abundant promise of the final deliverance of all men. To be more explicit, there is no good reason why we should not be open to this possibility [*CD*, IV.3.1, 478].

Nevertheless, Barth rejects any *a priori* assertion of *apokatastasis*. Advocacy of this doctrine is premature in that it denies or disarms evil and our own participation in it, even if that evil be described as absurd and

---

[9] Lash, 1994, 52.

irrational, and also (and more importantly for Barth) presumes on God's freedom since God *necessarily* must save all [*CD*, II.2, 418]. Missing this discussion of sin Bromiley, for example, mistakenly claims that

> it is not apparent why, in his view, the Holy Spirit in His ministry of calling should not positively fulfil in all individuals the one eternal will of the triune God.[10]

Recognising that we have no inherent claim to divine grace and cannot know the details of the future, Barth strongly emphasises that we should cautiously but yet distinctly hope and pray for the universal scope of the actual redemption in the Future [*CD*, IV.3.1, 478].[11] When this eschatological nescience is taken seriously (one that also forbids speculation about ultimate damnation), the singers of a Barthian *apokatastasis* lose their voices. Barth delivers only a *tacit* nod in its direction, and that directly *after* his warnings of the real possibility of ultimate damnation [*CD*, IV.3.1, 477f.]. The threat of damnation *may* finally be withdrawn, and if it is then this will be due not to any logical necessity (although Barth admits that his thoughts and utterances do seem to lead most clearly in this direction), but rather to God's free and gracious gift of Christ.

> To the man who persistently tries to change the truth into untruth, God does not owe eternal patience and therefore deliverance [*CD*, IV.3.1, 477].

To speak with confident prediction of the end of Christ's prophetic work is an illegitimate exercise, "For it has not yet reached the end" [*CD*, IV.3.1, 328]. Therefore, we may agree with Ford,

> Barth wants to keep open both sides [of the narrative's possibilities]: the gravity of sin and the overwhelming power of salvation.[12]

---

[10] Geoffrey W. Bomiley (1979), *Introduction to the Theology of Karl Barth*, Edinburgh, 97.

[11] On Barth's nescience, see *FC*, 140.

[12] Ford, 1981, 73.

A Barthian Threat to the Tragic Vision?

Barth's Unwelcoming of Theological Tragedy

The reading that Barth's *theo-logic* does not leave room for the occurrence of the unimaginable has been questioned in this study. Certainly God's 'yes' to the creature does establish the creature's 'yes' to God; but this does not so *overpower* contemporaneous existence that the absurd is completely extinguished from the phenomenal world.[13] That destruction of the 'unreal' has to take place through Christ's Prophetic work; and the shape of that Future remains future for us, and thereby unpredictable. Barth's eschatology *logically* requires both this nescience and the entertaining of the possibility of damnation.

Moreover, although Barth does not spend time explicitly reflecting on this matter, it is arguable that even in the positive resolution of the story of the world's redemption, however that may appear, the conclusion does not *necessarily* render this drama a comedy. Everything simply does not compensatingly work out all right in the end. There remains a form of discontinuity between the act of rebellion and the positive resolution, since God's act is the pure *destruction* of this rebellion and the conversion of the rebel on the other side of the caesura (will the rebel be caught in the fallout?).

Nevertheless, Barth's interest lies elsewhere: in the hope for universal eschatological redemption, in fulfilment rather than frustration.[14] This is why he perceives *some* truth in Leibnizian optimism, since here everything will be set right in the end [*CD*, IV.4, 408]. If left unqualified, as often occurs in the immediately relevant texts in Barth's *oeuvre*, this mood could unwittingly lean too heavily towards hope's premature over-confidence, and thereby border on an un-nescient certainty. Barth's refusal to explicitly entertain themes of 'tragedy' in his treatment of eschatology and hope creates a certain tension with his presentation of hope's fallibalism.

In contrast to von Balthasar, Barth's primary aesthetic interest lies less in the dramatic arts than in Mozart's music [e.g., *CD*, III.3, 297ff.]. When the names of Homer, Goethe, Dostoyevsky, Shakespeare, Ibsen, Shaw, amongst others, do appear, those of the Attic Tragedians are

---

[13] This distinction is missed by Highfield [139f.].

[14] See, e.g., Barth, 1963, 16.

conspicuous by their absence. The solitary reference to Euripides, for example, concerns the theme of *eros*, and not the tragic vision [*CD*, III.2, 279]. Shakespearean allusions also avoid the tragedies [*CD*, III.2, 233; IV.2, 214f.]. Indeed, Barth's references to tragedy or the tragic are, on the whole, scant.

His occasional use of the term 'tragedy' refers to the sinful human condition, or more accurately, to the active outworking of humanity's sin and guilt [*CD*, III.1, 406; IV.2, 230]. Echoing themes of tragic irony, Barth declares that it is "the tragedy of all other [forms of] mastery" than that of Christ that they produce "imitation" in the mastered, whereas Christ enables man "to be completely himself" [*CD*, I.2, 276]. However, on the whole, Barth prefers to speak of humanity's *sin* rather than her "tragic greatness" for fear that the latter may imply less than the former [*CD*, I.2, 430].

Moreover, human existence's 'tragedy' has been incarnationally negated. Hence Barth sets talk of tragedy in the context of a study of the kingdom's "total and absolutely victorious clash ... with nothingness" [*CD*, IV.2, 230]. Herein

> the tragedy of human existence is dissolved. There is something far more serious and tragic, viz., the fact that our distress - the anguish of our sin and guilt - is freely accepted by God, and that in Him, and only in Him, it becomes real agony. ... Jesus Christ ... breaks down this resistance to grace by Himself appearing as grace triumphant, as the royal removal of our sin and guilt by the action of God Himself [*CD*, II.1, 374].

The tragic has been, is being, and will be overcome. Consequently, its continuing relevance for theology is seriously limited in Barth's mind. The dramatic element in the conflict between God and sin itself thereby becomes spoken of in almost Homeric terms, without retention of any serious component of the tragic [*CD*, IV.3.1, 172].[15] The dramatic element here functions to avoid abstracting the God-sin conflict from Christ's history [*CD*, I.2, 376]. And for Barth, that story has only one direction. IV.3 roots talk of Christ as "the Subject of the action, the dominating Character in the drama, and the Hero in the conflict", as may be expected given the militaristically triumphant tone, in the discussion "that there can be no question of an equality between the two factors which here confront and conflict with one another" [*CD*, IV.3.1, 172, 171f.].

---

[15] For Barth's use of 'drama' to describe creation, reconciliation and redemption, see *CD*, I.2, 253.

Consequently, Barth warns of "the tragedy of an abstract *theologia crucis*" that changes the story of the cross and resurrection into joyless "Nordic morbidity" [*CD*, IV.1, 559].

This, of course, does not in any way mitigate the fact that the Christian suffers the present's contradiction between the 'old' and 'new'. "Sooner or later, in one way or another, we shall have to give ear to this sad voice" [*CD*, III.1, 373]. Barth's thoughts are too 'realistic' to exclusively permit the overwhelming joy of the divine success to undermine consciousness of eschatological provisionality, albeit that consciousness is of secondary importance. He acknowledges that "the heavens grow dark, that harmony is engulfed in disharmony and teleology obscured by senselessness" [*CD*, III.1, 372]. This awareness concretely and soberly recalls the "limits and the frailty and end of all things" [*CD*, III.1, 373]. And it is for this reason that Barth opposes Leibniz's over-optimism [*CD*, III.1, 388f.]. Hence, Barth suggestively claims that the act of hope in Christ is a "comforted despair" [*CD*, IV.1, 633]. It is something that stands in contrast to non-Christian forms of optimism and pessimism [e.g., *CD*, IV.1, 408].

Nevertheless, if unqualified, the triumphal discourse can all too easily tend toward eschatological prediction, since the character of the Future is confidently predicated from the knowledge of this victorious past-event. Therein the real Future would be imaginatively conceived with certainty before its universal manifestation, and its shape would thereby be blueprinted. As Chapter 2 earlier indicated, Barth would certainly not here be following the lines of the seventeenth-century Federal theologians, or of millennialist groups, by mapping the exact form of *future history*. However, 'victory' talk could lead down a similar path with respect to the *ultimate outcome* of the future. This is precisely the road that Berkouwer and others suggest that Barth is travelling on with their identification of a 'logical' Barthian nod toward the *apokatastasis*.

Barth's Simplifying the Manifold

According to Barth, Christ has reached his goal in one sense. In another sense, that goal has not yet been reached in us and by us. Potentially, therefore, Barth leaves open the question of the shape of the Future without feeling any need to qualify the expression of divine eschatological victory. "We can", Berkouwer cites Barth as saying, "be certain that God's lordship is and will be total in all, but what this signifies for us we must leave to

God" [*TG*, 114].   Nevertheless, as has already been suggested, this triumphal discourse can create certain tensions for a hope that remains aware of its nescience and fragility. The problem here is one of Barth's over-generalisation, and this occurs in two senses. Firstly, Barth frequently tends to generalise about history's direction by focusing almost exclusively on the victorious nature of Christ's history. Secondly, Barth's very approach to Christ's victory is itself too unspecific. Hence, in a Hegelianly inspired dialectic of creation, sin and redemption's drama, according to Barth God's redemptive plan cannot be thwarted.

He is certainly favourable to the potentially fruitful theme that "The multiplicity of his [God's] ways is endless" and his being and acts are infinitely rich, although "his will and resolve in all his ways is one and the same" [*CL*, 18]. However, one cannot escape the almost overwhelming theologically aesthetic feel of the drama; in other words, in practice he tends to underplay any informal and unsystematic description of any of those possible "ways", almost exclusively focusing on the content of the unity of this will and resolve in Christ. Barth's theology appears resistant, enigmatically so given his intention to provide space for creaturely becoming and avoid christomonism, to an incorporation of the differentiated voices of particular concrete human beings. Whatever his reasons for this - both the exaggerated reaction to Schleiermachian anthropocentrism and the contemplation of Christ's beauty, appear to be good contenders - he tells only half of the story, albeit the half that serves to direct the agency and consciousness of those created for, and elected in, the Son. Christ-talk cannot be an exclusive enterprise for a theology that seeks to take seriously the full range of God's grace in Christ, through creation.

In this way, Rogers, for example, speaks of Barth's christocentrism as suppressing and flattening narrative detail, and therefore neglecting the theologically enriching "overplus that the Spirit supplies".[16] Particularly in the reviewed areas of Judaism and gender, Rogers laments that "Barth is richly open for this sort of elaboration, though he does not pursue it."

Whatever the shortcomings of his pneumatology in relation to his anthropology, Barth certainly appears to undermine his desire to approach theology in more narrative terms through a theologically over-generalised christology.   Here, in what Frei names "a sort of epistemological monophysitism", he depreciates, through practical avoidance, what we may know about the historical Jesus.[17] Something more is occurring than

---

[16] Eugene F. Rogers (1998), 'Supplementing Barth on Jews and Gender: Identifying God by Anagogy and the Spirit', *Modern Theology* vol. 14, 43-81 (56).

[17] Frei, 1956, 574f.

what Colwell's suggestion that it constitutes "only" a question "of 'word space'" would imply, a rather perverse suggestion at that given the sheer quantitative immensity of Barth's *oeuvre*.[18]

An example of this can be found in his treatment of the cross. Barth recognises that knowledge of God must particularly be located in the cross, as understood in the light of his resurrection. And this is an understanding of the relation of these two events that does make significant reference to the darker side of the cross, that "dark event of Golgotha" [*CD*, IV.1, 343]. But Barth's account, in the main, emphasises the theme of "Jesus is Victor" [e.g., *CD*, IV.2, 290f.]. Indeed, although he can claim that Christ retains the wounds of the crucified, Barth later proceeds to undermine this by announcing that Christ now lives relieved of all the anguish, pain and despair [*CD*, IV.1., 305, 345].

Thus, at that place where the divine appears most mysteriously hidden, and human designs of self-grandeur perform their illusory victory dance, the face of the impaled victim in Barth strangely radiates with the resolving joy of Easter, and thereby verges on a domestication of the absurd [*CD*, IV.2, 311]. For according to Barth, the cross' significance is that "the eternal resolve of God ... became a historical event on Golgotha", thereby rendering it a salvific event in which the power of the *nihil* was broken [*CD*, IV.1, 409]. As "the *telos* of His whole existence" the cross "was not simply a catastrophe" [*CD*, IV.2, 164]. Neither was it "a tragic entanglement" nor a "misfortune which breaks over Him ... so that the initiative is wrested from Him and He ceases to be the Lord" [*CD*, IV.2, 251f.].

Friday's cataclysmic rupture of all forms of the harmony of meaning in speech, even those theological ones which attempt to humbly follow the *Deus dixit* itself, consequently appears to become domesticated by Barth's practical appeal to Sunday's eschatological redirection of human speech.[19] If, as Moltmann asserts, "Christian hope stands under the sign of the cross", then Barth's portrayal of the crucifixion supports a version of hope that could stand in tension with his notes of precariousness, fragility, etc. [*TH*, 195]. The work of Donald MacKinnon serves, here, as a necessary corrective to Barth's over-exuberant rhetoric.

---

[18] Colwell, 1989, 97.

[19] On the cross' rupture of all forms of speech, see Lewis, 335-362.

MacKinnon and the Undomesticability of Tragic Complexity

In a tribute to Cambridge's late Norris Hulse Professor of Divinity, Steiner speaks of "Donald's genius" particularly in terms of his post-Auschwitz fascination "by pain".[20] Here is a figure whose theology refuses to evade the interrogating dimensions of the tragic.

Although highly conscious of a debt to Barth, MacKinnon's style differs significantly from that of the former. Both the generally occasionalistic quality of his *oeuvre*, and the breadth of concern, suggest a thinker less enamoured by a systematic- and meta-perspective on everything than with an interrogation of specific themes, and a concern for the complexities of particulars. Indeed, it would not be unfair to say that MacKinnon's strength is in critiquing others' inadequacies, but his own positive theological work raises, and intends to do precisely that, more questions than it answers. He is deeply sensitive to the perspectival and fragile path followed in the process of thinking and describing, and yet simultaneously theologically convinced of the general viability of epistemological and ethical realism.[21] Consequently, he promotes, to an extent more becoming of Barth's theory than his practice, a theological discipline of silence to the extent of bordering on a "healthy agnosticism" before the inexhaustible reality of God.[22]

According to MacKinnon, there is an irreducibly tragic element in the Christian faith, particularly evidenced in the cross. Indeed, he goes so far as to acclaim it as "of central importance".[23] Although he does not press the theme of metaphysical villainy in a Nietzschean vein, MacKinnon does simply argue that under the influence of Plato came a "relegation of tragedy to a very secondary role around us".[24] An unfortunate situation has since developed in which Christians have lacked the courage to read the Gospels in the light of tragedy (and indeed also to read God in a modified kenotic *theopaschian* sense), and theologians have ultimately anaesthetised any sensitivity to the tragic by converting history into a ballet-dance of *ideas*, a process that MacKinnon detects in theodicies that unwarrantedly attempt to resolve the problem of evil.[25]

---

[20] Steiner, 1995, 6.
[21] See, e.g., MacKinnon (1979), *Explorations in Theology 5*, SCM Press, London, 138-165.
[22] Donald MacKinnon (1974), *The Problem of Metaphysics*, Gifford Lectures 1965-1966, Cambridge, 118.
[23] MacKinnon, 1968, 94.
[24] MacKinnon, 1969, 46.
[25] See, e.g., MacKinnon, 1968, 94; 104. On the Father's risking his own being in his suffering the loss of the Son, see MacKinnon (1976), 'The Relation of the Doctrines of the

Instead, MacKinnon reminds that Jesus was victorious over the temptation for an

> Heroic flight from the costly penetrating realities of Incarnation as that enfleshing is defined by the *theologia crucis*.[26]

Indeed, he even uses language of 'failure' to describe the cross, and the "dark inheritance of evil as well as good" that flows from Jesus' life, although such failure-talk is not generated from the same mood as Schweitzer, for instance.[27]   For the latter all Jesus' eschatologically couched hopes and expectations were never realised, although what is important for contemporaneity is not this husk but rather the kernel of his ethical teachings on love and brotherhood. MacKinnon's perspective, by contrast, qualifies his description in a somewhat trinitarian manner by adding that

> for him [Jesus'] acceptance of that failure could significantly be regarded as purposive and intentional, at least in the simple sense that he knew what he was doing, that here, and not elsewhere, he supposed the way appointed by his Father to lie.

Elsewhere the passion is spoken of as, in the language of the fourth gospel, something of a "burden laid on Jesus by his Father".[28] Surin explains:

> MacKinnon emphasizes that it is the Son who (as subject) embraces failure in his passion on the cross. In the event of the resurrection, however, it is the Father who (as subject) raises the dead Jesus to eternal life. And since the Father and Son occupy different 'logical spaces', so to speak, the failure

---

Incarnation and the Trinity', *Creation, Christ and Culture: Studies in Honour of T. F. Torrance*, ed. Richard W. A. McKinney, T&T Clark, Edinburgh, 92-107; 1968, 106.

[26] MacKinnon, 1979, 136.

[27] Ibid., 65. On the apparent failure of the messianic mission, see Lewis, 346-9; Moltmann, 1974, ch. 4.

[28] Donald M. MacKinnon and G.W.H. Lampe (1966), *The Resurrection: A Dialogue Arising from Broadcasts by G.W.H. Lampe and D.M. MacKinnon*, ed. William Purcell, A.R. Mowbray & Co. Ltd., London, 174.

of one need not necessarily be incompatible with the triumph accomplished by the other.[29]

In averting the theologian's gaze into the depths of the tragic, MacKinnon makes several moves, some of which correspond to aspects in Barth's thoughts, and others of which suggest ways of qualification and correction.

In a highly suggestive manner MacKinnon reads the story of Judas in a considerably different way from Barth. Barth holds out hope for Judas' salvation by God's grace, and provides rather exegetically tortuous warrants for this to the point of narrative distortion [*CD*, II.2, 458-506]. It is this move that leads Ford to acclaim for Barth, with some justification, a "knowledge in excess of the story".[30] In fairness to Barth, the narrative rendering of Judas' fate is to be placed within a more over-arching perspective of the universal love of God and human nescience of the future. Nevertheless, he almost over-reaches the bounds of his nescience in defence of the universal scope of grace. In contrast, for MacKinnon it is in this figure that Jesus' failure is focused, since it is here that the 'tragedy' of the cross is ineradicably exposed.[31] Although, there is here no speculation as to Judas' future, it does look as though the death and damnation of Judas are the price of salvation, and an indication of the irreducibly tragic.

Secondly, MacKinnon is profoundly sensitive to "the terrible sequel to the story of the cross" as being the open-ended horror of anti-Semitism, as well as to the fact that Jesus appeared to abdicate any responsibility for influencing the arrest of the Jewish move to self-destruction in A.D. 70.[32]

Barth, too, sought to take seriously the Jews in their particularity, and expressed a theological abhorrence of the growing anti-Semitism of the late 1920s and early 1930s Germany.[33] However, Barth's theology shows little of the sense of horror of Auschwitz that one would expect from someone concerned for the Jews' well-being. Even the Barmen Declaration, the framing of which was heavily influenced by Barth, does not express solidarity with the Jews, something for which Barth later

---

[29] Kenneth Surin (1986), 'Christology, Tragedy and "Ideology"', *Theology* vol. 89, 232-291 (287).

[30] Ford, 1981, 183.

[31] MacKinnon, 1969, 49f.

[32] MacKinnon, 1968, 103. On the latter, see 1979, 64.

[33] See the citations from Barth in Stephen R. Haynes (1991), *Prospects for Post-Holocaust Theology*, Scholars Press, Atlanta, Georgia, 55.

admitted culpability.[34]   Rather, for Barth, Israel's specific function becomes that of "representing the passing and setting aside of the 'old man', of the 'man' who resists his election" [*CD*, II.2, 61].   The *Judenfrage* tends to be reduced to existence in resistance to God's election; hence Barth's infamous over-generalised, rhetorically derogatory, description of the Jews as *Gotteskrank*, and *Spiritbereft*, "a hard and stiff-necked people" [*CD*, I.2, 510].   At the very least, again something that Barth later appeared ready to lament, as Marquardt claims,

> at times, Barth is tempted to reduce the Jews to a cipher, to a mirror that reflects life, but lives none of its own [cf. *CD*, III.3, 221].[35]

At the most, he appears, albeit unintentionally, as unmistakably sounding a theological anti-Semitism, and of abstracting "the Synagogue" from *actual* Jewish people.[36]   MacKinnon's refusal to escape the difficulties and complexities associated with focusing on concrete particularities and peoples, would seriously question Barth's treatment of the *Judenfrage*, and could also re-open possibilities for learning from themes within tragedy.

Finally and crucially, what remains in MacKinnon's reflections is a sense in which any language of 'victory' or the slogan that 'death is swallowed up' needs careful qualification.   If this is not done, such triumphal semantics operate

> as if the agony and delusion, the sheer monstrous reality of physical and spiritual suffering [of Gethsemane and Golgotha] which he bore were a mere charade.

This, for MacKinnon, would be the "bloodless victory" that "the scoffers" were tempting Jesus with.[37]   MacKinnon's concern is to prevent the vision of Easter Sunday from obscuring and undermining the narrative

---

[34] Barth, 1981, 250.

[35] Marquardt, cited in Katherine Sonderegger (1992), *That Jesus was Born a Jew: Karl Barth's "Doctrine of Israel"*, The University of Pennsylvania Press, University, Park, PA., 146. See Barth cited in Rogers, 1998, 46f.

[36] So Haynes, 65. On Barth's over-generalisation, see Haynes, 71; Rogers, 1998, 45f.

[37] MacKinnon, 1968, 92f.

of Good Friday and the divine's plumbing the depths of human life. As early as 1940 he declared, on

> the acclamation of *Christus Victor* that ... [t]he character of
> that victory is a paradox. Its trophy is a scaffold.[38]

This theme becomes more pronounced over the next three decades of his writings. Although Christians know how Jesus' incarnate story 'ends', MacKinnon comes to declare, they cannot allow this to obliterate the memory of the catastrophe, scandal, failure, etc., of the preceding events. Worn cliché, over-familiarity with the narrative, optimism's theoretical foreclosure, "refusal to recall the concrete detail of the event" in the generality of theory, undisciplined talk of 'victory', must all be prevented from blunting the *skandalon* of the crucifixion.[39] So the Passion cannot be properly conceived of as a descent from the cross postponed for thirty-six hours, a sudden dramatic Hollywood happy ending, or a reversal, all of which obliterate the memory of the preceding sombre and catastrophic events.[40] Ruled out also, or at least heavily modified, would be Moltmann's comment that the resurrection is the beginning and source of the abolition of the universal Good Friday [*TH*, 211].

By way of support, MacKinnon notes how the risen Christ retains the marks of his execution. Moreover, his post-Easter commerce with the disciples is elusive and restricted, as if to guard them against the mistake of supposing that they were witnesses of a reversal, and not a vindication, of those things which had happened. As the Father's Amen to the life of Christ, if the resurrection does anything it drives one back to find the secret of the order of the world in what Christ said and did, and the healing of its continuing bitterness in the place of his endurance.

Therefore, for MacKinnon, this victory is not free of the tragic quality which the Duke of Wellington insisted belonged necessarily to all victories.[41] The surd and ambiguous element remains.

> The light has shone in the darkness, which has failed to
> overcome it; but the darkness still remains, and of the end of
> the traitor there is no record.[42]

---

[38] MacKinnon (1940), *God the Living and the True*, Signposts 2, Dacre Press, Westminster, 20; cf. 1976, 92-107.

[39] MacKinnon, 1968, 102f.

[40] MacKinnon, 1976, 95; 1968, 101.

[41] MacKinnon, 1979, 192.

[42] MacKinnon, 1968, 91f.

It is only in the light of the resurrection that Christians can learn to say with Pascal, that Christ will indeed be in agony until the end of the world. Or, as Lash declares, alluding to the image of Rev. 5:6, "There are scars, it seems, in heaven".[43]

In chastising MacKinnon for promoting a Manichaean ultimate dualism of forces, Hebblethwaite overlooks the nature of the situatedness of MacKinnon's talk which refuses eschatological prediction or premature talk of 'ultimates'.[44] Hope, for MacKinnon, as much as for Barth, is reticent of the details of the shape of the Future. And yet, Christian hope is nothing less than "a message of which our world is in direst need", a world which swings from various forms of facile optimism to debilitating despair.[45] Although MacKinnon's main focus appears to lie in the contrasting perspective from that of Barth, he maintains that

> we need to be reminded of the ultimate sweetness of things, in a time of wrath to be recalled to mercy, and in a time of violence to be told again of persuasion. ... [o]ur greatest teachers are those who remind us that the law of God's being is pity and meekness, although a pity and meekness revealed in the Cross.[46]

Cited here is Barth as an example of this reminder of this joyous hope. The otherwise sympathetic Ford appears not to notice this voice in MacKinnon, albeit a barely audible one, when he contrasts the latter's emphasis on the darkness inherent within tragedy with both Paul's 'sorrowful yet always rejoicing', and Gardener's explication of the 'redemptive' quality and joy in Shakespeare's *King Lear*.[47]

And yet Ford's contrast is pertinent to the effect that there is little in MacKinnon that sounds the note of trintarian creative overflow, albeit remembering the Cross, which reaches its crescendo in the enraptured celebration of human doxological response.

---

[43] Lash, 1996, 207.
[44] So Brian Hebblethwaite (1989), 'MacKinnon and the Problem of Evil', *Christ, Ethics and Tragedy: Essays in Honour of Donald MacKinnon*, ed. Kenneth Surin, Cambridge, 131-145 (142f.).
[45] MacKinnon, 1968, 120.
[46] MacKinnon, 1968, 118.
[47] Ford (1989), 'Tragedy and Atonement', in Surin, 117-130 (123).

In saying this, however, MacKinnon himself comes to serve as a reminder to Barth of the theological complexity of the tragic dimension, of a hope without the secure enclaves of even pious talk of triumph. In MacKinnon is put into practice the profound sense of eschatological provisionality and hubristic brokenness of thought and action, culminating in the almost tortuous, tentative, and stammering bringing of Christ's reconciling action to speech and practice. The redeeming action of God in Christ has not yet been resolved, awareness of which does not lead MacKinnon into using 'cross' and the 'tragic' as purely interpretative categories, as West wrongly accuses MacKinnon of doing.[48] The recognition of the existential relevance of tragedy and *hubris* is not the same as fatalism, a distinction West fails to recognise along with the interrogative character of MacKinnon's *oeuvre*.

Correspondence, Sacramentality and the Place of Human Agency

It has been suggested above that Barth weakens the narrative complexity associated with Jesus' life, death and resurrection. However, there appears a further difficulty in his presentation which, if pressed, could serve to resist this MacKinnonian corrective of his optimistic-sounding tone of triumphal rhetoric: that of his attitude to the nature of human agency in the construction of the eschatological Future. Eschatological victory, albeit a painfully achieved one, could still be known by Barth if that Future is portrayed as coming irresistibly, something which Barth's personalistic language of encounter, the absurdity of sin, and the sinner's foolish self-closure against obedience, would all intentionally militate against. Nevertheless, there are a few indications of tension within such an account, i.e., elements that create the suspicion of a Barthian subverting of the nescience of the Future.

Chapter 7 argued for the importance of the theme of 'correspondence' in depicting the relation between the prior divine activity and the consequent constitution of the gratefully responsive human activity. This concept promotes the theme of obedient human action to the divine command, and maintains the concreteness of that activity by conceiving its proper relation to the divine act in Christ through a movement of analogy. Correspondence accurately depicts the obedient following *after* the divine example. However, there is a sense in which this category here appears as being too *formal*. By this description is intended not so much a suggestion of a Barthian undermining of the

---

[48] Philip West maintains [West (1985), 'Christology as "Ideology"', *Theology* vol. 88, 428-436 (434)].

novelty and spontaneity of human agency (although there is a very real sense in which this question is a valid one for the way in which Barth presents his theology in practice). Rather, the concern is that Barth fails to indicate *how* this model of correspondence can maintain God's kenotic and sacramental operating *through* the creaturely in order to construct the universally present kingdom.

Barth, in IV.3, does speak of God's choosing his people to be his witnesses, through whom he freely works and speaks [see, e.g., *CD*, IV.3.2, 607-610]. This aspect is potentially, and unfortunately, disregarded in IV.4 and *CL* wherein the concept of 'correspondence', rather than 'witness', assumes centre-stage. An example of what occurs here may be sought briefly in Barth's presentation of baptism in IV.4, since this discussion appears as a clarification of how the divine agency maintains and determines human agency.

IV.4 argues for the exclusive christological identification of the 'sacraments': Jesus Christ as the one and only *mysterion*, an odd move given the fact that in his earlier writings Barth had spoken of the single Word of God in three forms. His humanity alone is the bearer, means and instrument of grace, and therefore baptism cannot be named a 'sacrament' or identified with the 'baptism of the Spirit' [*CD*, IV.4, 102]. What results from this is a perspective in which Barth maintains humanity's agency in its *distinction* from the divine, but also in asymmetrical *unity* with it in the sense that one acts in baptism in correspondence to the one's prior constitution in having been baptised with the Spirit [see *CD*, IV.4, 128ff.].

There is no suggestion, however, of Christ as working mediatorily (even if the concept of mediation here remembers the divine freedom of choice) through the elements of water in baptism and the bread and wine in the Lord's Supper. But here, Barth is in danger of portraying Christ's action as being immediate and without contingent manifestation, what Molnar terms an unconscious slipping into "a docetic view".[49]

Jüngel claims that the problem lies in the fact that Barth does not have enough of a sense of soteriological passivity, and thereby that his stress on human activity in baptism, therefore, risks God's sole act (*Gottes Allwirksamkeit*) in redemption.[50] While there is certainly a problem with Barth's presentation, it is not obvious that Jüngel has solved it since he here underplays the relation between the baptisms of the Spirit (the

---

[49] Paul Molnar (1996), *Karl Barth and the Theology of the Lord's Supper: A Systematic Investigation*, Peter Lang, 305.

[50] Jüngel (1982), *Barth-Studien*, Gütersloh, Zürich, 202-206; cf. Spjuth, 136ff.

Christian's *passively* being determined) and that with water (the Christian's *active* response) in Barth. Nevertheless, Jüngel has highlighted an important sense of human passivity in baptism that Barth's account tends to neglect. This is because Barth unwittingly neglects baptism's christological focus: that Christ is vicariously baptised with the Spirit, and has died and been raised for us. In the latter position, infant baptism would thereby receive a more christological basis, recognising the Pauline "while we were still sinners Christ died for us".[51] The place of human agency as responsive gratitude would be protected in the administration of the rite, and also in the later 'becoming [of] what we are' in our baptism in Christ, and in eucharistic participation.[52]

The sense of immediacy could be prevented if Barth was to depict baptism as that 'witness' or 'parable' to the divine act in Christ *through which* Christ freely presents himself contemporaneously, as he does through the scriptures and preaching. Moreover, thematising God's *free* association with these witnesses would function to sustain Barth's protest against sacramentalism's imprisoning of the divine [see *CD*, IV.4, 106].

Barth's discussion of baptism as a *purely* human act, albeit in correspondence to the divine, tending toward a sacramental dualism as it does, parallels his omission of attending to the senses in which humanity shapes its future. In theory, he does not deny the contingent shaping of our intramundane futures; but he does, however, ignore the role of the creaturely in determining the *details* of the Absolute Future.

Certainly, with Barth one must affirm that one cannot repeat or create this Future, since that Future is Christ's coming. However, it may be tentatively suggested that our activity and inactivity must play a real, albeit unpredictable, constituent role in contributing to the exact shape that Christ's universal presence for our Future takes. After all, as Barth himself maintains, it is *this* world which will be universally eschatologically recreated in Christ. If this is the case, then imagining the universal Future cannot prematurely bypass the decisions, hopes, lives and absurd sinfulness of particular human beings.

While Meynell unduly is restrictive in his understanding of what Barth intends by 'proclamation', there is nevertheless something suggestive here in his complaint that

---

[51] Rom. 5:8, NRSV.

[52] See T.F. Torrance (1975), *Theology in Reconciliation: Essays Towards Evangelical and Catholic Unity in East and West*, Geoffrey Chapman, London, 99-105.

> For Barth, Jesus Christ has willed other men to be his free
> instruments or ministers only in the *proclamation of the word
> of* reconciliation, and not in reconciliation itself.[53]

Is this omitting to discuss such questions an instance in the
supposed weakness of Barth's doctrine of creation? Wingren certainly
misses Barth's christological account of creation when he too broadly
argues that Barth is the "spiritual father" of all "negation of the belief in
creation", and "for the flight from creation".[54] Erroneously Barth's
theology is presented as a mere inversion of Liberalism.[55] Nevertheless,
this is a problematic area in Barth in relation to the question of the
integration of creation and redemption, in the sense that the latter
could/should be conceived as operating under, through, and with the
conditions of the former. This is what gives a certain poignancy to
Berkhof's complaint that Barth still remains trapped within the view that
creation is "a theatre or stage" for the drama of redemption but it will
never be part of the drama itself.[56] A much richer picture of the
interactions and fluidities between human beings and their environment
appears to have been here too simplistically formalised.

Concluding suggestions

It is the failure to attend to the complexities of the eschatological nature of
the Christ-event, and thereafter its post-Pentecost commission, that leads
certain Barth-commentators too easily into misunderstanding the nature of
Barth's eschatological provisionality and nescience. For example, Ford
complains of the way

> in which [in Barth] his [i.e., Jesus'] identity is complete at the
> crucifixion and becomes the universal *Bildungsrman* through
> the resurrection.[57]

---

[53] Meynell, 1965, 277.

[54] Wingren, *The Flight from Creation*, 19, cited in Spjuth, 14.

[55] Wingren, 1958, 25.

[56] Hendrikus Berkhof, cited in Spjuth, 15. Spjuth links this to Barth's underestimation of
the divine imminence in creation by the Spirit [22f.].

[57] Ford, 1981, 169.

However, the nature of Barth's rhetoric and discourse of victory, if left unqualified, particularly points in the direction that a number of these commentators have taken. As Ford comments, albeit offering it in more of a Roberts-like vein than this study deems appropriate, it is difficult to see the "significance of history in progress now that everything has happened". Nevertheless, once the nature of Christ's 'victory' in his Easter work is itself qualified, hope retains its less optimistic, predictive and therefore potentially ideological sounding essence that Barth intends through his thematic of hope's fragile and interrogative character, but occasionally denies through triumphal rhetoric. The Barthian form of the theo-drama can too often unwittingly sound blind to the difficulties of a harmonious resolution that tragic drama creates for thought. Certainly one is aware that Christ was vindicated and 'saved' from death by the Father. But his scars remain, and his intercessory work retains the pain of the world's continuing forms of disobedience. The depths of the Father's love remains abyss-like in his Son who endured the destitution of cross and grave for the world's salvation.

Sharpening up this corrective device may not only lead one to clarify certain elements in Barth's thinking, but also, however, potentially distract (rather than ban) one from the exuberant hope for the Universal Future that is so vital to Barth. That is a risk worth taking, given one's remembering the pressures, temptations, and insecurities that hope has to endure in this Holy Saturday. As Tracy declares,

> any pure models of 'progress' unable and unwilling to face
> the tragedy and suffering in human existence fully deserve
> Christian theological suspicion, indeed contempt.[58]

The outcome could then be a theology with a different *feel* and *style* from that of Barth, albeit maintaining connections with the content of vast areas of his theology. Certainly, as with Barth in general, it would be a theology struggling to prevent the premature conceptual and dramatic foreclosure of the tragic fissures and abysses of human existence in a world generally ignorant of its Creator. Barth's admission of the brokenness of all theological speech, and his recollection that it remains a *theologia viatorum*, would be consciously appropriated in this move [*CD*, III.3, 293ff.]. For to state that our Future is in Christ is to remember that the shape of our future journeying is cruciform, that our hope is not for

---

[58] Tracy, 1994, 76.

some already predicted events, and that our business is "to fashion our finitude in the form of discipleship".[59]

One needs to be reminded that tragedy can remain only a *partial* hermeneutical category for the Christian, since for the spectators alone of the drama is the story known to be a tragedy. For the tragic protagonists, on the other hand, their future remains contingently open and therefore unknown, in some sense. Similarly, our particular endings remain our Future, albeit one hopes for one's End in God in Christ. In this time, one cannot speak of guaranteed happy endings. As Ford declares, taking his cue from the interaction between 2 Corinthians and MacKinnon's tragic vision, "There is a continuing possibility that can only be called tragic".[60] Tragic drama functions, therefore, as an interruption and interrogation of all forms of facile optimism, and glib generalisations in the face of painful particularities.

Hope nevertheless expects that the tragic will not have the *final* word, although it wanders necessarily *through* and *not yet beyond*, tragedy. Here Ford is correct to claim that

> the *in*adequacy of tragedy as a genre through which to [we must add, *solely*] understand the Gospel ... [suggesting that] tragedy has to be used but not allowed to dominate or obscure the uniqueness of what is presented here [in the Gospel].[61]

Christian hope is in our being placed within what Tracy describes as the

> final reality ... [of] the hard, unyielding reality of the pure Unbounded Love disclosed to us in God's revelation of who God is who we are commanded and empowered to be in Christ Jesus.[62]

The very suffering of God himself in his Son portrays the process of the redemptive renewal of creation, which in turn provides hope that our

---

[59] Lash, 1989, 24.
[60] Ford, 1989, 124.
[61] Ibid., 126.
[62] Tracy, 1994, 101.

sufferings will not be ultimate [see *CD*, IV.2, 357f.]. This is a hope which, as Lash observes, lifts us

> from the despair, [and] takes us also beyond optimism;
> secondly, it takes us beyond the fantasy of science fiction to a
> more sober vision of the future of the world; and thirdly, in
> liberating us from determinism, it enables us to live beyond
> control.[63]

---

[63] Lash, 1994, 49.

Select Bibliography

Works by Karl Barth

(1928) *The Word of God and the Word of Man*, trans. Douglas Horton, London: Hodder and Stoughton. German (1929), *Das Wortes Gottes und die Theologie*, Chr. Kaiser, Verlag, München.

(1933) *The Resurrection of the Dead*, trans. H.J. Stenning, Hodder and Stoughton, London.

(1933) *Theological Existence To-Day! A Plea for Theological Freedom*, trans. R. Birch Hoyle, Hodder and Stoughton, London.

(1936) *Credo: A Presentation of the Chief Problems of Dogmatics with Reference to the Apostles' Creed*, trans. James Strathern McNab, Hodder & Stoughton, London. German (1935), *Credo: Die Hauptprobleme der Dogmatik dargestellt im Anschluß an das Apostolische Glaubensbekenntnis*, Chr. Kaiser Verlag, München.

(1937) 'Revelation', in *Revelation*, ed. John Baillie; Faber and Faber Ltd., London, 41-81.

(1938) *The Holy Ghost and the Christian Life*, trans. R. Birch Hoyle, Frederick Muller Ltd., London.

(1939) *Church and State*, trans. G. Ronald Howe, SCM Press, London.

(1949) *Dogmatics in Outline*, trans. G.T. Thomson, SCM Press, London.

(1954) *Against the Stream: Shorter Post-War Writings*, ed. Ronald Gregor Smith, SCM Press, London.

(1956) *Wolfgang Amadeus Mozart*, Zollikon-Zürich.

(1956-1975) *Church Dogmatics*, 14 volumes, T&T Clark, Edinburgh. German (1932-1967), *Kirchliche Dogmatik*, Evangelischer Verlag A.G., Zollikon-Zürich.

(1958) *The Faith of the Church A Commentary on the Apostles Creed According to Calvin's Catechism*, trans. Gabriel Vahanian, Collins, London.

(1959) *Christmas*, trans. Bernhard Citron, Oliver and Boyd, Edinburgh and London.

(1959) *God, Grace and Gospel*, trans. James Strathern McNab, Oliver and Boyd, Edinburgh and London, 3-27.

(1960) *Anselm: Fides Quaerens Intellectum. Anselm's Proof of the Existence of God in the Context of his Theological Scheme*, trans. of 2nd edn. 1958 by Ian W. Robertson, SCM Press, London.

(1960) *Community, State and Church*, ed. Will Herberg, Doubleday Anchor Books, New York.

(1960) 'Foreword', in Pierre Maury, *Predestination and Other Papers*, trans. Edwin Hudson, SCM Press, London, 15-18.

(1961) 'On Theology', *SJT* vol. 14, 225-228.

(1962) *Theology and Church: Shorter Writings, 1920-1928*, trans. Louise Pettibone Smith, SCM Press, London.

(1963) *Evangelical Theology: An Introduction*, trans. Grover Foley, Collins, London.

(1963) *Karl Barth's Table Talk*, ed. John D. Godsey, Oliver and Boyd, Edinburgh and London.

(1964) *God Here and Now*, trans. Paul M. van Buren, Routledge and Kegan Paul, London.

(1967) *The Humanity of God*, trans. John Newton Thomas and Thomas Wieser, Collins, London.

(1968) *The Beginnings of Dialectical Theology*, ed. J.M. Robinson, trans. Part I by Keith R. Crim, Part II by Louis De Grazia and Keith R. Crim, John Knox Press, Richmond, Virginia.

(1968) *The Epistle to the Romans*, trans. of 6th ed. by Edwyn C. Hoskyns, Oxford University Press, Oxford.

(1969) *How I Changed My Mind*, ed. and trans. John Godsey, The Saint Andrew's Press, Edinburgh.

(1971) *Fragments Grave and Gay*, trans. Eris Mosbacher, ed. H. Martin Rumscheidt, Collins, London.

(1972) *Protestant Theology in the Nineteenth Century: Its Background and History*, trans. Brian Cozens and John Bowden, SCM Press, London.

(1976) 'Jesus Christ and the Social Movement (1911)', in *Karl Barth and Radical Politics*, ed. and trans. George Hunsinger, Westminster, Philadelphia, 19-45.

(1978) 'Concluding Unscientific Postscript on Schleiermacher', trans. George Hunsinger, *Studies in Religion* vol. 7, 117-135.

(1981) *Ethics*, trans. G.W. Bromiley, Seabury, New York.

(1981) *Karl Barth: Letters, 1961-1968*, ed. and trans. Geoffrey W. Bromiley, T&T Clark, Edinburgh.

(1981) *The Christian Life: Church Dogmatics IV.4, Lecture Fragments*, trans. G.W. Bromiley, T&T Clark, Edinburgh.

(1982) *Die christliche Dogmatik im Entwurf*, ed. Gerhard Sauter, TVZ, Zürich.

(1985) *Der Römerbrief*, 1st edn., 1919, ed. H. Stoevesandt, Theologische Verlag, Zurich.

(1986) 'Extra Nos - Pro Nobis - In Nobis', trans. George Hunsinger, *The Thomist* vol. 50, 497-511.

(1986) *Karl Barth-Rudolf Bultmann Letters, 1922-1966*, ed. Bernd Jaspert, trans. Geoffrey W. Bromiley, T&T Clark, Edinburgh.

(1986) *The Way of Theology in Karl Barth: Essays and Comments*, ed. H. Martin Rumscheidt, Pickwick Publications, Allison Park, Pennsylvania, 63-78.

(1986) *Witness to the Word: A Commentary on John 1. Lectures at Münster in 1925 and Bonn in 1933*, ed. Walther Fürst, trans. Geoffrey W. Bromiley, William B. Eerdmans Publishing Company, Grand Rapids, Michigan.

(1990) *The Göttingen Dogmatics: Instruction in the Christian Religion, Volume 1*, trans. Geoffrey W. Bromiley, William B. Eerdmans Publishing Company, Grand Rapids, Michigan.

Barth, Karl, and Brunner, Emil (1946), *Natural Theology*, trans. Peter Fraenkel, The Centenary Press, London.

Barth, Karl, and Thurneysen, Eduard (1964), *Revolutionary Theology in the Making: Barth-Thurneysen Correspondence, 1914-1925*, trans. James D. Smart, The Epworth Press, London.

Other Works

Abel, Lionel (1963), *Metatheatre: A New View of Dramatic Form*, Hill & Wang, New York.

Adkins, A.W.H. (1960), *Merit and Responsibility: A Study in Greek Values*, Oxford University Press.

Almond, Philip C. (1978), 'Karl Barth and Anthropocentric Theology', *SJT* vol. 31, 435-447.

Aloni, Nimrod (1991), *Beyond Nihilism: Nietzsche's Healing and Edifying Philosophy*, University Press of America, Lanham, New York and London.

Aristotle (1984), *Poetics*, trans. I. Bywater, in *The Complete Works of Aristotle Volume Two*, ed. Jonathan Barnes, Princeton University Press, Princeton and Oxford.

Auerbach, Eric (1953), *Mimesis: The Representation of Reality in Western Literature*, trans. Willard R. Trask, Princeton University Press.

Aung, Salai Hla (1998), *The Doctrine of Creation in the Theology of Barth, Moltmann and Pannenberg: Creation in Theological, Ecological and Philosophical-Scientific Perspective*, Roderer Verlag, Regensburg.

Avis, Paul D.L. (1979), 'Friedrich Schleiermacher and the Science of Theology', *SJT* vol. 32, 19-43.

Bailey, Joe (1988), *Pessimism*, Routledge, London and New York.

Baillie, D.M (1948), *God Was in Christ: An Essay on Incarnation and Atonement*, Faber, London.

Baillie, John (1934), *And the Life Everlasting*, Oxford University Press.

Baillie, John (1939), *Our Knowledge of God*, Oxford University Press.

Baillie, John (1964), *The Idea of Revelation in Recent Thought*, Columbia University Press, London.

Baldock, Marion (1989), *Greek Tragedy: An Introduction*, Bristol Classical Press.

von Balthasar, Hans Urs (1965), *Word and Spirit: Essays in Theology 2*, trans. A.V. Littledale, Herder and Herder, New York.

von Balthasar, Hans Urs (1972), *The Theology of Karl Barth*, trans. John Drury, Anchor, New York.

von Balthasar, Hans Urs (1990), *Mysterium Paschale: The Mystery of Easter*, trans. Aidan Nichols, T&T Clark, Edinburgh.

Baranowski, Shelley (1981), 'The primacy of theology: Karl Barth and Socialism', *Studies on Religion* vol. 10, 451-461.

Barbour, John D. (1983), 'Tragedy and Ethical Reflection', *Journal of Religion* vol. 63, 1-25.

Barr, James (1993), *Biblical Faith and Natural Theology: The Gifford Lectures for 1991 Delivered in the University of Edinburgh*, Clarendon Press, Oxford.

Bauckham, Richard (1987), *Moltmann: Messianic Theology in the Making*, Marshall Morgan and Scott, Basingstoke.

Bauckham, Richard (1995), *The Theology of Jürgen Moltmann*, T&T Clark, Edinburgh.

Bauckham, Richard (ed.) (1999), *God Will Be All in All: The Eschatology of Jürgen Moltmann*, T&T Clark, Edinburgh.

Bauckham, Richard, and Hart, Trevor (1999), *Hope Against Hope: Christian Eschatology in Contemporary Context*, Darton, Longman and Todd, London.

Bauckham, Richard, and Hart, Trevor (1999), 'Salvation and Creation: "All Things New"', in *The Scope of Salvation: Theatres of God's Drama. Lincoln Lectures in Theology 1998*, Lincoln Cathedral Publications, 40-54.

Beasley-Murray, G.R. (1974), 'How Christian is the Book of Revelation?', in *Reconciliation and Hope: New Testament Essays in Atonement and Eschatology Presented to L.L. Morris on his 60th Birthday*, ed. Robert J. Banks, Eerdmans, Grand Rapids, 275-84.

Beasley-Murray, G.R. (1986), *Jesus and the Kingdom of God*, Eerdmans, Grand Rapids.

Bentley, James (1973), 'Karl Barth as a Christian Socialist', *Theology* vol. 76, 349-356.

Berkouwer, G.C. (1956), *The Triumph of Grace in the Theology of Karl Barth*, trans. H. R. Boer, Paternoster Press, London.

Berkouwer, G.C. (1972), *The Return of Christ*, trans. James van Oosterom, William B. Eerdmans Publishing Company, Grand Rapids, Michigan.

Bettis, Joseph D. (1967), 'Is Karl Barth a Universalist?', *SJT* vol. 20, 424-436.

Biggar, Nigel (1993), *The Hastening that waits: Karl Barth's Ethics*, Clarendon Press, Oxford.

Biggar, Nigel (ed.) (1988), *Reckoning With Barth: Essays in Commemoration of the Centenary of Karl Barth's Birth*, Mowbray, Oxford.

Bonhoeffer, Dietrich (1962), *Act and Being*, trans. Bernard Noble, Collins, London.

Bouchard, Larry (1989), *Tragic Method and Tragic Theology: Evil in Contemporary Drama and Religious Thought*, Pennsylvania State University Press.

Bradley, A.C. (1957), *Shakespearean Tragedy*, Macmillan, London.

Bradley, A.C. (1962), 'Hegel's Theory of Tragedy', in *Hegel on Tragedy*, eds. Anne and Henry Paolucci, Harper Torchbooks, New York, Evanston, San Francisco and London, 367-88.

Bradshaw, Timothy (1986), 'Karl Barth on the Trinity: A Family Resemblance', *SJT* vol. 39, 145-164.

Brecher, Robert (1983), 'Karl Barth: Wittgensteinian Theologian Manqué', *Heythrop Journal* vol. 24, 290-300.

Bridges, James T. (1987), *Human Destiny and Resurrection in Pannenberg and Rahner*, Peter Lang, New York, Bern, Frankfurt am Main, Paris.

Bromiley, Geoffrey W. (1986), 'The Authority of Scripture in Karl Barth', in *Hermeneutics, Authority and Canon*, eds. D.A. Carson and John D. Woodbridge, Inter Varsity Press, Leicester, 275-294.

Brown, Colin (1962), 'Karl Barth's Doctrine of Creation', *Churchman* vol. 76, 99-105.

Brown, Robert (1980), 'On God's Ontic and Noetic Absoluteness: A Critique of Barth', *SJT* vol. 33, 533-549.

Brunner, Emil (1939), *Man in Revolt: A Christian Anthropology*, trans. Olive Wyon, Lutterworth Press, London.

Brunner, Emil (1949), *Dogmatics Volume I: The Christian Doctrine of God*, trans. Olive Wyon, Lutterworth Press, London.

Brunner, Emil (1951), 'The New Barth: Observations on Karl Barth's *Doctrine of Man*', *SJT* vol. 4, 123-35.

Brunner, Emil (1952), *Dogmatics Volume II: The Christian Doctrine of Creation and Redemption*, trans. Olive Wyon, Lutterworth Press, London.

Brunner, Emil (1954), *The Eternal Hope*, trans. Harold Knight, Lutterworth Press, London.

Buckley, James J. (1986), 'Christological Inquiry: Barth, Rahner, and the Identity of Jesus Christ', *The Thomist* vol. 50, 586-598.

Buckley, James. J., and Wilson, William McF. (1985), 'A Dialogue with Barth and Farrer on Theological Method', *Heythrop Journal* vol. 26, 274-293.

Bultmann, Rudolf (1952), *Theology of the New Testament Volume 1*, trans. Kendrick Grobel, SCM Press, London.

Bultmann, Rudolf (1957), *History and Eschatology. The Gifford Lectures 1955*, The University Press, Edinburgh.

Bultmann, Rudolf (1958), *Jesus and the Word*, trans. Louise Pettibone Smith and Erminie Huntress Lantero, Collins, London.

Bultmann, Rudolf (1961), *Existence and Faith. Shorter Writings of Rudolf Bultmann*, trans. Schubert Ogden, London.

Busch, Eberhard (1976), *Karl Barth: His Life from Letters and Autobiographical Texts*, trans. John Bowden, SCM Press, London.

Butler, G.A. (1974), 'Karl Barth and Political Theology', *SJT* vol. 25, 441-456.

Caird, G.B. (ed.) (1970), *The Christian Hope*, SPCK, London.

Cameron, Nigel M. de S. (ed.) (1989), *Issues in Faith and History*, Rutherford House, Edinburgh.

Cameron, Nigel M. de S. (ed.) (1992), *Universalism and the Doctrine of Hell. Papers Presented at the Fourth Edinburgh Conference on Christian Dogmatics*, Paternoster Press, Carlisle.

Cane, Anthony William (1996), 'Ontology, Theodicy and Idiom - The Challenge of Nietzschean Tragedy to Christian Writing on Evil', *New Blackfriars* vol. 77, 84-91.

Cavell, Stanley (1969), *Must We Mean What We Say? A Book of Essays*, Charles Scribner's Sons, New York.

Clouse, Robert G. (ed.) (1977), *The Meaning of the Millennium*, Inter Varsity Press, Downers Grove.

Collins, Alice (1988), 'Barth's Relationship to Schleiermacher: A Reassessment', *Studies in Religion* vol. 17, 213-224.

Colwell, John (1989), *Actuality and Provisionality: Eternity and Election in the Theology of Karl Barth*, Rutherford House Books, Edinburgh.

Copleston, Frederick (1963), *A History of Philosophy, Volume VII, Fichte to Nietzsche*, Search Press, London.

Cousins, Ewert H. (ed.) (1972), *Hope and the Future of Man*, Fortress Press.

Crawford, R.G. (1971), 'The Atonement in Karl Barth', *Theology* vol. 74, 355-358.

Crawford, R.G. (1972), 'The Theological Method of Karl Barth', *SJT* vol. 25, 320-336.

Crouter, Richard (1988), 'Introduction', in *On Religion: Speeches to Its Cultured Despisers*, trans. Richard Crouter, Cambridge University Press, 1-73.

Cullmann, Oscar (1951), *Christ and Time: The Primitive Conception of Time and History*, trans. Floyd V. Filson, SCM Press, London.

Cullmann, Oscar (1958), *Immortality of the Soul or Resurrection of the Dead? The Witness of the New Testament*, The Epworth Press, London.

Cushman, Robert E. (1981), *Faith Seeking Understanding: Essays Theological and Critical*, Duke University Press, Durham, N. Carolina.

Dalferth, Ingolf U. (1995), 'The Eschatological Roots of the Doctrine of the Trinity', in *Trinitarian Theology Today: Essays on Divine Being and Act*, ed. Christoph Schwöbel, T&T Clark, Edinburgh, 147-170.

Davison, James E. (1984), 'Can God Speak a Word to Man? Barth's Critique of Schleiermacher's Theology', *SJT* vol. 37, 189-211.

Deddo, Gary (1994), 'The Grammar of Barth's Theology of Personal Relations', *SJT* vol. 47, 183-222.

Deegan, Dan L. (1961), 'The Christological Determinant in Barth's Doctrine of Creation', *SJT* vol. 14, 119-135.

Devanny, Christopher (1997), 'Truth, Tragedy and Compassion: Some Reflection on the Theology of Donald MacKinnon', *New Blackfriars* vol. 78, 33-42.

Dickinson, Charles C. (1981), 'Church Dogmatics IV/4', in *Karl Barth in Re-View: Posthumous Works Reviewed and Assessed*, ed. H. Martin Rumscheidt, The Pickwick Press, Pittsburgh, Pa., 43-53.

Dorrien, Gary (2000), *The Barthian Revolt in Modern Theology: Theology Without Weapons*, Westminster John Knox Press, Louisville.

Duthie, Charles (1969), 'Providence in the Theology of Karl Barth', in *Providence*, ed. Maurice Wiles, SPCK Theological Collections 12, SPCK, London.

Edwards, Philip (1987), *Shakespeare: A Winter's Progress*, Oxford and New York.

Ellis-Fermer, Una (1945), *The Frontiers of Drama*, London.

Else, Gerald F. (1986), *Plato and Aristotle on Poetry*, ed. Peter Burian, University of North Carolina Press, Chapel Hill and London.

Emmet, Dorothy (1994), *The Role of the Unrealisable: A Study in Regulative Ideals*, St. Martin's Press, New York.

Euripides (1954), *The Bacchae and Other Plays*, trans. Philip Vellacott, Penguin Books.

Exum, J. Cheryl (1992), *Tragedy and Biblical Narrative: Arrows of the Almighty*, Cambridge University Press.

Fergusson, David (1997), 'Eschatology', in *The Cambridge Companion to Christian Doctrine*, ed. Colin E. Gunton, Cambridge University Press, 226-244.

Feuerbach, Ludwig (1989), *The Essence of Christianity*, trans. George Eliot, Prometheus Books, New York.

Fisher, Simon (1986), *Revelatory Positivism? Barth's Earliest Theology and the Marburg School*, Oxford University Press.

Fitzgerald, Ross (ed.) (1979), *The Sources of Hope*, Pergamon Press.

Flew, Anthony, and MacIntyre, Alasdair (eds.) (1955), *New Essays in Philosophical Theology*, SCM Press, London.

Ford, David F. (1981), *Barth and God's Story   Biblical Narrative and the Theological Method of Karl Barth in the Church*, Peter Lang, New York.

Ford, David F. (ed.) (1997), *The Modern Theologians*, 2nd edn., Blackwells, Oxford.

Frei, Hans (1956), 'The Doctrine of Revelation in the Thought of Karl Barth, 1909-1922', unpublished Ph.D thesis, Yale University.

Frei, Hans (1957), 'Niebuhr's Theological Background', in *Faith and Ethics: The Theology of H. Richard Niebuhr*, ed. Paul Ramsey, Harper and Row, New York, 9-64.

Frei, Hans (1992), *Types of Christian Theology*, Yale University Press, New Haven and London.

Frei, Hans (1993), *Theology and Narrative: Selected Essays*, eds. George Hunsinger and William C. Placher, Oxford University Press.

Frykberg, E. (1994), 'The Child as Solution: The Problem of the Superordinate-Subordinate Ordering of the Male-Female relation in Barth's Theology', *SJT* vol. 47, 327-354.

Fuchs, Ernst (1971), 'The Hermeneutical Problem', in *The Future of Our Religious Past*, ed. J.M. Robinson, London.

Georgopoulos, N. (ed.) (1993), *Tragedy and Philosophy*, Macmillan, London.

Godsey, John (1956), 'The Architecture of Karl Barth's *Church Dogmatics*', *SJT* vol. 9, 236-250.

Gorringe, Timothy J. (1999), 'Eschatology and Political Radicalism.   The Example of Karl Barth and Jürgen Moltmann', in *God Will Be All in All: The Eschatology of Jürgen Moltmann*, ed. Richard Bauckham, T&T Clark, Edinburgh, 87-114.

Gorringe, Timothy J. (1999), *Karl Barth: Against Hegemony*, Oxford University Press.

Green, Garrett (1995), 'Challenging the Religious Studies Canon: Karl Barth's Theory of Religion', *Journal of Religion* vol. 75, 473-486.

Green, Joel B., McKnight, Scot and Marshall, I.H. (eds.) (1992), *Dictionary of Jesus and the Gospels*, Inter Varsity Press, Leicester.

Gunton, Colin (1972), 'Karl Barth and the Development of Doctrine', *SJT* vol. 25, 171-180.

Gunton, Colin (1974), 'Barth's Doctrine of Election as Part of His Doctrine of God', *JTS* vol. 25, 381-392.

Gunton, Colin (1978), *Becoming and Being: The Doctrine of God in Charles Hartshorne and Karl Barth*, Oxford University Press.

Gunton, Colin (1986), 'Barth, the Trinity, and Human Freedom', *Theology Today* vol. 43, 316-330.

Gustafson, James M. (1984), *Ethics from a Theocentric Perspective, Volume II. Ethics and Theology*, Chicago.

Hanson, P.D. (ed.) (1983), *Visionaries and their Apocalypses*, SPCK, London.

von Harnack, Adolf (1904), *What is Christianity?*, trans. T.B. Saunders, 3rd edn., Putnam, New York.

Hart, Trevor A. (1993), 'A Capacity for Ambiguity? The Barth-Brunner Debate Revisited', *Tyndale Bulletin* vol. 44, 289-305.

Hart, Trevor A. (1999), *Regarding Karl Barth: Essays Toward a Reading of His Theology*, Paternoster Press, Carlisle.

Hart, Trevor A. (ed.) (1995), *Justice the True and Only Mercy: Essays on the Life and Theology of Peter Taylor Forsyth*, T&T Clark, Edinburgh.

Hart, Trevor A., and Thimell, Daniel P. (eds.) (1989), *Christ in Our Place: The Humanity of God in Christ for the Reconciliation of the World*, eds. Trevor A. Hart and Daniel P. Thimell, Paternoster, Exeter.

Hartwell, Herbert (1964), *The Theology of Karl Barth: An Introduction*, Duckworth.

Hartwell, Herbert (1969), 'Karl Barth on Baptism', *SJT* vol. 22, 10-29.

Harvey, van A. (1996), 'Projection: A Metaphor in Search of a Theory?', in *Can Religion Be Explained Away?*, ed. D.Z. Phillips, Macmillan, London, 66-82.

Hausmann, William John (1969), *Karl Barth's Doctrine of Election*, Philosophical Library, New York.

Haynes, Stephen, R. (1991), *Prospects for Post-Holocaust Theology*, Scholars Press, Atlanta, Georgia.

Hebblethwaite, Brian (1984), *The Christian Hope*, Marshall Morgan and Scott, Basingstoke.

Hegel, G.W.F. (1920), *The Philosophy of Fine Art*, 4 vols., trans. F.P.B. Omaston, London, selections in Anne and Henry Paolucci (eds.) (1962), *Hegel on Tragedy*, Harper Torchbooks, New York, Evanston, San Francisco and London.

Heilman, Robert Bechtold (1968), *Tragedy and Melodrama. Versions of Experience*, University of Washington Press, Seattle and London.

Hellwig, Monica K. (1991), 'Eschatology', in *Systematic Theology: Roman Catholic Perspectives Volume 2*, eds. Francis Schüssler Fiorenza and John P. Galvin, Fortress Press, Minneapolis, 349-372.

Helme, Mark (1981), 'Notes and Comments: Barth and Philosophy', *Heythrop Journal* vol. 22, 285-9.

Hendry, George S. (1978), 'The Freedom of God in the Theology of Karl Barth', *SJT* vol. 31, 229-244.

Hendry, George S. (1982), 'Nothing', *Theology Today* vol. 39, 274-289.

Hendry, George S. (1984), 'The Transcendental Method in the Theology of Karl Barth', *SJT* vol. 37, 213-227.

Hepburn, R.W. (1982), 'Optimism, Finitude and the Meaning of Life', in *The Philosophical Frontiers of Christian Theology: Essays Presented to D.M. MacKinnon*, eds. Brian Hebblethwaite and Stewart Sutherland, Cambridge University Press, 119-144.

Hick, John (1976), *Death and Eternal Life*, Collins, London.

Hick, John (1977), *Evil and the God of Love*, 2nd edn., Macmillan, London.

Hick, John (1981), 'An Irenaean Theodicy', in *Encountering Evil: Live Options in Theodicy*, ed. Stephen T. Davis, T&T Clark, Edinburgh, 39-52.

Hick, John (ed.) (1966), *Faith and the Philosophers*, ed. John Hick, St. Martin's Press, New York.

Highfield, Ron (1989), *Barth and Rahner in Dialogue: Toward an Ecumenical Understanding of Sin and Evil*, Peter Lang, New York, Bern, Frankfurt am Main, Paris.

Higton, Michael Anthony (1997), 'The Identity of Jesus Christ in the Church: An Exploration in the Theology of Hans Frei', unpublished Ph.D. Thesis, University of Cambridge.

Hoekema, Anthony A. (1978), *The Bible and the Future*, Paternoster Press, Exeter.

Hood, Robert E. (1985), *Contemporary Political Orders and Christ: Karl Barth's Christology and Political Praxis*, Pickwick Publications, Allison Park, Pensylvannia.

Houlgate, Stephen (1986), *Hegel, Nietzsche and the Criticism of Metaphysics*, Cambridge University Press.

Hunsinger, George (1978), 'Karl Barth and Radical Politics: Some Further Considerations', *Studies in Religion* vol. 7, 167-191.

Hunsinger, George (1983), 'Karl Barth and Liberation Theology', *Journal of Religion* vol. 63, 247-263.

Hunsinger, George (1986), 'The Harnack/Barth Correspondence: A Paraphrase with Comments', *The Thomist* vol. 50, 599-622.

Hunsinger, George (1986-7), 'Beyond Literalism and Expressivism: Karl Barth's Hermeneutical Realism', *Modern Theology* vol. 3, 209-223.

Hunsinger, George (1991), *How to Read Karl Barth: The Shape of His Theology*, Oxford University Press.

Hunsinger, George (1993), 'Article Review: Karl Barth's *The Göttingen Dogmatics*', *SJT* vol. 46, 371-382.

Hunsinger, George (1993), 'Truth as Self-Involving: Barth and Lindbeck on the Cognitive and Performative Aspects of Truth in Theological Discourse', *Journal of the American Academy of Religion* vol. 61, 41-56.

Hunsinger, George (ed.) (1976), *Karl Barth and Radical Politics*, Westminster, Philadelphia.

Hunter, G.K. (1972), 'Introduction', in *King Lear*, New Penguin Shakespeare, ed. G.K. Hunter, Penguin Books, Harmondsworth, 7-55.

Ingraffia, Brian D. (1995), *Postmodern Theory and Biblical Theology: Vanquishing God's Shadow*, Cambridge University Press.

Jaspers, Karl (1969), *Tragedy is not Enough*, trans. Harald A.T. Reiche, Harry T. Moore, Karl W. Deutsch, Archon Books.

Jenson, Robert W. (1969), *God After God: The God of the Past and the God of the Future, Seen in the Work of Karl Barth*, Bobbs-Merrill, Indianapolis, New York.

Jenson, Robert W. (1993), 'You Wonder Where the Spirit Went', *Pro Ecclesia* vol. 2, 296-305.

Jüngel, Eberhard (1975), *Death: The Riddle and the Mystery*, trans. Iain and Ute Nicol, The Saint Andrew Press, Edinburgh.

Jüngel, Eberhard (1976), *The Doctrine of the Trinity: God's Being is in Becoming*, trans. Horton Harris, Monographic Supplements to the Scottish Journal of Theology, eds. T. F. Torrance and J.K.S. Reid, Edinburgh and London.

Jüngel, Eberhard (1976), 'The Truth of Life: Observations on Truth as the Interruption of the Continuity of Life', in *Creation, Christ and Culture: Studies in Honour of T.F. Torrance*, ed. Richard W.A. McKinney, T&T Clark, Edinburgh, 231-236.

Jüngel, Eberhard (1982), *Barth-Studien*, Gütersloh, Zürich.

Jüngel, Eberhard (1983), *God as the Mystery of the World: On the Foundation of the Theology of the Crucified One in the Debate between Theism and Atheism*, trans. Darrell L. Guder, T&T Clark, Edinburgh.

Jüngel, Eberhard (1986), *Karl Barth, a Theological Legacy*, trans. by Garrett E. Paul, Westminster, Philadelphia.

Jüngel, Eberhard (1989), *Theological Essays Volume 1*, trans. J.B. Webster, T&T Clark, Edinburgh.

Jüngel, Eberhard (1995), *Theological Essays Volume 2*, trans. J.B. Webster, T&T Clark, Edinburgh.

Kasper, Walter (1985), *Faith and the Future*, trans. Robert Nowell, Burns & Oates, London.

Kaufmann, Walter (1969), *Tragedy and Philosophy*, Doubleday, New York.

Kaufmann, Walter (1974), *Nietzsche: Philosopher, Psychologist, Antichrist*, 4th edn., Princeton University Press, Princeton, N.J.

Kekes, John (1990), *Facing Evil*, Princeton University Press.

Kelsey, David H. (1975), *The Uses of Scripture in Recent Theology*, SCM Press, London.

Kelsey, David H. (1986), 'Aquinas and Barth on the Human Body', *The Thomist* vol. 50, 643-689.

Kerr, Fergus (1996), 'Cartesianism According to Karl Barth', *New Blackfriars* vol. 77, 358-368.

Kerr, Fergus (1997), *Immortal Longings: Versions of Transcending Humanity*, SPCK, London.

Kitchen, Martin (1991), 'Karl Barth and the Weimar Republic', *Downside Review* vol. 109, 183-201.

Kitto, H.D.F. (1956), *Form and Meaning in Drama*, Methuen.

Klemm, David (1987), 'Towards a Rhetoric of Postmodern Theology Through Barth and Heidegger', *Journal of the American Academy of Religion* vol. 55, 443-469.

Knox, Bernard M.W. (1966), *Oedipus at Thebes. Sophocles' Tragic Hero and His Time*, 2nd edn., Yale University Press.

König, Adrio (1989), *The Eclipse of Christ in Eschatology: Toward a Christ-Centered Approach*, Marshall Morgan and Scott, London.

Krieger, Murray (1960), *The Tragic Vision*, Chicago and Toronto.

Küng, Hans (1984), *Does God Exist?: An Answer for Today*, trans. Edward Quinn, SCM Press, London.

Küng, Hans (1984), *Eternal Life?*, trans. Edward Quinn, Collins, London.

Ladd, George Eldon (1974), 'Apocalyptic and New Testament Theology', in *Reconciliation and Hope: New Testament Essays in Atonement and Eschatology Presented to L.L. Morris on his 60th Birthday*, ed. Robert J. Banks, Eerdmans, Grand Rapids, 285-96.

Ladd, George Eldon (1974), *The Presence of the Future*, Eerdmans, Grand Rapids.

Lash, Nicholas (1981), *A Matter of Hope: A Theologian's Reflections on the Thought of Karl Marx*, Darton Longman and Todd, London.

Lash, Nicholas (1986), *Theology on the Way to Emmaus*, SCM Press, London.

Lash, Nicholas (1989), 'Incarnation and Determinate Freedom', in *On Freedom*, ed. Leroy S. Rouner, University of Notre Dame Press, 15-29.

Lash, Nicholas (1990), 'Friday, Saturday, Sunday', *New Blackfriars* vol. 71, 109-119.

Lash, Nicholas (1991), 'Conversation in Gethsemane', in *Pluralism and Truth: David Tracy and the Hermeneutics of Religion*, eds. Werner G. Jeanrond and Jennifer L. Rike, Crossroad Publishing Co., New York, 51-61.

Lash, Nicholas (1994), 'Beyond the End of History', *Concilium* vol. 5, 47-55.

Lash, Nicholas (1996), *The Beginning and End of Religion*, Cambridge University Press.

Lee, Jung Young (1969), 'Karl Barth's Use of Analogy in his Church Dogmatics', *SJT* vol. 22, 129-151.

Leech, Clifford (1969), *Tragedy: The Critical Idiom*, Methuen & Co. Ltd., London.

Lewis, Alan E. (1987), 'The Burial of God: Rupture and Resumption as the Story of Salvation', *SJT* vol. 40, 335-362.

Loades, Ann (1996), 'On Tearing the Darkness to Tatters: Hope for this World?', in *Essentials of Christian Community: Essays for Daniel W. Hardy*, eds. David F. Ford and Dennis L. Stamps, T&T Clark, Edinburgh, 296-304.

Loughlin, Gerard (1996), *Telling God's Story: Bible, Church and Narrative*, Cambridge University Press.

Louth, Andrew (1969), 'Barth and the Problem of Natural Theology', *Downside Review* vol. 87, 268-277.

Lovin, Robin W. (1984), *Christian Faith and Public Choices: The Social Ethics of Barth, Brunner, and Bonhoeffer*, Fortress Press, Philadelphia.

Lowe, Walter (1988), 'Barth as the Critic of Dualism: Re-Reading the *Römerbrief'*, *SJT* vol. 41, 377-395.

Lucas, D.W. (ed.) (1968), *Aristotle: Poetics*, Clarendon Press, Oxford.

Lucas, F.L. (1946), *Tragedy in relation to Aristotle's Poetics*, London.

Lynch, William F. (1965), *Images of Hope: Imagination as Healer of the Hopeless*, University of Notre Dame Press.

McCormack, Bruce L. (1995), *Karl Barth's Critically Realistic Dialectical Theology*, Clarendon Press, Oxford.

McCormack, Bruce L. (1997), 'Beyond Nonfoundational and Postmodern Readings of Barth: Critically Dialectical Theology', *Zeitschrift für dialektische Theologie* vol. 13, 67-95.

McCormack, Bruce L. (1998), 'Revelation and History in Transfoundationalist Perspective: Karl Barth's Theological Epistemology in Conversation with a Schleiermachian Tradition', *Journal of Religion* vol. 78, 18-37.

McGrath, Alister E. (1986), *The Making of Modern German Christology. From the Enlightenment to Pannenberg*, Oxford.

Macken, John (1990), *The Autonomy Theme in the Church Dogmatics: Karl Barth and His Critics*, Cambridge University Press.

McKinney, Richard W.A. (ed.) (1976), *Creation, Christ and Culture: Studies in Honour of T.F. Torrance*, T&T Clark, Edinburgh.

MacKinnon, Donald M. (1940), *The Church of God*, Signposts 7, Dacre Press, Westminster.

MacKinnon, Donald M. (1940), *God the Living and the True*, Signposts 2, Dacre Press, Westminster.

MacKinnon, Donald M. (1962), 'Revised Reviews: XIII - Barth's Epistles to the Romans', *Theology* vol. 65, 3-7.

MacKinnon, Donald M. (1966), 'Subjective and Objective Conceptions of Atonement', *Prospect for Theology: Essays in Honour of H. H. Farmer*, ed. F. G. Healey, James Nisbet & Co. Ltd., Digswell Place, 169-182.

MacKinnon, Donald M. (1968), *Borderlands of Theology and Other Essays*, Lutterworth Press, London.

MacKinnon, Donald M. (1969), *The Stripping of the Altars: The Gore Memorial Lecture Delivered on 5 November 1968 in Westminster Abbey, and Other Papers and Essays on Related Topics*, Collins, London.

MacKinnon, Donald M. (1974), *The Problem of Metaphysics*, Cambridge University Press.

MacKinnon, Donald M. (1979), *Explorations in Theology 5*, SCM Press, London.

MacKinnon, Donald M. (1986), 'Some Reflections on Hans Urs von Balthasar's Christology with Special Reference to Theodramatik II/2, III and IV', *The Analogy of Beauty: The Theology of Hans Urs von Balthasar*, ed. John Riches, T&T Clark, Edinburgh, 164-174.

MacKinnon, Donald M. (1987), *Themes in Theology: The Three-Fold Cord. Essays in Philosophy, Politics and Theology*, T&T Clark, Edinburgh.

MacKinnon, Donald M. (ed.) (1953), *Christian Faith and Communist Faith: A Series of Studies by Members of the Anglican Communion*, Macmillan, London.

MacKinnon, Donald M., and Lampe, G.W.H. (1966), *The Resurrection: A Dialogue Arising from Broadcasts by G. W. H. Lampe and D. M. MacKinnon*, ed. William Purcell, A.R. Mowbray & Co. Ltd., London.

Mackintosh, H.R. (1937), *Types of Modern Theology: Schleiermacher to Barth*, Nisbet, London.

McLean, Stuart D. (1975), 'The Humanity of Man in Karl Barth's Thought', *SJT* vol. 28, 127-147.

McLean, Stuart D. (1981), *Humanity in the Theology of Karl Barth*, T&T Clark, Edinburgh.

Mallow, Vernon R (1983), *The Demonic. A Selected Study. An Examination into the Theology of Edwin Lewis, Karl Barth, and Paul Tillich*, University Press of America, Lanham, New York, London.

Marquardt, Friedrich-Wilhelm (1972), *Theologie und Sozialismus. Das Beispiel Karl Barths*, Kaiser, München.

Marshall, Bruce D. (1987), *Christology in Conflict: The Identity of a Saviour in Rahner and Barth*, Basil Blackwell, Oxford.

Marshall, Bruce D. (1994), 'Rhetoric and Realism in Barth', *Toronto Journal of Theology* vol. 10, 9-16.

Marty, Martin E., and Peerman, Dean G. (eds.) (1968), *New Theology No. 5*, Collier-Macmillan, London and New York.

Matheney, Paul D. (1990), *Dogmatics and Ethics: The Theological Realism and Ethics of Karl Barth's Church Dogmatics*, Verlag Peter Lang, Frankfurt am Main, Bern, New York, Paris.

May, Keith M. (1990), *Nietzsche and the Spirit of Tragedy*, Macmillan, London.

Meynell, Hugo (1965), *Grace Versus Nature: Studies in Karl Barth's* Church Dogmatics, Sheed and Ward, London and Melbourne.

Miell, David K. (1989), 'Barth on Persons in Relationship: A Case for Further Reflection?', *SJT* vol. 42, 541-555.

Migliore, Daniel L. (1991), 'Karl Barth's First Lectures in Dogmatics: *Instruction in the Christian Religion*', in Karl Barth, *The Göttingen Dogmatics: Instruction in the Christian Religion Volume 1*, trans. Geoffrey W. Bromiley, William B. Eerdmans Publishing Company, Grand Rapids, Michigan, xv-lxii.

Molnar, Paul (1989), 'The Function of the Immanent Trinity in the Theology of Karl Barth: Implications for Today', *SJT* vol. 42, 367-399.

Molnar, Paul (1995), 'Some Problems with Pannenberg's Solution to Barth's "Faith Subjectivism"', *SJT* vol. 48, 315-339.

Molnar, Paul (1996), *Karl Barth and the Theology of the Lord's Supper: A Systematic Investigation*, Peter Lang, New York, Washington, D.C./Baltimore, Boston, Bern, Frankfurt am Main, Berlin, Vienna, Paris.

Molnar, Paul (1996), 'Toward a Contemporary Doctrine of the Immanent Trinity: Karl Barth and the Present Discussion', *SJT* vol. 49, 311-357.

Moltmann, Jürgen (1967), *Theology of Hope: On the Ground and Implications of a Christian Eschatology*, trans. James W. Leitch, SCM Press, London.

Moltmann, Jürgen (1974), *The Crucified God: The Cross of Christ as the Foundation and Criticism of Christian Theology*, trans. R.A. Wilson and John Bowden, SCM Press, London.

Moltmann, Jürgen (1975), *The Church in the Power of the Spirit: A Contribution to Messianic Eschatology*, trans. Margaret Kohl, SCM Press, London.

Moltmann, Jürgen (1979), *The Future of Creation*, trans. Margaret Kohl, SCM Press, London.

Moltmann, Jürgen (1981), *The Trinity and the Kingdom of God: The Doctrine of God*, trans. Margaret Kohl, SCM Press, London.

Moltmann, Jürgen (1984), *On Human Dignity: Political Theology and Ethics*, ed. and trans. D.M. Meeks, SCM Press, London.

Moltmann, Jürgen (1985), *God in Creation: An Ecological Doctrine of Creation*, trans. M. Kohl, SCM Press, London.

Moltmann, Jürgen (1996), *The Coming of God: Christian Eschatology*, trans. Margaret Kohl, SCM Press, London.

Mounce, Robert H. (1977), *The Book of Revelation*, Eerdmans, Grand Rapids.

Mueller, David L. (1990), *Foundation of Karl Barth's Doctrine of Reconciliation: Jesus Christ Crucified and Risen*, Toronto Studies in Theology Volume 54, The Edwin Mellen Press, Lewiston/Queenston/Lampeter.

Muir, Kenneth (1986), *Shakespeare: King Lear*, Penguin Books, London.

Muller, Richard A. (1994), 'Barth's *Göttingen Dogmatics (1924-26):* A Review and Assessment', *Westminster Journal of Theology* vol. 56, 115-132.

Nietzsche, Friedrich (1967), *The Birth of Tragedy*, trans W. Kaufmann, Vintage Books, New York.

Nietzsche, Friedrich (1974), *The Gay Science*, trans. Walter Kaufmann, Vintage Books, New York.

Nussbaum, Martha Craven (1986), *The Fragility of Goodness: Luck and Ethics in Greek Tragedy and Philosophy*, Cambridge University Press.

O'Collins, Gerald (1968), 'The Principle and Theology of Hope', *SJT* vol. 21, 129-144.

O'Donovan, Joan E. (1986), 'Man Made in the Image of God: The Disagreement Between Barth and Brunner Reconsidered', *SJT* vol. 39, 433-459.

O'Grady, Colm (1969), *The Church in Catholic Theology: Dialogue with Karl Barth*, Geoffrey Chapman, London, Dublin, Melbourne.

O'Grady, Colm (1970), *The Church in the Theology of Karl Barth*, Geoffrey Chapman, London, Dublin, Melbourne.

Oden, Thomas C. (1969), *The Promise of Barth: The Ethics of Freedom*, J.B. Lippincott Company, Philadelphia and New York.

Osborn, Robert T. (1983), 'A "Personalistic" Appraisal of Barth's Political Ethics', *Studies in Religion* vol. 12, 313-324.

Pannenberg, Wolfhart (1969), *Theology and the Kingdom of God*, trans. Richard John Neuhaus, Westminster, Philadelphia.

Pannenberg, Wolfhart (1971), *Basic Questions in Theology, Volume 2*, trans. George H. Kehm, SCM Press, London.

Pannenberg, Wolfhart (1977), *Faith and Reality*, trans. John Maxwell, Search Press, London.

Pannenberg, Wolfhart (1984), 'Constructive and Critical Functions of Eschatology', *Harvard Theological Review* vol. 77, 119-139.

Pannenberg, Wolfhart (1991), *Systematic Theology Volume 1*, trans. Geoffrey W. Bromiley, T&T Clark, Edinburgh.

Pannenberg, Wolfhart (1994), *Systematic Theology Volume 2*, trans. Geoffrey W. Bromiley, T&T Clark, Edinburgh.

Pannenberg, Wolfhart (1998), *Systematic Theology, Volume 3*, trans. Geoffrey W. Bromiley, T&T Clark, Edinburgh.

Parker, T.H.L (1960), 'Barth on Revelation', *SJT* vol. 13, 366-381.

Phan, Peter C. (1988), *Eternity in Time: A Study of Karl Rahner's Eschatology*, Associated University Press, London and Toronto.

Poon, Wilson and McLeish, Tom (1999), 'Real Presences: Two Scientists' Response to George Steiner', *Theology* vol. 102, 169-177.

Prenter, Regin (1967), 'Dietrich Bonhoeffer and Karl Barth's Positivism of Revelation', in *World Come of Age: A Symposium on Dietrich Bonhoeffer*, ed. Ronald Gregor Smith, Collins, London, 93-130.

Rahner, Karl (1961-72), *Theological Investigations*, 23 volumes, Darton, Longman and Todd, London.

Rahner, Karl (1978), *Foundations of Christian Faith. An Introduction to the Idea of Christianity*, trans. William V. Dych, Darton Longman & Todd, London.

Raphael, D. Daiches (1960), *The Paradox of Tragedy: The Mahlon Powell Lectures 1959*, George Allen and Unwin Ltd., London.

Reist, Jr., John S. (1983), 'Barthian Ostraca: Ethical and Epistolary Fragments', *Journal of Religion* vol. 63, 281-289.

Reist, Jr., John S. (1987), 'Commencement, Continuation, Consummation: Karl Barth's Theology of Hope', *Evangelical Quarterly* vol. 87, 195-214.

Richards, I.A. (1924), *Principles of Literary Criticism*, Routledge & Kegan Paul, London.

Richmond, James (1966), *Faith and Philosophy*, Hodder and Stoughton, London.

Richmond, James (1970), *Theology and Metaphysics*, SCM Press, London.

Richmond, James (1986), 'God and the Natural Orders: Is there Permanent Validity in Karl Barth's Warning to Natural Theology', in *Being and Truth: Essays in Honour of John Macquarrie*, eds. Alistair Kee and Eugene T. Long, SCM Press, London, 393-409.

Ricoeur, Paul (1985), 'Evil, a Challenge to Philosophy and Theology', *Journal of the American Academy of Religion* vol. 53, 635-648.

Ricoeur, Paul (1986), *Fallible Man*, rev. trans. Charles A. Kelbey, Fordham University Press, New York.

Ricoeur, Paul (1992), *Oneself as Another*, trans. Kathleen Blamey, University of Chicago Press, Chicago and London.

Ritschl, Albrecht (1902), *The Christian Doctrine of Justification and Reconciliation*, trans. H.R. Mackintosh and A.B. Macaulay, 2nd edn., T&T Clark, Edinburgh.

Roberts, Richard H. (1979), 'Karl Barth's Doctrine of Time: Its Nature and Implications', in *Karl Barth: Studies of his Theological Method*, ed. S.W. Sykes, Clarendon Press, Oxford, 88-146.

Roberts, Richard H. (1980), 'The Ideal and the Real in the Theology of Karl Barth', in *New Studies in Theology 1*, eds. Stephen Sykes and Derek Holmes, Duckworth, London, 163-180.

Roberts, Richard H. (1991), *A Theology on its Way? Essays on Karl Barth*, T&T Clark, Edinburgh.

Rodin, R. Scott (1997), *Evil and Theodicy in the Theology of Karl Barth*, Peter Lang, New York, Washington, D.C., Boston, Bern, Frankfurt am Main, Berlin, Vienna, Paris.

Rogers, Eugene F. (1995), *Thomas Aquinas and Karl Barth: Sacred Doctrine and the Knowledge of God*, University of Notre Dame Press.

Rogers, Eugene F. (1998), 'Supplementing Barth on Jews and Gender: Identifying God by Anagogy and the Spirit', *Modern Theology* vol. 14, 43-81.

Roochnik, David (1990), *The Tragedy of Reason: Toward a Platonic Conception of Logos*, Routledge, New York and London.

Rosato, Philip J. (1981), *The Spirit as Lord: The Pneumatology of Karl Barth*, T&T Clark, Edinburgh.

Rosset, Clement (1993), *Joyful Cruelty: Towards a Philosophy of the Real*, trans. and introduction by David F. Bell, Oxford University Press.

Rowland, Christopher (1982), *The Open Heaven: A Study of Apocalyptic in Judaism and Early Christianity*, SPCK, London.

Rowland, Christopher (1993), *Revelation*, Epworth Press, London.

Rumscheidt, H. Martin (ed.) (1972), *Revelation and Theology: An Analysis of the Barth-Harnack Correspondence of 1923*, Cambridge University Press.

Runia, Klaas (1982), 'Karl Barth's Christology', in *Christ the Lord Studies in Christology Presented to Donald Guthrie*, ed. Harold H. Rowdon, Inter Varsity Press, Leicester, 299-310.

Russell, D.S. (1992), *Divine Disclosure: An Introduction to Jewish Apocalyptic*, SCM Press, London.

Russell, John (1988), 'Impassibility and Pathos in Barth's Idea of God', *Anglican Theological Review* vol. 70, 221-232.

Sallis, John (1991), *Crossings. Nietzsche and the Space of Tragedy*, The University of Chicago Press.

Sauter, Gerhard (1999), 'Why is Karl Barth's Church Dogmatics Not a 'Theology of Hope'? Some Observations on Barth's Understanding of Eschatology', *SJT* vol. 52, 407-429.

Schacht, Richard (1983), *Nietzsche*, Routledge, London and New York.

Schleiermacher, Friedrich (1998), *On Religion: Speeches to Its Cultured Despisers*, trans. Richard Crouter, Cambridge University Press.

Schmitt, Keith Randall (1985), *Death and After-Life in the Theologies of Karl Barth and John Hick*, Rodopi, Amsterdam.

Schwarz, Hans (1984), 'Eschatology', in *Christian Dogmatics volume 2*, eds. Carl E. Braaten and Robert W. Jenson, Fortress Press, Philadelphia, 477-587.

Schweitzer, Albert (1910), *The Quest of the Historical Jesus*, A&C Black, London.

Scott, David A. (1986), 'Karl Barth and the "Other" Task of Theology', *The Thomist* vol. 50, 540-567.

Scott, J.L. (1964), 'The Covenant in the Theology of Karl Barth', *SJT* vol. 17, 182-198.

Scott, Jr., Nathan A., and Sharp, Nathan A. (eds.) (1994), *Reading George Steiner*, The John Hopkins University Press, Baltimore and London, 1-13.

Sewall, Richard (1959), *The Vision of Tragedy*, Yale University Press, New Haven.

Shakespeare, William (1972), *King Lear*, ed. G.K. Hunter, New Penguin Shakespeare, eds. T.J.B. Spencer and Stanley Wells, Penguin Books, Harmondsworth.

Silk, M.S., and Stern, J.P. (1981), *Nietzsche on Tragedy*, Cambridge University Press.

Sim, David C. (1986), *Apocalyptic Eschatology in the Gospel of Matthew*, Cambridge University Press.

Smart, Ninian, Sherry, Patrick, and Katz, Steven T. (eds.) (1985), *Nineteenth Century Religious Thought in the West, Volumes I-III*, Cambridge University Press.

Smith, Molly (1991), *The Darker World Within: Evil in the Tragedies of Shakespeare and His Successors*, University of Delaware Press, Newark, London and Toronto.

Smith, Steven G. (1983), *The Argument to the Other: Reason Beyond Reason in the Thought of Karl Barth and Emmanuel Levinas*, Scholars Press, Chicago.

Smith, Steven G. (1984), 'Karl Barth and Fideism: A Reconsideration', *Anglican Theological Review* vol. 66, 64-78.

Sophocles (1954), *Three Tragedies 1*, trans. David Grene, Robert Fitzgerald, Elizabeth Wyckoff, The University of Chicago Press.

Spjuth, Roland (1995), *Creation, Contingency and Divine Presence in the Theologies of Thomas F. Torrance and Eberhard Jüngel*, Lund University Press.

Steiner, George (1961), *The Death of Tragedy*, Oxford University Press.

Steiner, George (1969), *Language and Silence: Essays 1958-1966*, Penguin Books, Harmondsworth.

Steiner, George (1975), *After Babel: Aspects of Language and Translation*, Oxford University Press.

Steiner, George (1989), *Real Presences: Is there Anything in What we Say?*, Faber and Faber, London and Boston.

Steiner, George (1995), 'Tribute to Donald MacKinnon', *Theology* vol. 98, 2-9.

Steiner, George (1996), *No Passion Spent: Essays 1978-1996*, Faber and Faber, London.

Steiner, George (1996), 'Tragedy, Pure and Simple', in *Tragedy and the Tragic: Greek Theatre and Beyond*, ed. M.S. Silk, Clarendon Press, Oxford, 534-546.

Stern, J. P. (1978), *Nietzsche*, Fontana, London.

Surin, Kenneth (1986), 'Christology, Tragedy and "Ideology"', *Theology* vol. 89, 283-291.

Surin, Kenneth (1989), *The Turnings of the Darkness and Light: Theological Essays*, Cambridge University Press.

Surin, Kenneth (ed.) (1989), *Christ, Ethics and Tragedy: Essays in Honour of Donald MacKinnon*, Cambridge University Press.

Sutherland, Stewart (1990), 'Christianity and Tragedy', *Journal of Literature and Theology* vol. 4, 157-168.

Sykes, Stephen W. (1984), *The Identity of Christianity: Theologians and the Essence of Christianity from Schleiermacher to Barth*, SPCK, London.

Sykes, Stephen W. (ed.) (1979), *Karl Barth: Studies of His Theological Method*, Oxford.

Sykes, Stephen W. (ed.) (1989), *Karl Barth: Centenary Essays*, Cambridge University Press.

von Szeliski, John (1961), *Tragedy and Fear: Why Modern Tragic Drama Fails*, The University of North Carolina Press, Chapel Hill.

Tanner, Michael (1994), *Nietzsche*, Oxford University Press.

Taubes, Jacob (1954), 'Theodicy and Theology: A Philosophical Analysis of Karl Barth's Dialectical Theology', *Journal of Religion* vol. 34, 231-243.

Thiemann, Ronald F. (1991), *Constructing a Public Theology: The Church in a Pluralistic Culture*, John Knox Press, Louisville, Westminster.

Thiselton, Anthony C. (1994), 'Barr on Barth and Natural Theology: A Plea for Hermeneutics in Historical Theology', *SJT* vol. 47, 519-528.

Thiselton, Anthony C. (1995), *Interpreting God and the Postmodern Self: On Meaning, Manipulation and Promise*, T&T Clark, Edinburgh.

Thomas, J. (1977), 'The Epistemology of Karl Barth', *Heythrop Journal* vol. 18, 383-398.

Thompson, Geoff (1995), '... As Open to the world as any theologian could be ...'? Karl Barth's Account of Extra Ecclesial Truth and its Value to Christianity's Encounter with Other Religious Traditions', unpublished Ph.D Thesis, University of Cambridge.

Thompson, John (1976), 'The Humanity of God in the Theology of Karl Barth', *SJT* vol. 29, 249-269.

Thompson, John (1978), *Christ in Perspective in the Theology of Karl Barth*, T&T Clark, Edinburgh.

Thompson, John (1991), *The Holy Spirit in the Theology of Karl Barth*, Pennsylvania.

Thompson, John (1994), 'Barth and Balthasar: An Ecumenical Dialogue', in *The Beauty of Christ: An Introduction to the Theology of Hans Urs von Balthasar*, eds. Bede McGregor and Thomas Norris, T&T Clark, Edinburgh, 171-192.

Thompson, John (ed.) (1986), *Theology Beyond Christendom: Essays on the Centenary of the Birth of Karl Barth*, Princeton Theological Monograph Series 6, Pickwick Publications, Allison Park, Pennsylvania.

Torrance, Alan (1996), *Persons in Communion: An Essay on Trinitarian Description and Human Participation, With Special Reference to Volume One of Karl Barth's* Church Dogmatics, T&T Clark, Edinburgh.

Torrance, James B. (1956), 'The Priesthood of Jesus. A Study in the Doctrine of the Atonement', in *Essays in Christology for Karl Barth*, ed. T.H.L. Parker, Lutterworth Press, London, 155-173.

Torrance, James B. (1981), 'The Vicarious Humanity of Christ', in *The Incarnation: Ecumenical Studies in the Nicene-Constantinopolitan Creed*, ed. T.F. Torrance, Handsel Press, Edinburgh, 127-147.

Torrance, Thomas F. (1949), 'Universalism or Election?', *SJT* vol. 2, 310-318.

Torrance, Thomas F. (1962), *Karl Barth: An Introduction to His Early Theology, 1910-1931*, SCM Press, London.

Torrance, Thomas F. (1966), 'Service in Jesus Christ', in *Service in Christ: Essays Presented to Karl Barth on His 80th Birthday*, eds. James I. McCord and T.H.L. Parker, Epworth Press, London, 1-16.

Torrance, Thomas F. (1990), *Karl Barth: Biblical and Evangelical Theologian*, T&T Clark, Edinburgh.

Tracy, David (1987), *Plurality and Ambiguity: Hermeneutics, Religion, Hope*, SCM Press, London.

Tracy, David (1990), 'On Naming the Present', *Concilium* 1990/1, SCM Press, London, 66-85.

Tracy, David (1994), *On Naming the Present: Reflections on God, Hermeneutics and Church*, SCM Press, London.

Trapp, Michael (1996), 'Tragedy and the Possibility of Moral Reasoning: Response to Foley', in *Tragedy and the Tragic: Greek Theatre and Beyond*, ed. M.S. Silk, Clarendon Press, Oxford, 74-84.

Travis, Stephen H. (1980), *Christian Hope and the Future of Man*, Inter Varsity Press, Leicester.

Veitch, J. A. (1971), 'Revelation and Religion in Karl Barth', *SJT* vol. 24, 1-22.

Vickers, Brian (1973), *Towards Greek Tragedy: Drama, Myth, Society*, Longman, London and New York.

Villa-Vicencio, Charles (ed.) (1988), *On Reading Karl Barth in South Africa*, William B. Eerdmans, Grand Rapids, Michigan.

Wallace, Mark I. (1990), *The Second Naiveté: Barth, Ricoeur, and the New Yale Theology*, Mercer University Press, Macon.

Walsh, Brian J. (1987), 'Theology of Hope and the Doctrine of Creation: An Appraisal of Jürgen Moltmann', *Evangelical Quarterly* vol. 59, 53-76.

Ward, Graham (1993), 'Barth and Postmodernism', *New Blackfriars* vol. 74, 550-556.

Ward, Graham (1993), 'George Steiner and the Theology of Culture', *New Blackfriars* vol. 74, 98-105.

Ward, Graham (1993), 'The Revelation of the Holy Other as Wholly Other. Between Barth's Theology of Word and Levinas' Philosophy of Saying', *Modern Theology* vol. 9, 159-180.

Ward, Graham (1995), *Barth, Derrida and the Language of Theology*, Cambridge University Press.

Watson, Gordon (1977), 'Karl Barth and St. Anselm's Theological Programme', *SJT* vol. 30, 31-45.

Watson, Gordon (1989), 'A Study in St. Anselm's Soteriology and Karl Barth's Theological Method', *SJT* vol. 42, 493-512.

Webb, Stephen H. (1991), *Refiguring Theology: The Rhetoric of Karl Barth*, State University of New York Press.

Webster, John (1987), '"On the Frontiers of What is Observable": Barth's *Römerbrief* and Negative Theology', *Downside Review* vol. 105, 169-180.

Webster, John (1991), 'Eschatology, Ontology and Human Action', *Toronto Journal of Theology* vol. 7, 4-18.

Webster, John (1994), '"Assured and Patient and Cheerful Expectation": Barth on Christian Hope as the Church's Task', *Toronto Journal of Theology* vol. 10, 35-52.

Webster, John (1995), *Barth's Ethics of Reconciliation*, Cambridge University Press.

Webster, John (1998), *Barth's Moral Theology: Human Action in Barth's Thought*, T&T Clark, Edinburgh.

Webster, John (ed.) (1994), *The Possibilities of Theology: Studies in the Theology of Eberhard Jüngel in his Sixtieth Year*, T&T Clark, Edinburgh.

Weiss, Johannes (1971), *Jesus' Proclamation of the Kingdom of God*, trans. R.H. Hiers and D.L. Holland, London.

Werpehowski, William (1986), 'Narrative and Ethics in Barth', *Theology Today* vol. 43, 334-353.

West, Charles (1958), *Communism and the Theologians*, SCM Press, London.

West, P. (1974), 'Professor MacKinnon on the Atonement', *Theology* vol. 77, 232-238.

West, P. (1985), 'Christology as "Ideology"', *Theology* vol. 88, 428-436.

Whitehouse, W. A. (1949), 'The Christian View of Man: An Examination of Karl Barth's Doctrine', *SJT* vol. 2, 57-82.

Whitehouse, W. A. (1951), 'Providence: An Account of Karl Barth's Doctrine', *SJT* vol. 4, 241-256.

Wigley, Stephen D. (1993), 'Karl Barth on St. Anselm: The Influence of Anselm's "Theological Scheme" on T.F. Torrance and Eberhard Jüngel', *SJT* vol. 46, 79-97.

Wignall, P. G. (1980), 'D.M. MacKinnon: An Introduction to his Early Theological Writings', *New Studies in Theology 1*, eds. Stephen Sykes and Derek Holmes, Duckworth, London, 75-94.

Wilburn, Ralph G. (1969), 'Some Questions on Moltmann's Theology of Hope', *Religion in Life* vol. 38, 578-595.

Williams, Bernard (1966), *Modern Tragedy*, Chatto and Windus, London.

Williamson, René de Visme (1976), *Politics and Protestant Theology: An Interpretation of Tillich, Barth, Bonhoeffer, and Brunner*, Louisiana State University Press.

Willis, Robert E. (1970), 'Some Difficulties in Barth's Development of Special Ethics', *Religious Studies* vol. 6, 147-155.

Willis, Robert E. (1971), *The Ethics of Karl Barth*, E.J. Brill, Leiden.

Willis, W. Waite (1987), *Theism, Atheism and the Doctrine of the Trinity: The Trinitarian Theologies of Karl Barth and Jürgen Moltmann in response to protest Atheism*, Scholars Press, Atlanta, Georgia.

Wingren, Gustaf (1958), *Theology in Conflict: Nygren, Barth, Bultmann*, trans. Eric H. Wahlstrom, Oliver and Boyd, Edinburgh and London.

Wisnefske, Ned (1990), *Our Natural Knowledge of God: A Prospect for Natural Theology After Kant and Barth*, Peter Lang, New York, Bern, Frankfurt am Main, Paris.

Young, Julian (1992), *Nietzsche's Philosophy of Art*, Cambridge University Press.

Zahrnt, Heinz (1969), *The Question of God: Protestant Theology in the Twentieth Century*, trans. R. A. Wilson, Collins, London.

Index of Names